D0583683

CORPORATIONS
VS.
THE COURT

POWER AND SOCIAL CHANGE: STUDIES IN POLITICAL SOCIOLOGY

CORPORATIONS VS. THE COURT

Private Power, Public Interests

David Sciulli

LYNNE
RIENNER
PUBLISHERS

BOULDER
LONDON

Published in the United States of America in 1999 by
Lynne Rienner Publishers, Inc.
1800 30th Street, Boulder, Colorado 80301

and in the United Kingdom by
Lynne Rienner Publishers, Inc.
3 Henrietta Street, Covent Garden, London WC2E 8LU

Library of Congress Cataloging-in-Publication Data
Sciulli, David.
    Corporations vs. the court : private power, public interests /
    David Sciulli.
    (Power and social change—studies in political sociology)
    Includes bibliographical references and index.
    ISBN 1-55587-688-9 (hc : alk. paper)
    1. Corporation law—Social aspects—United States—States.
    2. Corporate governance—United States—States. 3. Judicial power—
    Social aspects—United States—States. I. Title. II. Series.
    KF1416.S397   1998
    346.73'066—dc21   98-7512
                                                                  CIP

British Cataloguing in Publication Data
A Cataloguing in Publication record for this book
is available from the British Library.

Printed and bound in the United States of America

        The paper used in this publication meets the requirements
   ∞   of the American National Standard for Permanence of
        Paper for Printed Library Materials Z39.48-1984.

    5 4 3 2 1

Contents

Acknowledgments

I benefited greatly from written comments on earlier drafts of chapters of this book from Steven Brint, Mark Mizruchi, Donald Black, Jim Burk, and Deborah DeMott. I also benefited from more general discussions with Gideon Sjoberg, Bill D'Antonio, Amitai Etzioni, Uta Gerhardt, Bernard Barber, Erwin Scheuch, Masamichi Sasaki, and David Frankford.

I thank in particular Isabelle Corbisier, a graduate of the Law Faculty at Catholic University in Louvain, Belgium, for commenting at length on an early draft of this manuscript. I also thank Catherine Riegle, a graduate student at the University of Chicago, who methodically read this entire manuscript as well as a related one, titled "Corporate Power in Civil Society." At the time, Riegle was a senior at Texas A&M; the next year she entered the graduate program at Chicago. For the purposes of improving the book's accessibility, she was an ideal reviewer: She brought the insights and criticisms of an interested, talented general reader to the manuscript. I have no doubt that some readers will wish that I had adopted more of her suggestions for improvement. An anonymous reviewer for Lynne Rienner Publishers gave me excellent, lengthy written comments, and I thank Bridget Julian, associate editor, for her encouragement, helpfulness, and editorial assistance.

I have presented parts of this book at the following scholarly meetings, where I benefited from comments by panelists and attendees: the 32nd Congress of the International Institute of Sociology at the University of Trieste in July 1995 (at a plenary session chaired by Pierpaolo Donati of the University of Bologna and presided over by IIS host Alberto Gasparini); the Sociology Institute at Heidelberg University in June 1995 (at a seminar hosted by Uta Gerhardt and attended by Wolfgang Schluchter and Gianfranco Poggi); the American Sociological Association annual meetings at Toronto in August 1997 (at a session organized by Neil Fligstein and chaired by Linda Brewster Stearns) and at Washington, D.C., in August 1995 (at a session I chaired on Corporations and Community); a faculty colloquium at the School of Law at Washington and Lee University in March 1996 (organized by David Millon and Lyman Johnson); and the Midwest Sociological Society annual meeting in April 1993 (at a session organized by Robert Antonio).

Finally, I thank my colleagues at Texas A&M for general support and, more particularly, I thank my department chair, Dudley Poston, for his exemplary commitment to research and scholarly integrity.

Introduction

Corporations are more than profit-driven commercial enterprises. They are also private governments in civil society. When top managers or shareholder majorities advance their interests against bondholders, long-term suppliers, middle managers, line employees, and local communities, they exercise collective power over them. As these power plays become patterned or institutionalized, top managers in particular develop what legal scholars call a corporation's "governance structure."[1] Once we appreciate that corporate managers exercise power through a structure of private governance, some significant sociological questions come to the fore: How is corporate power actually structured and exercised in the United States? More generally, are there identifiable limits to corporate power, both legal and normative, that are found in democratic societies and not in more imposed social orders? What is the status of these legal and normative limits in the United States today? Have they been maintained, despite intensifying global competition, or have they been exceeded, thereby potentially enervating U.S. democracy?

Since the founding of the U.S. government, first state legislatures and then state courts—not the Supreme Court, Congress, or any regulatory agency—have overseen how corporations govern themselves and exercise their collective power in civil society. Today, the state courts of Delaware, California, New York, and New Jersey in particular comprise what legal scholars call the "corporate judiciary." Even as these state courts handle all matter of civil and criminal cases (the exception being Delaware's Chancery, which specializes in trusts and intracorporate disputes), they bear ultimate responsibility for limiting corporate power in the United States. Thus, the corporate judiciary in general, including Delaware's Chancery in particular, qualifies uniquely as an "environmental agent," to use a term from the new institutionalism in the sociology of organizations. The corporate judiciary imposes on top managers and shareholder majorities norms of behavior that are institutionalized in corporations' "environment," the larger society.

1

To what purpose does the corporate judiciary normatively mediate corporate power? The U.S. corporate judiciary endeavors to accomplish more than the protection of particular shareholders, bondholders, suppliers, middle managers, employees, retirees, and local communities from harm by particular corporate policies. In a grander sense, it also endeavors to protect the larger U.S. society from being harmed by corporate power. Put more specifically, the corporate judiciary considers whether particular exercises of corporate power can potentially harm the larger social order. It asks: When does corporate power potentially challenge institutional arrangements in U.S. civil society that can be seen as basic to democracy in the United States?

The terms *basic* and *institutional* are both important in describing the corporate judiciary's mission. For instance, we may demonstrate that certain contemporary exercises of U.S. corporate power disrupt an existing balance between economic institutions (such as labor, capital, and commodity markets) and noneconomic institutions (such as families, communities, and voluntary associations). We could therefore say that existing institutional arrangements in U.S. civil society are being altered. But we have not established that the particular balance that is thus altered, or any other balance, is in itself basic to this democracy. The corporate judiciary at times explores this grander issue: Which institutional arrangements in U.S. civil society must it preserve in the face of any challenges by corporate power? We can see already that this grand mission qualifies the U.S. corporate judiciary as a particularly important institution. More technically, this is what qualifies the U.S. corporate judiciary as an "environmental agent" that tries to identify and advocate for the interests of the whole (the environment, the larger social order), not only the interests of the parts (the corporations in this environment, or particular constituents in particular corporations).

When U.S. state courts consider whether corporate power challenges basic institutional arrangements, they clearly move far beyond economists' narrower way of thinking about corporations. Economists portray corporations as power-neutral, profit-seeking commercial enterprises that, as such, are incapable of harming their constituents, let alone the larger social order. State courts, by contrast, think about corporations in broader terms: They treat corporations as "intermediary associations." Intermediary associations bear this name because they are powerful private bodies in civil society that stand between the state and the individual. As powerful bodies, they help to limit the state's power. By the same token, they are nearly as capable as the state of exercising their power in abusive or arbitrary ways.

For instance, when the state enforces laws retroactively, it acts arbitrarily. Retroactive laws not only harm particular individuals or groups but also affront norms and practices that truly are "basic" to U.S. democracy. Corporate managers can act just as arbitrarily. This means that corporations can also cause harm and can also affront the same basic norms and practices. For instance, when corporate managers respond to a hostile takeover bid by offering to buy the shares of stock held by a shareholder majority without extending the same offer to other shareholders, they act arbitrarily. Similarly, when managers abruptly change longstanding corporate policies—covering pension funds, for example, or their obligations to long-term suppliers—without announcing the change in advance (or without offering a credible business reason for doing so, let alone demonstrating its credibility), they also act arbitrarily. The courts do not permit such exercises of corporate power. The courts monitor corporate power, therefore, because even though corporations are private bodies, they are capable, like the state, of acting in ways that challenge norms and practices that distinguish a democratic society from more imposed social orders.

What is curious, however, is that this broader approach to corporate power, this institutional or constitutional approach, has to be constructed from the behavior of the U.S. corporate judiciary from the Founding to the present. Although this broader approach does indeed orient the corporate judiciary, typically sitting judges do not explicitly identify it even when they act on it, nor do observing legal scholars when they comment on it.[2] Moreover, there is no theory in the sociological study of corporations (or of organizations) that adequately describes and explains this broader approach by the U.S. corporate judiciary. Sociologists fail to capture the corporate judiciary's role as an environmental agent even as they seek examples of institutions that perform the role of holding organizations to norms and practices in their environments.

For example, Malcolm Waters notes this gap in Daniel Bell's groundbreaking effort in the 1970s to characterize a postindustrial society:

> Nowhere does Bell view corporate economic power as arbitrary or as a source of class formation. Indeed he takes the view that corporations are so internally differentiated and so subject to external controls that it is difficult if not impossible to locate any site of power within them. For Bell, power resides in concrete individual persons and groups rather than in abstract structures. Arbitrary economic power can therefore only occur under entrepreneurial or family capitalism in which an identifiable elite can own and inherit property.[3]

Bell's view of corporations, accurately described by Waters, does not differ significantly from portrayals of corporations that we might find in the works of the most narrowly trained economists.

To their credit, sociologists who study organizations appreciate that corporations (and other organizations) wield economic and political power. Yet these sociologists, too, do not study the mediating role performed by the corporate judiciary. For that matter, they do not study large, profit-seeking corporations as frequently as they study governmental agencies and nonprofit organizations. Those that do study corporations focus on the multidivisional form, interlocking directorates, directors' scanning for information, "corporate learning," and corporate participation in politics. They do not explain why (let alone predict when) state courts intervene into how corporations govern themselves.[4] As a result, even these sociologists ignore what economists and legal scholars ignore. They fail to take note at a conceptual level of the U.S. corporate judiciary's broader, more institutional or constitutional approach to corporate power. As a result, they fail to address the issue of how corporations and other intermediary associations govern themselves within fully institutionalized democracies, and how this differs empirically in more imposed social orders.

Still, we will see that this gap in the literature can be filled by drawing on an existing theoretical approach in the sociology of organizations: the "new institutionalism."[5] Institutionalists draw attention to how norms institutionalized in the larger social order frame or mediate the otherwise rational or economizing behavior of organizations. However, because institutionalists rarely study law or courts,[6] they have been reluctant to identify who or what maintains institutionalized norms, rules, and practices. They also acknowledge that they cannot identify, let alone predict and explain, the relationship between changes in the behavior of organizations and changes in the social order, that is, in basic institutional arrangements in civil society. We will trace the workings of the corporate judiciary since the Founding with an eye to assessing the strengths and weaknesses of the new institutionalism in accounting for the behavior of corporations, as one important subset of organizations. We will also endeavor to answer a central question driving political sociology more generally: How is collective power exercised in civil society, and when, where, and how do democratic societies in particular limit these exercises?

The historical study of the corporate judiciary in the interior chapters of this volume is designed to help advance the institutional approach to organizations both in substance and at a conceptual level. In substance, it draws attention to the importance of the U.S. corporate judiciary as an environmental agent, maintaining existing *normative* mediations on corporate power. At a conceptual level, this historical study also draws attention to the importance of distinguishing intermediary associations from the larger category of organizations. Changes in the governance of intermediary associations can either support or challenge institutional arrangements in civil society and thereby alter the direction of social change. By contrast, changes in how other organizations make decisions or settle disputes typically fail to carry such grand, institutional consequences. When institutionalists focus on organizations as their unit of analysis instead of intermediary associations, therefore, they already complicate their own efforts to link the study of organizations to larger questions about social change.

Corporations are more like hospitals, universities, and other sites of professional practice than like restaurants, retail stores, and other sites of strictly commercial activity. As intermediary associations, they "intermediate" between the state and the individual. We have already considered how corporations, as powerful private bodies, help to limit the state's power. After all, their very presence in civil society means that the state does not monopolize collective power, as is the case in more authoritarian social orders.

But we can also consider the other side of corporations' intermediary position in civil society. Corporate entities are capable of broadening individuals' loyalties beyond their families and primary groups (including their ethnic, gender, religious, and class affiliations). They are therefore capable of mediating individuals' prejudices—what sociologists call their particularism, their narrow identities. Consider, however, what this means. If corporate managers exercise power over other corporate constituents in abusive ways, they can just as easily encourage these individuals to "hunker down," that is, to engage more exclusively in the particularism that marks less institutionalized democracies as well as authoritarian regimes. Moreover, when corporate managers exercise their power in abusive ways, they do more than harm particular constituents, particular middle managers, employees, bondholders, suppliers, and local communities. They also potentially enervate institutional arrangements that are basic to any democratic social order.

This concern about the cumulative potential of corporations to challenge basic institutional arrangements in the United States is what state judges have in mind, albeit typically implicitly, when they adopt an institutional or constitutional approach to corporate power. After all, individuals who are subjected to abuse in everyday life as corporate constituents are hardly likely to form the vigilant citizenry that the Founders believed was the ultimate guarantor of a democratic republic. They are hardly likely to recognize as a body when the state has exceeded its bounds and then to mobilize collectively to return the state to its proper place. They are more likely to act strictly self-interestedly, to endeavor to secure their own families' and groups' protections and privileges within both private and public spheres of life.[7]

*   *   *

As noted earlier, corporate law in the United States is a domain of the state courts. Why this is the case may be traced quite literally to the founding and framing of the U.S. government, when it was left to state legislatures and state courts to develop the substantive norms of corporate law and of family law. The law of professions and nonprofit organizations essentially developed by analogy to corporate law.[8]

Just as constitutional law identifies the proper scope of state power, corporate law identifies the proper scope of corporate power. Indeed, it is not an exaggeration to say that in particular Delaware's Chancery Court and Supreme Court together function as the constitutional court of the United States for intermediary associations, for powerful private bodies in civil society. How corporations exercise their collective power, the means that corporate managers employ as they endeavor either to maximize investors' dividends or else to maximize their companies' growth, are matters that ultimately the Delaware courts decide.

The Delaware courts and other state courts face a problem today. They are pressured both by systemic forces in today's global economy and by impressive arguments of legal and economic "contractarians" to treat corporations as strictly commercial enterprises rather than intermediary associations. They are pressured, in essence, to adopt Daniel Bell's "postindustrial" view of corporations as essentially power-neutral sites of individual contracting. In this view, managers and investors endeavor benignly to maximize either dividends or growth. Their efforts may on occasion harm particular constituents, such as employees or local communities, but their efforts cannot possibly harm the larger social order.[9]

State courts are pressured, therefore, to abandon the idea that corporations function not only as commercial enterprises but also as powerful intermediary associations in civil society that, as such, bear institutional or constitutional responsibilities—beyond their contractual obligations to particular corporate constituents. The Delaware courts in particular continue to resist adopting this narrower, more strictly economistic, approach to corporate power. But Delaware's courts, like those in other states, have already been cast adrift from those moorings in corporate law doctrine that had once oriented them to consider the broader consequences of corporate power. Like other state courts, the Delaware courts now have great difficulty pinpointing when the governance of corporations carries what I call "institutional externalities." I identify as institutional externalities exercises of corporate power that disrupt institutional arrangements in civil society basic to maintaining a democratic society. Like other state courts, the Delaware courts are focusing more exclusively now on what I call the "immediate externalities" of corporate power—exercises of corporate power that harm particular individuals and groups (whether employees and retirees, or local communities and consumers) but do not disrupt or challenge basic institutional arrangements in civil society.

One purpose of this volume is to identify the moorings in corporate law doctrine that once oriented the corporate judiciary to recognize and endeavor to mediate the institutional consequences of corporate power. The goal here is to explore how state legislatures and then state courts once enforced *normative* mediations of corporate power, and then to consider whether these normative mediations are indeed basic to maintaining a democratic social order.

A second purpose of this volume is to identify and highlight that moment in the mid-1970s when the corporate judiciary began to lose its way, when it began to experience drift as an institution. As this process of institutional drift continues to unfold today, the corporate judiciary is simultaneously leaving the governance of U.S. corporations "available" for greater drift away from any moorings in democratic civil society. Thus, two major U.S. institutions, one economic and one legal, are adrift today. They no longer broadly and consistently support institutional arrangements basic to a democratic social order. Rather, both institutions are in the process of becoming ever more "available" to tolerate challenges to basic norms and practices of U.S. democracy.

A third purpose of this volume is to explore the promise and limits of the institutional approach in the sociology of organizations. Beyond discussing concepts and findings from this approach's major proponents, we will see why it is important to distinguish intermediary associations from other organizations and also to identify the corporate judiciary as a particularly important agent of norms institutionalized in the larger society, the "environment" in which organizations conduct their affairs.

Finally, this volume has yet a fourth purpose. I am interested in bringing the literatures of political sociology, organization theory, and legal scholarship into dialogue. For sociologists, this book is designed to open access to the often arcane language of law journals. For legal scholars, it offers a social theory designed to identify the institutional consequences of ongoing changes in corporate law, judicial practice, and corporate governance.

Notes

1. Corporate governance refers to how corporate decisions are made and to how intracorporate disputes are resolved.

2. For a lengthy discussion of this point, see my related manuscript titled "Corporate Power in Civil Society."

3. Waters (1995:41–42).

4. For sociological studies of corporations, see Fligstein (1990), Mizruchi (1982, 1992), Burt (1983), Useem (1984, 1993), Morrill (1995), and Roy (1997). Also see an exchange between sociologists of organizations on the evolution of European automobile manufacturers: Hannan et al. (1995), Baum and Powell (1995), and Hannan and Carroll (1995); and see Powell's work on biotechnology companies (Powell, Koput, and Smith-Doerr 1996).

5. See Powell and DiMaggio (1991) for an important collection.

6. The 1994 collection edited by Sim Sitkin and Robert Bies, *The Legalistic Organization,* is designed to move institutionalism in this direction. See the opening chapter by Richard Scott for an assessment of organization theorists' failure to follow Max Weber's lead in bringing law to the study of organizations. The 1994 article by Sutton, Dobbin, Meyer, and Scott, "The Legalization of the Workplace," explores how due process guarantees are extended to employees. It does not address

how corporations are governed more generally, and it says not a word about the corporate judiciary.

7. See Bellah et al. (1985) more generally; see also Putnam (1993).

8. See Lowi (1995) for an insightful, general account of the role of state legislatures in U.S. democracy.

9. The most formidable and unambiguous statement of this position may be found in Easterbrook and Fischel (1991).

PART 1

An Institutional Approach to Corporations and Courts

1

The Promise and Limits of Institutionalism

The new institutionalism in the sociology of organizations holds the greatest promise for explaining why the U.S. corporate judiciary continues to impose normative obligations on corporate managers and shareholder majorities. However, institutionalists typically study nonprofit organizations, including educational institutions and administrative agencies, rather than for-profit corporations. One consequence of their research strategy is that institutionalists have said literally nothing about the contributions that the corporate judiciary makes to the "institutional environment" of corporations or its more indirect influence upon the environment of other organizations.

One purpose of this book is to extend the institutionalist approach to organizations to these substantive areas, that is, to corporate governance and the judiciary's oversight of corporate power. In doing so, we uncover a basic limitation in institutionalism at the conceptual level: Institutionalists fail to distinguish intermediary associations within the larger set of organizations. We will see that this is one reason why they fail to identify any clear interrelationship between organizational behavior and institutional change. A second purpose of this book is thus to overcome this limitation, so as to connect the institutional approach to organizations to the larger concerns of sociology and political science.[1] In the process, we will endeavor to bring sociologists and political scientists into a dialogue with legal scholars, a dialogue that has the potential to counterbalance economists' growing influence over the corporate judiciary.[2] We begin by placing institutionalism into context by reviewing briefly the evolution of social theory over the past century.

Social Theory, Institutionalism,
and the Problem of Social Order

From the seventeenth century to the mid-1970s, social theory revolved broadly around the problem of social order—that is, around theorists' efforts to answer the following question: What holds society together? In the mid-nineteenth century, Karl Marx offered an updated version of Hobbes's (and Thrasymachus's) answer to this question, namely that society is held together by power. Marx insisted that capitalist society is held together by three major factors: the solidarity of the owners of productive property, the ideology of capitalism (whereby the rich merit their wealth, and the poor their poverty), and the lack of solidarity (and revolutionary ideology) of workers.

At the turn of the century, Emile Durkheim offered an updated version of Locke's answer to the problem of social order, that society is held together by voluntary agreement. Thinking sociologically, however, Durkheim replaced Locke's allegory of individuals in a "state of nature"— who agree voluntarily to support a state—with an emphasis on the precontractual norms and interests that bind individuals together well before they act so formally. Durkheim held that certain norms span a society as a whole, comprising what he called a collective conscience. He then proposed that shared sentiments hold society together despite systematic forces of "anomie" to the contrary, forces that cut some individuals loose from shared feelings of solidarity.[3] Individuals may experience anomie or "normlessness" when their routines and practices are disrupted, whether by sudden changes in the economy or by the general mobility and uprootedness of contemporary social life.

Working independently of Durkheim, Max Weber despaired over the future of modern societies, ultimately returning to Hobbes's answer to the problem of social order. Rather than sharing Durkheim's faith that sentiments were, and would remain, shared, Weber saw systemic forces of social change (manifested in ongoing industrialization and urbanization) disrupting people's lives much more fundamentally. Weber saw a marked tendency for individuals in modern societies to experience a literal "fragmentation of meaning," a breakdown of once shared beliefs and practices. Weber believed that this ongoing breakdown could only be stemmed by relying more and more frequently on formal mechanisms of social control, including police and courts. Where Durkheim saw that systemic forces of anomie would dislodge some individuals from their earlier solidarities, and yet believed that a collective conscience would nonetheless remain in place, Weber was less sanguine. In his view, systemic forces of rationalization— of purposeful calculation and economizing—would ultimately result in most individuals being subjected to formal controls by large, impersonal organizations, that is, bureaucracies. Against Lockean or voluntaristic answers to the problem of social order, therefore, Weber held that order is likely to be maintained in modern societies only by formal controls and bureaucratic organizations. He feared that these controls and organizations would become ever more constricting and authoritarian.

Talcott Parsons appreciated Durkheim's and Weber's points about the disruptive consequences of systemic forces. He built on their respective insights of anomie and rationalization by pointing to a tendency for even bureaucratic organizations to experience "functional differentiation," to become specialized by task or function. One need only consider the number of departments and units in hospitals today, as compared to the number in 1920 or 1950 or even 1970, to appreciate Parsons's point. Functions or tasks are broken down over time into more and more distinct parts; individuals are thus trained to perform narrower, often increasingly complicated, specialties. The question for Parsons, then, was whether there are countervailing forces to functional differentiation—forces not only of social control but also of social integration (which Durkheim treated as shared sentiments)—that can thereby maintain social order short of breakdown or an authoritarian outcome.

Even as Parsons appreciated that differentiation and specialization exacerbate the fragmentation of meaning that had concerned Weber, he rejected Weber's pathos. He believed that individuals internalize in common sets of substantive normative beliefs—sentiments—in modern societies that are "functional," that is, orderly, competitive, and at least somewhat integrative (rather than controlling). However, he converted into a more analytical and abstract framework Durkheim's perception of shared norms and of the stabilizing influence of routines and practices. Parsons saw all "functional" societies resting, at the very least, on institutionalized "media of interchange" (money, power, influence, and value commitments) and, more particularly, on individuals sharing *some* substantive normative basis for evaluating the legitimacy (or lack of legitimacy) of existing social arrangements.

However, while Parsons was developing his more abstract, substantive normative account of social order, symbolic interactionists (as well as ethnomethodologists and phenomenologists) began to push even further Weber's understanding of the fragmentation of meaning and, ironically, Parsons's own theory of functional differentiation. Based on their findings from field research, they have questioned the relevance of Durkheim's and Parsons's normativist responses to the classic problem of social order as such. They question the very effort to account for social order in terms of any overarching substantive norms or shared sentiments.[4] Rather than endeavoring to account for how order is established and maintained across an entire society, interactionists focus their attention on the structure and dynamics of individuals' everyday interactions, their local orders. They explore how people who act on competing material interests and different normative beliefs nonetheless come to share understandings in their every-day lives, how they negotiate "shared meanings of the situation" in their interpersonal encounters.

By emphasizing that people share understandings only in particular, often fleeting encounters, interactionists question the likelihood that people share any set of substantive normative beliefs more generally. In many regards interactionists see society as an abstract concept, not as a lived reality. In essence, they say to us: "You can participate in any number of inter-personal encounters in the United States; you can enter and leave any num-ber of local orders. But on what basis can you conclude that particular values and norms found in particular encounters somehow span 'American society,' and thereby help to integrate people into the larger social order?"[5]

Meanwhile, as Parsons was developing his mature social theory and interactionists were calling his efforts into question, Marx's materialist response to the problem of social order was being replaced by a decidedly non-Marxist alternative. Rational choice theorists (and neoclassical econo-mists) do not accept that a small group dominates society as a whole. They do insist, however, that all groups, including entire societies, are held together on the basis of members' material interests, not on the basis of members' normative beliefs. Coupling this essentially materialist position with interactionists' skepticism about the likelihood that any set of values and norms spans an entire society, rational choice theorists today make a strong case for their view. They argue that at the moment that the material interests of the members of a group begin to diverge (due to functional dif-ferentiation), group leaders will have to turn increasingly to material incen-tives, and ultimately to coercion, to maintain solidarity.[6] In a group as large as an entire society, we can expect to see countless instances where some combination of material incentives and coercion accounts for order. Where such incentives are not available, or where they are used ineffectively (that is, where they are not backed up by force), we can expect to find disorder or group conflict.

Here is where proponents of the "new institutionalism" in the sociolo-gy of organizations enter the picture. They challenge both interactionists and rational choice theorists by updating Durkheim's and Parsons's norma-tivist response to the problem of social order, and thus fight on two fronts simultaneously. On one front, they attempt to reinstate the classical prob-lem of social order against interactionists' more narrow focus on everyday encounters. Here, however, they run up against the problem of identifying the relationship between changes in organizations on the one hand and increases or decreases in social order on the other. On their second front, institutionalists bring substantive norms into their account of social order—against rational choice theorists' more narrow focus on material incentives and coercion.[7] Here they have made their greatest contribution to theory and research. They have done so by departing significantly from the way that Durkheim and Parsons characterized the contribution that shared substantive norms or sentiments make to social order. In essence, they take a middle ground between interactionists' emphasis on the importance of local order and Durkheim's concept of collective conscience; in addition, they build creatively on Parsons's notion of functional differentiation.

Institutionalists argue, against Weber and rational choice theorists, that shared sentiments do mediate individuals' self-interested behavior short of a breakdown of order and meaning. But they also argue, against Durkheim and Parsons, that these sentiments or substantive norms neither are internalized by individuals in common nor necessarily span society as a whole. Finally, against interactionists, institutionalists insist that the mediating force of sentiments or substantive norms can and does span a scope considerably broader than individuals' fleeting interpersonal encounters or strictly local orders. Their central argument is that substantive norms can be institutionalized across a "field," a functional sector of society (whether banking, manufacturing, education, or entertainment and the arts). The most successful organizations in each field typically exhibit fidelity to the substantive norms distinctive to that field, as opposed to acting more rationally or more directly on their own material interests. The most successful banks, for example, adopt certain architectural designs and position their tellers and managers in certain ways. No one orders organization agents to conform to these ways of doing things. Rather, the agents of the most influential banks in a field cognitively recognize the norms institutionalized in their field *without necessarily internalizing those norms as their own personal, affective beliefs.*

This fits well with legal scholars' and network analysts' efforts to distinguish what they call "positional interests" from individuals' self-interests.[8]

> Individual incumbents of the top command positions in various institutional hierarchies are usually constrained in their roles as fiduciaries, or agents, of the organization to behave in ways unrelated to their personal biographies or personal interests (although the two sets of interests undoubtedly coincide extensively).[9]

When agents bring their organizations into conformity with institutionalized norms, they typically do so strictly cognitively, in their position's best interests, not more affectively or emotionally, in their own self-interests. They decide for themselves whether and when it is in their organization's and their position's best interests to conform. They do not feel guilt or suffer pangs of conscience when they decide, for whatever reason, that it is no longer in their organization's or position's best interests to conform. But they remain always aware that violating institutionalized norms, while an option, is more likely to carry costs than to be cost-free.

This stakes out an important normativist response to the problem of social order. According to the institutionalists' account, the factor that mediates the behavior of organization agents is a field's substantive norms of behavior, not simply immediate material incentives or immediate threats of coercion. That is, the organizations that conform with the substantive norms institutionalized in their sector do not act strictly rationally or in "market-mimicking" ways. Their conforming behavior is not the most instrumentally rational means by which to advance their immediate material interests. To the contrary, institutionalized norms, like internalized norms, are by definition nonrational. They mediate how organization agents define organizational success and then act on their positional interests, just as internalized norms mediate how individuals define personal success and then act on their self-interests.

A Closer Look at Institutionalism

Institutionalists share a basic approach to the study of organizations that clearly distinguishes their work from that of population ecologists and proponents of resource dependence, the two other major approaches in the sociology of organizations.[10] They focus on how routines, rules, and procedures institutionalized in social sectors broadly alter organizational behavior in these domains. Yet, institutionalists differ among themselves in their approach to sectoral or "environmental" pressures. They characterize these pressures differently and offer differing descriptions of the ways they alter organizational behavior. In addition, institutionalists say little about whether and how changes in the governance and behavior of organizations might either support or challenge the larger social order—that is, either anticipate, initiate, or reflect a coming institutional change. This particular gap in their work accounts for why they pay little attention to state courts' interventions into the governance of corporations and other intermediary associations.[11] In the following sections, I explore in greater depth each of these aspects of the institutionalist approach.

Sectoral or Environmental
Pressures on Organizational Behavior

Describing the sectors or environments that normatively mediate organizations' behavior, Paul DiMaggio and Walter Powell use the term "isomorphism," a term first employed in sociology by social ecologist Amos Hawley in 1968.[12] Isomorphism refers to situations in which organizations within a sector come to resemble each other because they respond to the same environmental pressures as they compete for power, influence, and especially legitimacy within their sectors. Early in the development of the institutional or environmental approach to organizations, DiMaggio and Powell distinguished analytically between three mechanisms of isomorphism, which, presumably, are found in different combinations in different social sectors.[13]

First in their classification, "coercive isomorphism" occurs when either the success of particular organizations in a sector or else general cultural expectations spanning sectors literally compel the agents of other organizations to conform to certain patterns of behavior. This occurs, for example, when organizations are denied credentials or other signs of legitimacy or credibility when they fail to conform. Second, "mimetic isomorphism" occurs when organization agents broadly copy the behavior of those organizations in their sector that seem most successful, even as much of the behavior they copy is not really economizing or instrumentally rational. For instance, the managers of computer software companies may see that the most successful organizations in their sector tend to have a certain kind of landscaping, or tend to occupy buildings with a certain architectural design. They copy this along with these organizations' strategies for research and marketing.

DiMaggio and Powell are somewhat vague in discussing the third mechanism of isomorphism. They say simply that "normative isomorphism" occurs when, for example, organizations contain increasing numbers of professional employees who simultaneously exhibit a commitment to their organizations as well as fidelity to professional norms of behavior. We will see in the next chapter that this third type of isomorphism is problematic in current institutionalist accounts, and yet it holds the key to accounting empirically for the behavior of the corporate judiciary.

Powell has conceded that "this formulation [of the three types of isomorphism] is too broad." He now believes that the specific *qualities* of the norms and practices institutionalized in a given sector matter. One needs to consider (1) whether institutionalized norms and practices "are based on recognized sources of authority"; (2) whether they are fiscally based or more broadly programmatic; and (3) whether they are accepted or resisted by organization leaders.[14] We will see in the next chapter that the qualities of the norms and practices institutionalized in sectors of democratic social orders will differ in identifiable ways from the qualities found in the same sectors of more imposed social orders. *To the extent that this is the case, we can identify shifts in the direction of social change by monitoring whether the norms and practices institutionalized in particular sectors either gain or lose those qualities found uniquely in democratic social orders.*

With respect to the capacity of environmental pressures to alter organizational behavior, Powell and DiMaggio argued in 1983 that regardless of which of the three mechanisms of isomorphism comes into play in a given sector, the result is invariant. Organizations become more homogeneous in structure or "form." DiMaggio and Powell feared that this increasing homogeneity signified an ominous decline in the substantive pluralism of U.S. society.[15] Writing just before the turbulence of hostile takeovers and leveraged buyouts that swept across "Corporate America" beginning in late 1983, DiMaggio and Powell essentially predicted a secular decline in organizational diversity and innovation in the United States.[16] Other institutionalists disagreed then, and some certainly do today. They point out that even when the norms and practices institutionalized in particular sectors are highly constricting, this does not mean that organizations will invariably become more homogeneous.[17] Rather, constricting norms and practices may accelerate specialization both within and across organizations, through the process Parsons called functional differentiation. The result might be greater heterogeneity among organizations—a pattern of organizational change more consistent with increasing diversity and innovation than with any vision of an iron cage.

Apart from this difference of opinion among institutionalists, what is most revealing about their exchange is that both sets of theorists have acknowledged that their concepts do not allow them—or researchers—to resolve the issue empirically. That is, their approach to organizations fails to offer researchers the conceptual distinctions they need to identify whether organizations are in fact becoming either more homogeneous or more heterogeneous in form or structure. The changing positions that DiMaggio and Powell have staked out on this issue over the last decade in response to their critics illustrate the problem that they and other institutionalists face at a conceptual level.

For example, in 1983 DiMaggio and Powell articulated their fear that increasing organizational homogeneity was leading the social order of the United States in the direction of a Weberian "iron cage." Even then they hedged, however, saying that "organizations in a field may be highly diverse on some dimensions yet extremely homogeneous on others."[18] Five years later, DiMaggio expressed regret for using the term "iron cage" as well as for the vagueness of Meyer and Rowan's similar characterizations in 1977 of the social consequences of "institutionalized organizations."[19] Three years after that, Powell largely repudiated the homogenization thesis by exploring six "sources of heterogeneity"; in discussing the first of these, he asserts that even within "tightly bounded organizational fields, no two firms will have the exact same pattern of resource flows."[20]

This hedging and repudiating reflect the fact that institutionalists cannot resolve the homogeneity/heterogeneity issue until they become clearer about two points. First, they must clarify the level of analysis at which they are operating.[21] Are they following ecologists in studying whole sets ("populations") of organizations, or are they instead studying individual organizations—or, for that matter, particular divisions within organizations? Second, and more important for present purposes, institutionalists must become clearer about whether and how changes at the level of organizations (or divisions) affect the larger social order. Do all changes in organizations automatically support the institutional design of the larger social order? Or do some challenge it, thereby contributing to institutional change?[22]

Institutional Consequences of Organizational Change

Institutionalists have difficulty identifying institutional change.[23] This is so because, as we saw in the debate over homogenization and heterogeneity, their concepts currently orient them to identify qualities of organizations and environments found in all modern social orders. Institutionalists see organizations in all modern societies becoming either more homogeneous or more heterogeneous. What they fail to identify are the differences in the relationship between organizational change and institutional change that distinguish democratic social orders from more imposed social orders. This failure leaves them with a major problem: Institutionalists lack the concepts with which to identify the relationship between organizational change and *shifts* in the direction of institutional change, either from a democratic social order to a more imposed social order or vice versa.

In short, institutionalists' concepts do not allow us to identify when organizational behavior helps to institutionalize democratic norms and practices in civil society or when organizational behavior challenges such norms and practices across sectors. Yet, we will see in this volume that the U.S. corporate judiciary has always monitored corporate power with this very issue in mind (albeit often implicitly). The question we may pose to institutionalists even at this early point in our discussion is: Why would we assume that the relationship between organizational behavior and institutional change will be the same in democratic social orders as it is in more imposed social orders? Is it not more logical to assume the opposite, that the relationship will be identifiably different?[24]

Institutionalism and Economic
Accounts of Organizational Behavior

Open Systems Theory

Institutionalists' indirect or environmental approach to the study of organizations was presaged from the 1950s through the mid-1970s by "open systems theory."[25] Proponents of this theory emphasized that some organizations are typically more "open" to external pressures than insulated (or "decoupled") from them. Such organizations are typically neither narrowly "rational systems," which economize irrespective of what other organizations are doing, nor "natural systems," which maintain some valued way of life despite environmental pressures to the contrary.[26]

Open systems theorists appreciated that organizations can become less rational when they are riven by internal divisions. They added to the literature the insight that organizations can also become less rational, and certainly less "natural" or closed, when they become exposed to influences from the wider society, the "environment." Thus, open systems theorists held that an organization is "a coalition of shifting interest groups that develops goals by negotiation," and that "the structure of the coalition, its activities, and its outcomes are strongly influenced by environmental factors."[27]

Still, there was a basic weakness in the open systems approach. Proponents tended to define an organization's "environments" narrowly, as institutionalized *techniques,* as pressures to economize, to secure the "resources required by the organization's production system to transform inputs into outputs."[28] Thus, open systems theorists followed rational systems theorists in portraying organizations as essentially dedicated to economic production and material exchange. They were vague whenever they referred to the response of organizations to norms institutionalized in the environment.

Equally important, they failed to portray organizations as intermediary associations that exercise collective power in the larger social order.[29] As a result, open systems theorists had difficulty distinguishing their approach, both at a conceptual level or in its empirical findings, from rational choice theory and neoclassical economics generally.[30] Economists emphasize how competitive pressures from domestic and international markets "rationalize" organizations. Open systems theorists simply added that state and industry trade associations typically contribute to this same process of "rationalization." They identified state- and association-sanctioned "routines" at a conceptual level as market mimicking—as augmenting and possibly accelerating, rather than normatively mediating, organizations' rational responses to competitive pressures.

In short, at the conceptual level, open systems theorists ended up departing from rational systems theory and neoclassical economics only by drawing attention to group competition within organizations. Rational systems theorists do downplay the significance of this factor in altering how organizations compete in markets. They insist that intra-organizational dynamics, whatever they might be, are secondary to the respects in which all modern organizations differ from primary groups (and "natural systems" generally): Modern organizations develop formalized practices—standard operating procedures—dedicated to attaining relatively specific goals in instrumentally rational ways.[31]

The New Institutionalism

This convergence around principles of neoclassical economics seemingly ended in 1977 with the publication of a groundbreaking article in *American Journal of Sociology* by John Meyer and Brian Rowan. This article marked the birth of the new institutionalism in sociology.[32] Meyer and Rowan turned organization theorists' attention to the manner in which *cultural* routines, rules, and procedures—that is, externally sanctioned *symbols,* as opposed to material pressures to economize—alter the behavior of organizations.[33] In focusing, however, on nonprofit organizations, educational institutions, and public agencies to highlight the importance of culturally sanctioned symbols, Meyer and Rowan's ultimate distinction between institutionalism and neoclassical economics came down to a partitioning of the universe of organizations: Institutionalism appeared to endeavor to describe and explain the behavior of nonprofit organizations, whereas neoclassical economics would be left to account for the behavior of corporations, for-profit organizations. That is, Meyer and Rowan were still conceding, however broadly or elliptically, that *corporate* behavior falls more or less exclusively within the domain of neoclassical economics.[34]

Today, institutionalists gloss over this concession by characterizing the institutional environments of all organizations in broad and, as they openly admit, vague terms.[35] They note that the constraints and opportunities institutionalized in organizations' environments are both material and cultural.[36] On the one hand, some constraints can be traced to the power of the state or industry trade associations, and some opportunities can be traced to the material rewards available in certain markets. This set of institutionalized pathways orients organization leaders to find and then follow those instrumentally rational modes of behavior that have helped other organizations to economize. On the other hand, some constraints and opportunities institutionalized in organizations' environments are social constructions of meaning, including those that identify whether any particular organization's behavior is "legitimate" or not. These institutionalized pathways orient organization leaders quite differently from the first set. They orient them to find and then follow those normatively acceptable modes of behavior that have helped other organizations to gain legitimacy in the eyes of influential outsiders (including industry leaders, investment bankers, state officials, and public influentials). In addition, these pathways may also help the constituents of organizations to attach some shared meaning to what they are doing, particularly when they are not acting in ways that are strictly economizing or instrumentally rational.[37]

In 1977 Meyer and Rowan called this second set of pathways "myths." Ever since, institutionalists have frequently implied that "myths" institutionalized in organizations' environments account in some part for the behavior of for-profit organizations and, in larger part, for the behavior of nonprofits. More important, institutionalists insist that organization agents and constituents can cognitively grasp the content of the myths institutionalized in their sector—irrespective of whether this content is symbolic or instrumental, ritualistic or economizing. Organization agents can recognize and understand the responsibilities or obligations that institutionalized myths impose on anyone in their position, even when the pathways of organizational behavior that capture their attention have little affective or emotional impact on them personally.[38]

Indeed, the single greatest contribution that institutionalists have made to the study of organizations and to the social sciences generally is this "cognitive turn" in accounting for organizations' fidelity to cultural or normative factors in their environments.[39] By broadening the concept of organization environments to include rituals of behavior that organization agents can cognitively recognize and understand in common—and that allow them to bear responsibilities or obligations in the absence of any immediate economic payoff—institutionalists finally opened up a way of distancing their approach to organizations from that of neoclassical economists. They also opened up a way of returning theorists of culture to the dialogue, by refining the contributions of Durkheim, Parsons, and others who had attributed orderly relations of social and economic exchange to individual internalization of commonly held, appropriate norms and values.[40]

As we have seen, then, institutionalists hold that the ritual content of modern social orders, to say nothing of the instrumentally rational content, presents the occupants of organizational positions with standards of behavior that they can recognize and understand *in common* without having to internalize the same substantive normative beliefs. With this cognitive turn, institutionalists have indeed carved out an area of empirical study distinct from existing "culturalist" or "normativist" approaches to social order. Today, institutionalists concentrate on how organization agents adapt the behavior of their organizations to institutionalized myths and rituals within particular social sectors. Institutionalists do not hold that norms institutionalized within a sector are so constraining that all particular organizations in this sector adopt the same routines in response. Rather, they see the effects of these norms being more diffuse, either broadly constraining all organization agents in a sector or else broadly opening legitimate opportunities to all of them. Because this view of the relationship between sectoral myths and organizational behavior is so general, Meyer, Scott, and Deal acknowledged in 1981 that the institutional approach is "often vague and ambiguous," offering researchers more "an interpretation than precise direction."[41]

Institutionalists' Four Difficulties

Despite the promise of their cognitive turn and the importance of their effort to provide a normativist account of social order, institutionalists still face the difficulty that they inherited from open systems theory. That is, they must still distinguish the qualitative, ritualistic effects of cultural and normative pressures institutionalized in environments from the quantitative, economizing effects of competitive and coercive pressures that come from markets as well as from the state and industry associations. That this remains a problem for institutionalists is clear by the indiscriminate ways in which they use the terms "rational" and "rationalization."[42] For example, they frequently associate with institutionalized environments "rationalized rules and requirements" that "closely resemble technical rules."[43] Here they try to convey two points simultaneously: First, they suggest that organization agents typically want their organizations to appear rational in a narrow, technical sense because this appearance conveys to influential outsiders (such as investment bankers) that their organizations are economically competitive. They suggest as well, however, that organization agents believe that this appearance simultaneously (1) provides organization constituents with a shared sense of purpose or meaning, and (2) enhances the organization's legitimacy in the eyes of other influential outsiders—in this case, for example, the accreditation committees of professional associations.[44]

Institutionalists are therefore hindered in drawing any distinctions between the consequences that these two sets of external pressures have on organizational behavior in practice.[45] They lack the concepts with which to rule out neoclassical economists' competing explanation for all organizational behavior, namely that organization agents adopt *only* those "rituals" or models of behavior that prove over time to increase their organization's economic competitiveness.[46] This is why Scott concluded in 1987 that even though institutional theory is no longer in its infancy, it is still seeking its bearings in adolescence. We can see this absence of concepts clearly in Powell's recent discussion of "networks of learning" in and around biotechnology companies.[47] These companies establish and maintain ties (both contractual and informal) with researchers in related organizations (universities, independent research laboratories, pharmaceutical companies) because this keeps them competitive economically in their field. Whatever "legitimacy" this also brings these companies, in the eyes of other researchers, is very much a secondary consideration. That is, at the moment that these companies' managers find that it is sounder on economic grounds to restrict research activity to in-house divisions, these networks will end; concerns about "legitimacy" will not be sufficient to sustain them.

Beyond this difficulty that institutionalists inherited from open systems theory, they face three other difficulties that pose even greater problems for researchers who wish to work within this approach. Only by overcoming all three difficulties can institutional theory mature, and thereby orient methodical historical and crossnational studies of the relationship between organizational behavior and institutional change.

Institutionalists' first difficulty speaks to the issue we just raised about Powell's recent work. Institutionalists need to identify the specific contexts in which organization agents' concerns about their organization's "legitimacy" take precedence over their more immediate (and material) interests in increasing their organization's economic competitiveness. When exactly do organization agents opt to enhance their organization's legitimacy even when this compromises their organization's economic performance? Furthermore, can social scientists identify when the "legitimacy" of a particular organization either increases or decreases over time? Are all standards of legitimacy relative to time, place, and organization function or task? Or is there some general standard of legitimacy that social scientists may credibly apply to organizations in the United States and other advanced societies in historical and crossnational perspective?

Institutionalists' second difficulty is to explain why the state or, certainly, any industry association ever rewards organization agents for insulating or "decoupling" divisions of their organizations from the "rationalizing" pressures of domestic and international markets. As did Meyer and Rowan in 1977, institutionalists tend to see all such strategies as "ritualistic." They see such organizational behavior as driven by "myths" rather than by systemic pressures to economize. The term "myths" conveys that when norms are institutionalized in a sector, they yield rituals or cultural practices that are more idiosyncratic than general. They are idiosyncratic to particular organizations, or to this one sector, or, possibly, to one particular national culture; they are not found elsewhere.[48] *The term conveys that organizational and sectoral rituals are driven by substantive norms of behavior, idiosyncratic to time and place or culture, rather than by procedural norms of behavior that span all democratic social orders but are absent in other social orders.*

The term "myths" thus conveys that existing rituals, whatever their content, likely advance the informal, largely hidden agendas of particular organization agents and constituents. After all, it is difficult to imagine that the rituals of organizations—as behavioral responses to "myths" institutionalized in their environments—advance any organizational goal that agents would willingly discuss openly with shareholders or, say, investment bankers. If any behavioral responses to "myths" actually do advance publicly defensible organizational or institutional purposes, institutionalists have yet to identify at a conceptual level (1) what those "myths" are, (2) what their purposes might be, and (3) which "environmental agents" publicly support those purposes and myths.

Finally, we will see in this volume that the U.S. corporate judiciary functions as a critically important "environmental agent" for corporations and other major intermediary associations in U.S. civil society. It has endeavored to specify the corporation's legitimate place and purpose in U.S. civil society. To this end, it has endeavored to justify imposing norms of behavior—what judges call "fiduciary duties"—on corporate managers and other corporate agents that clearly cannot be reduced, either in principle or in practice, to their efforts to economize. We will see that these norms are not "myths." They are not idiosyncratic to time and place; their institutionalization within and across social sectors is precisely what distinguishes a fully institutionalized democracy from formal democracies, to say nothing of more imposed social orders. We will also see that this process of institutionalization is not guaranteed by isomorphic pressures of any kind but is contingent in the United States and in every other advanced society. Furthermore, as I have indicated, the U.S. corporate judiciary is currently "drifting" away from contributing to this process of institutionalization for the first time in its history. Thus, we will see that the United States is in the midst of a process of institutional change that is eluding institutionalists' attention because of the concepts they employ.

The third difficulty for institutionalists is even broadly to characterize the *direction* of change of organizations, social sectors, institutionalized routines, or the larger social order. That is, ironically, they have difficulty establishing why either organizational homogeneity or organizational heterogeneity really matters. They may suggest in broad strokes that organizational heterogeneity is consistent with a democratic social order and that organizational homogeneity presages an "iron cage." But they fail to identify thresholds of organizational heterogeneity that distinguish democratic social orders from more imposed social orders. Therefore, their calls for greater organizational heterogeneity do not follow logically from their own characterizations of isomorphism. These calls are instead ad hoc appeals, strictly subjective or ideological.[49]

On the other hand, it is logical to suggest, as they do, that isomorphism with respect to institutionalized routines is consistent with orderliness, with orderly relations of social and economic exchange as such. Yet, even here they face a problem. They appreciate that the institutional environments of specifically democratic social orders are not only differentiated by function but are also dynamic in substance. They change not only across a generation but often within shorter time periods. Because of this, however, organizational isomorphism with respect to the substantive rituals or the "culture" of a social sector at one moment in time may very well limit the capacity to adapt later to domestic and international competition. Isomorphism is as likely to presage institutional and organizational crises as it is to guarantee orderly relations of social and economic exchange, let alone relations that contribute automatically to institutionalizing democracy more fully in civil society.

We will see in the next chapter that social scientists may distinguish a fully institutionalized democracy from more imposed social orders by finding out whether a particular form of organization is present within intermediary associations. This approach is advantageous since social scientists cannot draw this distinction directly, in substance, by pointing to whether an organization's economic competitiveness is increasing or decreasing, to whether organizational "rituals" common to all modern societies are being followed or not, or to whether the state is effective or ineffective in "handling the [purported] basic problems of the country."[50] After all, patently authoritarian regimes can contain economically competitive organizations that also mimic the architectural design and landscaping of their counterparts in democratic social orders, and their states can also solve basic problems (as defined popularly by the vast majority of their populations).

Notes

1. See two collections, by Elkin and Soltan (1993) and Soltan and Elkin (1996), on the "new constitutionalism" in political science, an effort to return that discipline to the larger concerns of earlier generations.

2. See Chancellor Allen (1993).

3. Durkheim's contemporary Maurice Halbwachs posed what today sounds like the more correct position about substantive social norms, namely that they are more group-specific than society-wide. See Halbwachs (1992) for a collection of works edited by Lewis Coser. See also essays by Iwona Irwin-Zarecka (1996) and Suzanne Vromen (1996) for applications of Halbwachs's ideas to the contemporary study of groups' different "collective memories" of historical events and national monuments.

4. For a clear statement regarding why ethnomethodologists criticized Parsons and why today they have greater affection for Bourdieu's social theory, despite its structural and functional elements, see Cicourel (1993).

5. Sheldon Stryker (1980) is an important exception in the literature because he argues that interactionists have to find some way to accommodate broader contributions to order—"structural" factors—at a theoretical level. Close to Stryker is Anselm Strauss's notion (1978) that order is "negotiated" even when it appears to be structurally driven. Cicourel (1993) finds promise in Bourdieu's work precisely because he endeavors to synthesize structural and interactionist accounts of order rather than cutting as many bridges to interactionism as Parsons had done. Bourdieu (1979, 1989), however, ends up with an account of social order that revolves around power and "symbolic violence," the power to manipulate symbols of prestige or "distinction." Anthony Giddens argues (1979, 1984) that people gain a sense of "ontological security" by participating in everyday routines, and this accounts— somehow—for social order overall. Giddens is not clear about the linkage and, like the classic social theorists earlier and Bourdieu today, he offers no answer to the problem of democratic social order in a global economy. Murray Milner (1996) notes that even otherwise iconoclastic postmodern theorists accept the lived reality of local understandings. How postmodernists account for social order overall is anyone's guess.

6. The most succinct statement remains that by Hechter (1987). He attributes group solidarity to two factors: the controls that leaders exercise over members, and members' degree of dependence on the group for access to valued goods. See Coleman (1990) for a grander elaboration of rational choice theory.

7. See the collection edited by Powell and DiMaggio (1991).

8. Legal scholars use the terms "positional interests," "positional power," and "positional conflicts" in ways that are quite consistent with sociologists' uses of these and related concepts. For instance, network analyst David Knoke emphasizes

that individuals may exercise "positional power" even when they are not subjectively aware that they are doing so (Knoke 1990:9–10). Mark Granovetter (1990:99) prefers the term "embeddedness" to the term "position," but his point is consistent with Knoke's: He studies individuals' "relational embeddedness" within their local settings, and then he studies the latter's "structural embeddedness" within larger organizational and institutional contexts. See Powell and Smith-Doerr (1994) for a masterful review of network approaches in economic sociology. French sociologist Pierre Bourdieu also uses the term "position" in ways that Knoke, Granovetter, and U.S. legal scholars can support. He refers often to a "relationally defined position" (1979, 1989). Given that he explicitly distinguishes "position" from the broader terms "field" and "market," he would certainly accept that "position" must also be distinguished from the narrower terms "self-interest" and "subjective interest."

   9. Knoke (1981:308–309, quoted by Jepperson and Meyer 1991:230–231, note 5).

   10. I do not explore either of these alternative approaches here because neither departs as dramatically from principles of neoclassical economics. Neither approach deals as centrally as does the new institutionalism with the norms that frame organizational behavior. See Sciulli (1997b) on how population ecologists and institutionalists use the term "organization form."

   11. See Scott (1994) more generally on "law and organizations." Consider Scott's opening (1994:3): "Although the godfather of organization theory, Max Weber, pointed to the close association of law and organizations nearly a century ago, the great bulk of theory and research on organizations has failed to honor or build on this legacy. Only occasionally have analysts sought to link organizational and legal scholarship, and until quite recently, such efforts have not been regarded as mainstream but as marginal."

   12. DiMaggio and Powell (1983:149).

   13. DiMaggio and Powell (1983:150–152).

   14. Powell (1991:195). See Chapter 3, page 53 for critical comments on institutionalists' concern with "recognized sources of authority."

   15. DiMaggio and Powell (1983:147–149).

   16. DiMaggio and Powell (1983:158; also 1991:8).

   17. Scott and Meyer (1991); Scott (1991:171–172).

   18. DiMaggio and Powell (1983:147–149, 156).

   19. DiMaggio (1988:10).

   20. Powell (1991:195).

   21. See Stinchcombe (1990:2–3, 345–347).

   22. Victor Perez-Diaz (1993:39, 50) uses the term "institutional design" similarly, but without defining it. One definition is an amended version of Charles Anderson's "criteria of good design in the creation of political forms" (1979:275). I amend Anderson by inserting "social order" in brackets where he uses "political structure" and "political construction": "What we are looking for are principles of [social order] that have essentially the same standing as principles of design in architecture, canons of good practice that are not beyond criticism, that necessarily will reflect diverse schools of thought, but that nonetheless stand as a basis for appraising . . . any [social order]." More generally, see the collections edited by Elkin and Soltan (1993) and Soltan and Elkin (1996).

   23. The same criticism was leveled at Parsons in the 1950s, and today it is leveled at Bourdieu. See the collection edited by Calhoun, LiPuma, and Postone (1993), plus Calhoun (1995:132–161).

   24. Social scientists who study "civil society" share the same conceptual limitation, e.g., Perez-Diaz (1993), Seligman (1992), and Keane (1988). John Keane is

typical in the general way that he defines civil society, namely as "an aggregate of institutions whose members are engaged primarily in a complex of non-state activities—economic and cultural production, household life and voluntary associations—and who in this way preserve and transform their identity by exercising all sorts of pressures or controls upon state institutions" (1988:14). The issue is whether *democratic* social orders contain unique "aggregates of institutions," those not found in other modern social orders. See Schmitter (1983) for what he acknowledges is an unsuccessful effort to identify the *quality* of the relationship between rulers and ruled within Western democracies.

25. Some earlier institutionalists (such as Philip Selznick and Alvin Gouldner) treated organizations as open systems but also adopted a more critical stance toward the larger social order (see Chapter 3, pages 53–58). Thus, in many respects, there have been three periods of postwar institutionalism in the sociology of organizations: First, during the immediate postwar period, institutionalists retained a critical stance toward the larger social order by seeing a "mass society" or "working-class authoritarianism" potentially threatening democracy. Second, during the rise of open systems theory from the early 1960s to the mid-1970s, institutionalists replaced this broader concern with a narrower emphasis on group conflict within organizations. Finally, in the current period that began in 1977, institutionalists de-emphasize the importance of intra-organizational disputes and assume at a conceptual level, with neoclassical economists, that existing democracies are immutable.

26. See Scott (1981:18–23) for more elaborate definitions. Organizations that are natural systems typically fail to articulate clear goals or to operate with written rules. Scott's examples (from Rothschild-Witt 1979) are free medical clinics, alternative schools, rape counseling centers, and legal collectives (1981:21).

27. Scott (1981:22–23).

28. Scott (1991:165).

29. I distinguish intermediary associations from the larger category of organizations in the next chapter.

30. Scott (1987:507).

31. See note 26 for how this differs from "natural systems."

32. Scott (1991:165).

33. Scott (1987:507).

34. Powell (1991:183–185).

35. For example, see Meyer, Scott, and Deal (1981/1983:60).

36. This is like Bourdieu holding (1989) that the "field of power" revolves around two poles, one anchored by economic capital and the other anchored by symbolic capital.

37. Friedland and Alford (1991:243).

38. Zucker (1977/1991:85); Friedland and Alford (1991:249); Jepperson (1991:143, 147). We will see in Chapter 3 that institutionalists' presupposition that established practices can be recognized and understood in common by organizational leaders moves far beyond the scope of application of their own concepts.

39. Meyer, Scott, and Deal (1981/1983:46–48); DiMaggio and Powell (1991:19).

40. See Warner (1978) for an early call for Parsons to take a cognitive turn.

41. Meyer, Scott, and Deal (1981/1983:60). Endeavoring in 1987 to be more specific, Richard Scott presents seven ways in which environmental influences can affect organizations (1987:501–507). Scott's listing does not advance the present discussion. For more recent applications of the institutional approach, see Kamens, Meyer, and Benavot (1996) on secondary schools, and Powell, Koput, and Smith-Doerr (1996) on biotechnology firms.

42. See Sciulli (1997c).

43. Scott (1983:160).

44. Ibid.

45. See DiMaggio (1994) on the difficulty of identifying "cultural" influences on economic structures and practices.

46. Scott (1987:504–505); also Zucker (1977/1991:104).

47. Powell, Koput, and Smith-Doerr (1996).

48. See the Ouchi and Wilkins (1985) review of the literature on organization cultures. Institutionalists, following Bourdieu, probably prefer the term "organization habitus" to "organization culture," but both terms refer to the substantive normative beliefs that constituents share within particular organizations.

49. For example, see DiMaggio and Powell (1983:158). The same is true of John Keane's treatment of pluralism as an ultimate end of civil society (1988:preface). Aside from failing to identify thresholds of group pluralism that distinguish democratic social orders from more imposed social orders, Keane's call for greater diversity as an end in itself leaves him with three insurmountable problems at a conceptual level. First, he defines the ideal democracy—that is, a socialist democracy—as "a differentiated and pluralistic system of power, wherein decisions of interest to collectivities of various sizes are made *autonomously* by *all* their members" (1988:3, my emphasis). This definition runs counter to Michels's well-established iron law of oligarchy. Second, Keane contradicts his own reference to group "autonomy" when he refers to civil society on the same page as a "realm of social activities that are legally organized and guaranteed by the state." What does group autonomy then mean? Autonomy from whom or what? Third, citing Walzer (1983), Keane argues that "a pluralist conception of equality" means that different institutional mechanisms distribute different goods to different people in different ways and for different reasons (1988:13). Going further, he labels as "neo-conservative" *any* suggestion that a democratic civil society is marked by particular forms and practices (1988:14). I show in the next two chapters that institutionalized democracies are distinguished from more imposed social orders by the presence of intermediary associations that contain collegial formations or deliberative bodies.

50. Perez-Diaz (1993:54); see also Streeck and Schmitter (1985), and Schmitter (1983:895–896).

2

Overcoming
Conceptual Limitations

The significance of the efforts of institutionalists to bring the classical problem of social order back into the center of social theory cannot be overstated.[1] As we have seen, they insist that substantive norms of behavior can be institutionalized across a social sector without being internalized in common by the individuals occupying organizational positions. They thus advance social theory beyond Durkheim's and Parsons's emphasis on the importance of socialization and internalization.[2] Institutionalists do not go far enough, however, in updating the project of classical social theory. Ironically, the obstacle they face today is the classics' own problem of social order itself—that is, the question, "What holds society together?" This question is too broad or too crude to orient social theory beyond the classics' materialist and normativist responses.[3] If a theory of social order and social change is to advance today, and in particular in the face of the challenges posed to Durkheim and Parsons by interactionists and rational choice theorists, then it must be oriented by a more sharply stated problem.

I propose that the problem of social order can fruitfully be recast as the problem of democratic social order in a global economy. We are no longer asking: What holds society together? Now we are asking: What qualities in organizational environments, what institutionalized norms and practices, if any, distinguish social orders that (1) institutionalize democracy most fully across sectors of civil society, and (2) compete most effectively in a global economy?[4] The first part of this question links the problem of social order explicitly and specifically to the issue of institutional change; the second part retains a connection to the concerns of neoclassical economics. The point of combining both questions, as the problem of democratic social order in a global economy, is that institutionalists in particular should be able to tell social scientists (and legal scholars) more than neoclassical economists tell them about when organizational change either challenges or supports the institutional design of a democratic social order. When do changes in the governance and behavior of organizations exhibit fidelity to

31

institutionalized norms found uniquely in sectors of democratic societies? When do such changes encroach unambiguously against these norms, thereby challenging a democratic society's institutional design?

Institutionalists have yet to address effectively institutional change because they have yet to distinguish their approach to organizations sufficiently at a conceptual level from that of neoclassical economics (see note 3). Institutionalists tell us more about the economic competitiveness and political influence of organizations than about the contributions organizations are able to make—as governance structures and wielders of collective power in civil society—to the institutional design of a democratic society. At the same time, institutionalists themselves say repeatedly that they wish to broaden their sights, to address more methodically the issue of institutional change. They say that they wish to connect their findings regarding the relationship between organizations and institutionalized environments to the "larger concerns of sociology."[5]

Identifying Institutional Change

Formal and Institutionalized Democracies

The potential of institutionalism to account for institutional change on the basis of changes in the behavior of organizations may be realized by amending how institutionalists characterize advanced societies. Social scientists can identify shifts in the direction of institutional change if they appreciate that advanced societies may institutionalize democracy more or less fully in civil society over time. They cannot identify such shifts by wondering, instead, whether advanced societies institutionalize "modernity" more or less fully over time.[6]

By definition, as democracy becomes more fully institutionalized in civil society, norms, routines, and practices in more and more sectors broadly support not only limited government but also citizen vigilance over arbitrary exercises of collective power. As Princeton political scientist Amy Gutman puts the issue: "Constitutional democracy does not advise endless participation among citizens, but it does advise eternal vigilance."[7] Maryland political scientist Stephen Elkin likewise writes: "Limiting political power is at the heart of a constitutional regime. Moreover, in considering how this may be done, the character of the citizenry will prove to be crucial, so that the formative effects of political institutions will receive attention."[8]

Rather than attempting to define directly, in ideal typical terms, the two basic qualities of democratic social orders—limited political power and citizen vigilance—social scientists can focus their attention on a single factor irreducible to either quality. As democracy becomes more fully institutionalized in civil society, norms of behavior will be institutionalized in more and more sectors that, *at the very least,* mediate public *and private* exercises of collective power short of abuse and arbitrariness. *This* normative mediation in organizations' institutionalized environments not only keeps government limited. It also provides dispersed citizens with the types of routines and practices in their everyday lives that makes it possible for them to remain vigilant, to develop and maintain the character unique to a democratic citizenry.

Clearly, any sector of society in which private corporations tolerate or encourage arbitrariness by management (or shareholder majorities) can hardly be said to support, merely by the fact of its existence, the institutional design of a democratic social order. We cannot assume that this sector necessarily contributes to the character formation of a democratic citizenry and thereby helps to keep government limited and responsible.[9] Nevertheless, this same sector may well be eminently "modern," may well contribute to a society's economic competitiveness.

Spanish social scientist Victor Perez-Diaz comes closest to identifying democratic social orders in this way. He distinguishes "consolidated democracies" (formal democracies) from "institutionalized democracies" (democratic social orders).[10] In his view, democracy is consolidated when a social order no longer contains any credible threats to formally democratic government; that is, when regularly held elections, competing political parties, pluralist or corporatist group competition for influence, and government's general fidelity to the rule of law can all be expected to proceed unhindered.[11] A democracy is institutionalized, on the other hand, when most individuals in society internalize basic democratic rules of the game, thereby becoming self-disciplining.[12]

This distinction is promising, but Perez-Diaz's way of defining institutionalized democracy, like Elkin's characterization, needs to be amended in light of our discussion of institutionalism's advance beyond Durkheim and Parsons. Perez-Diaz defines institutionalized democracy by turning immediately to a social psychological factor, namely whether individuals internalize appropriate norms of behavior. The social psychological turn, however, makes it unnecessarily difficult for social scientists to distinguish democratic social orders from formal democracies in historical and cross-national perspective. It makes it literally impossible for them to recognize transitions between democratic social orders and more imposed social orders, beyond observing whether the formalities of democratic government remain in place or not.

After all, social scientists have no way of identifying when a sufficient number of individuals in any given generation actually internalize the appropriate norms of behavior. Nor can they identify when putatively successful patterns of primary socialization either continue over time or are disrupted by events (whether by increasing rates of divorce and single-parent families, accessibility and quality of child care, vagaries of popular culture, or unemployment, underemployment, and general disruptions in the economy).[13] Moreover, why is it not possible for more and more individuals who have been socialized "properly" nonetheless to be subjected to arbitrariness in a growing number of private organizations in civil society? If this is possible, on what basis can we simply assume that such individuals will somehow automatically retain the qualities of a vigilant citizenry?

We may amend Perez-Diaz's approach by substituting a quality unique to the institutional design of democratic social orders, one that social scientists can identify in historical and crossnational perspective. This same quality is consistent with institutionalists' important cognitive turn in thinking about how norms institutionalized in environments mediate organizational behavior. We will see, however, that the institutionalized norms now at issue are procedural and span democratic social orders: They are not "myths" (substantive norms) idiosyncratic to particular sectors or to particular societies. In short, we propose that an identifiable set of procedural norms distinguishes the institutional design of democratic social orders from the institutional designs of formal democracies and, even more so, of more authoritarian or imposed orders. In democratic social orders *the behavior* of individuals who hold public and private positions of power exhibits fidelity to this set of norms. Their behavior does not challenge or violate this set of norms, and their behavior matters far more than whether these same individuals have internalized those norms in common, or any other set of norms, as beliefs that members of a vigilant citizenry putatively share personally and affectively.

Illustrating the Institutional Design of Democratic Societies

The following example illustrates the importance of the conceptual distinction we are drawing between the procedural norms that distinguish democratic social orders and the "myths" or substantive norms that keep a particular modern society orderly. Consider a situation in which the managers overseeing a corporate research division ask chemists to lower their professional standards in testing a product that the corporation is under a tight deadline to develop. Managers approach chemists by appealing to chemists' "team loyalty" and also by offering them bonuses or other pecuniary incentives.[14] Moreover, let's quickly add that the product in question is not toxic; everyone knows it poses no direct or indirect harm to any consumer. Let's also add that even though the product is inadequately tested by professional standards, it nonetheless ends up meeting consumer expectations, as projected by corporate managers.

We propose that in this situation managers exercise power arbitrarily over chemists. Put more technically, they exercise their positional power arbitrarily over the corporation's research division. The arbitrariness of their exercise of power is indicated by the fact that they are not likely to publicize their appeal to the chemists even within the corporation, let alone outside it. In this instance, then, managers exercise positional power arbitrarily even if most (or all) chemists in the division accept management's legitimacy, consider managers' request to be consistent with their own subjective desires, and receive compensation for complying, both materially and symbolically.

It is the corporate judiciary that monitors generally how directors and top managers structure the governance of corporations. It does not monitor the behavior of particular managers at particular moments—for example, the governance of corporate research divisions as in the illustration at hand. In this case the managers' behavior is more likely to be brought to the attention of regulatory agencies (particularly the Food and Drug Administration) than to state courts. Nonetheless, our illustration begins to reveal one of the central concerns of the corporate judiciary. At times it intervenes into what judges and legal scholars call "governance disputes," disputes between corporate boards and sitting management teams, on one side, and shareholders and other corporate constituents (called stakeholders), on the other. Put more specifically, the corporate judiciary monitors how managers structure the relationship between their own positions of power and the positions occupied by shareholders, bondholders, middle managers, and long-term suppliers. The corporate judiciary appreciates that corporate managers act not only self-interestedly, endeavoring to advance their own personal interests and beliefs. Corporate managers also act on what judges and legal scholars call "positional interests."[15]

We can appreciate how the corporate judiciary views management by considering an analogy to the presidency of the United States. Irrespective of any particular president's personal beliefs and sense of self-interest, any individual occupying this position is aware that its current relationship to positions of power in other branches of government is not immutable. It can change over time. Any president, therefore, endeavors at least to maintain, if not to increase, the relative power of the position he occupies vis-à-vis Congress and the courts.

The situation is similar when we consider the relationship between top managers and other corporate constituents. Any member of a corporate board and sitting management team also endeavors at least to maintain, if not to increase, the power of the position that he or she occupies vis-à-vis shareholders and stakeholders.[16] This holds true even when particular top managers personally are "corporate statesmen," willing to subordinate their self-interests to the interests of the corporate entity. Even these managers will typically endeavor to advance their positional interests against those of other constituents.[17] Our point is that state courts at times intervene into the governance of corporations when top managers go too far, when they set up a governance structure in which only their positional interests can possibly prevail against shareholders and stakeholders.

The courts have declared that corporate managers exercise positional power unfairly or arbitrarily in various situations, including the following five:[18] (1) when managers make it exceedingly difficult for shareholders, bondholders, or long-term suppliers objectively to monitor their performance; (2) when managers erect high barriers to their own removal for poor performance; (3) when managers endeavor to increase the size of the corporation, thereby increasing their position's power, prestige, and salary, as opposed to increasing shareholders' wealth; (4) when managers otherwise maximize the capital and resources at their control rather than distributing corporate wealth to shareholders as dividends; and (5) when managers diversify their corporations' divisions at shareholders' expense in order to ensure the importance of their positions in their firms. The courts intervene in these situations and in others not because they think they know better how to manage corporations. They intervene because they appreciate that managers' positional interests inherently diverge from those of shareholders and stakeholders, and the courts do not want managers to "have the power to unilaterally determine or materially vary the rules that govern those divergencies of interest."[19]

This principle of corporate governance accounts for the decision by Delaware's Supreme Court in 1985 to impose a multimillion dollar *personal* liability on the directors of Trans Union Corporation. This corporation's board approved a merger seemingly in shareholders' interests.[20] The court feared, however, that Trans Union's CEO, Van Gorkom, had initiated the merger in order to cash in his own shares in the company before he retired—not in order to advance the interests of shareholders, other constituents, or the corporate entity. The court's point was not to deny that shareholders generally had benefited. Its point in sanctioning the board was that directors had not kept informed about what the CEO was doing. The board had violated a basic norm of corporate law doctrine, what judges and legal scholars call the board's "fiduciary duty of loyalty" to the corporate entity as a distinct "person" in civil society. Like other persons, the corporate entity has "its" own interests and the board had failed, as one part of the corporation's governance structure, to maintain the integrity of its deliberations in identifying and then serving those interests, against the CEO's exercise of positional power.[21] Put more technically, the board had failed, as we will see in the next chapter, to maintain its own collegial form of organization.

Identifying the Institutional Design of Democratic Societies

Whether a corporate governance structure permits top managers to exercise their positional power arbitrarily is a matter of institutional design. It is not a matter of the social psychology of particular managers or of the local culture in which particular managers (or other corporate constituents) operate.[22] Permission to exercise power in a certain way in a certain instance is a matter of the *quality* of the rules or duties that managers impose on corporate constituents *through the corporation's governance structure*. Thus, constituents' social constructions of meaning, of their opinions about the legitimacy of managers' behavior or of the rules and duties sanctioned by the corporation's governance structure, are irrelevant. How managers and corporate constituents come to see things intersubjectively is ultimately a substantive normative issue and, therefore, a social psychological issue. This latter question thus involves (1) how managers and constituents were raised, what their personal beliefs happen to be; and (2) their local cultures, their subjective senses of "honor."[23] By contrast, whether a corporation's governance structure permits managers to advance their positional interests against shareholders and stakeholders in ways that are unfair or arbitrary is, on the other hand, ultimately a procedural normative issue. It is a matter of how the relationship between corporate positions is structured, irrespective of the personal beliefs, constructions of meaning, and senses of honor of the individuals occupying these positions.

We propose that social scientists (and judges) can use a threshold of procedural norms as a fixed standard by which to identify when the governance structures of corporations either support or challenge the institutional design of a democratic social order. A corporation supports the institutional design of a democratic social order when, as managers advance their positional interests through its governance structure, the rules or duties that managers impose on shareholders and stakeholders share the following attributes: They are publicly declared, intelligible, enforced generally rather than unevenly, prospective, capable of being performed, relatively constant rather than more ad hoc, compatible with each other rather than contradictory, and consistent with managers' actual behavior.[24]

These eight procedural norms can provide a useful, reliable standard. At the moment that a corporation's governance structure permits a sitting management team to impose rules or duties on shareholders or stakeholders that lack any one of these qualities, this corporate entity has crossed an identifiable *threshold*. The corporation's constituents can no longer take steps within the corporate entity to protect themselves from management's exercises of positional power. Individual shareholders, of course, can exit the corporation rather easily, by selling their stock. But new shareholders, whether wittingly or not, enter the same structured relationship among positions that the sellers left.

More important for present purposes, individual middle managers often cannot exit as easily or costlessly, by securing employment elsewhere. This difference in principle between shareholders and middle managers (and, as we will see, other stakeholders) is important and merits closer inspection.

Seen from the shareholder's position, a corporation appears to be a site of fluid contracting. But seen from the position of middle managers and other stakeholders, the same corporation appears to be a site of structured situations. This is the case because the *situation* in which a middle manager (or other stakeholder) finds himself or herself is more *structured* than the situation in which any shareholder finds himself or herself. Any middle manager is more dependent than any shareholder on the protections accorded to his or her position in the corporation's governance structure. The middle manager's position, that is, is inherently one of greater dependence and trust. Irrespective of whatever protections any particular middle manager may gain explicitly from top management, by "contract," all middle managers occupy positions of dependence. Ultimately, they have no alternative other than to trust top managers to act in good faith or disinterestedly in identifying the best interests of the corporate entity, as opposed to acting more unilaterally, in their own positional interests.

The same thing is even more true of bondholders, long-term suppliers, and retirees (and, of course, local communities, which are also corporate constituents). These constituents cannot exit a corporation even as costlessly as middle managers; their situations are even more structured. This means that any bondholder, supplier, or retiree is even more dependent on whatever protections their positions are accorded in the corporation's governance structure.

The corporate judiciary, then, sees the corporation as a site of structured situations, and not exclusively as a site of fluid contracting. This approach to corporate power accounts for why the corporate judiciary intervenes into governance disputes.

In light of the eight procedural norms just presented, we may consider again out illustrations of possible arbitrariness in corporate governance. In the case of the corporate research division, these managers are not likely to declare publicly what they are asking chemists to do. Moreover, their treatment of the chemists appears to be ad hoc, more site-specific than constant, and thereby atypical of their treatment of other professionals employed by the corporation. In the case of the managers who ensure that their positional interests prevail over those of shareholders and stakeholders, these managers too are not likely to declare publicly that they have effectively insulated themselves from oversight. Furthermore, in the absence of a public declaration of how they intend to exercise their positional power, including a formal declaration by the board, it is not possible for shareholders and particularly for stakeholders to recognize and understand *prospectively* how they might protect their positions.

It is relevant here that shareholders can exit on short notice by selling their shares, but that stakeholders find themselves in situations of greater dependence and trust. It is significant that stakeholders are also citizens. As citizens of democratic social orders, they are relied upon to develop and maintain a shared recognition and understanding of when collective power is exercised arbitrarily. If they experience arbitrariness routinely in their everyday lives, can they be said to recognize it and understand it? If so, can we assume that they share this recognition and understanding with other citizens?

The quality of vigilance that presumably distinguishes the citizens of democratic social orders from the citizens of other social orders is a product of institutional design, the relationship that extends from the state to civil society. It is not a product of any shared social psychology or shared culture capable of spanning citizens (and organizations) irrespective of a society's institutional design. This is why it is misleading to think of this quality as being a product of "myths" institutionalized in organizational environments. The term "myths" applies more appropriately to substantive normative beliefs that particular people share in a particular setting—about acceptable ways to raise children, the importance of education or career, preferred cuisines, or styles of music and dance. Such shared beliefs are more or less idiosyncratic to time and place, and Bourdieu captures this idiosyncrasy well with his term "habitus." A habitus is a local culture that particular people find familiar and that outsiders (anthropologists) might come to understand but can never truly "live."

By contrast, because the quality unique to democratic social orders is a matter of institutional design, it spans all such orders. The norms in question are institutionalized in civil society such that, at the very least, they mediate both public and private exercises of collective power short of arbitrariness. Democracy is formal or consolidated—and not institutionalized—in civil society when procedural norms (and then corporate governance structures) fail to mediate private arbitrariness by large organizations. Indeed, as the examples above illustrate, it is likely that all advanced societies today are unevenly institutionalized in this sense. No advanced society, including the United States, yet institutionalizes democracy fully, across all sectors of civil society. In sum, advanced social orders will differ in the extents to which the procedural norms in question are institutionalized in each sector of their civil societies.[25]

Consolidated and Institutional Democracies Revisited

We have grounded our discussion in Perez-Diaz's distinction between consolidated democracy and institutional democracy, replacing his social psychological orientation with an institutional standard. We may now distinguish democratic social orders from formal democracies and more imposed social orders. A democratic social order contains corporations whose internal governance, *at the very least,* supports those procedural norms already institutionalized in their environments that mediate private exercises of collective power short of arbitrariness. By contrast, the corporations of a formal democracy (to say nothing of a more imposed social order) lack governance structures of *this* type. Equally important, the procedural normative mediation we have noted is not institutionalized in corporations' environments in formal democracies and imposed orders. As we have seen, as the managers of corporations in formal democracies endeavor to maximize either growth or dividends, their governance structures fail to mediate their exercises of positional power short of arbitrariness. In turn, stakeholders experience an arbitrariness in their everyday lives that enervates rather than supports the shared sense of vigilance that purportedly distinguishes the citizens of democratic social orders. The behavior of corporate managers and others who hold positions of power in civil society, we propose, tells us more about impending shifts in the direction of institutional change than do individuals' subjective beliefs regarding their situation or their intersubjective constructions of meaning.

Whether corporate governance structures become isomorphic with institutionalized procedural norms that mediate managers' exercises of positional power short of arbitrariness is, for each sector of a modern civil society, an eminently empirical issue. This line of empirical inquiry can inform historical and crossnational comparisons across advanced societies as well as across each sector of a particular society. "Procedural rules for political decisions, in order to exist at all, have to be 'really sociologically' compatible with and supported by the cultural and economic structures of a society." That is, "they must continuously stand the test of their real recognition."[26] By applying the threshold of the eight procedural norms discussed earlier to the ways that corporate boards and sitting management teams exercise positional power, social scientists can identify whether arbitrariness is increasing or decreasing in corporate governance structures—independently of the more speculative issues of whether an increasing or decreasing number of individuals have internalized appropriate substantive norms of behavior.

Does this approach demand too much of corporate managers? Is managers' fidelity to the threshold of procedural norms an ideal, or is it a standard of actual behavior that can truly inform empirical research? An anonymous reviewer posed exactly this point when reading an earlier draft of this chapter, and this counterargument merits attention:

> The list of laws and other sanctioned duties that remain consistent with the threshold . . . seems unusually heroic given the confusions, misinterpretations, misunderstandings, and implicit contradictions that occur in all organizational actions. The list demands general prescriptions, not particular or ad hoc demands. But does this mean that particular rather than general prescriptions are irrelevant, when particular ones are frequent and commonplace? . . . [T]here is considerable support for the so-called "garbage can" model of organizations from the seminal work of James March, following insights of Herbert Simon, and developed by March,

Olsen and Cohen. These processes assume that goals cannot be given stable ranks, cannot be clearly defined, that information as to reaching them is seriously incomplete, and the means of reaching them, even with good information, are often not known. It would be an extaordinary organization if laws and sanctioned duties were always, or even very often, congruent with actual enforcement or administration. . . . Agents may not think that they are behaving arbitrarily and may not want to behave arbitrarily, but have no clear way of knowing what is arbitrary and what is not under these circumstances. The criteria may set an impossibly high standard of nonarbitrary power, achievable only in the mythic situation of complete routine, complete information, complete rationality and complete transparency.[27]

Bearing this objection in mind, let us return to our first illustration of arbitrary corporate governance, the management of a research division. Regardless of all of the confusions, contingencies, and misunderstandings that might beset corporate managers in such a situation, it is simply not normative in democratic social orders for them to ask chemists to feign professional behavior. If it were normative, corporate managers would be willing to publicize their request within the corporation and then outside. On the other hand, consider the breadth of options that the threshold of procedural norms permits managers, consistent with any democratic social order. Corporate managers are free to ask chemists to test any product they wish, including ones that are potentially toxic (but meet with regulatory approval). They may change their minds about these products in midstream and call upon chemists to move entirely to a new line of research and development. They may promote or demote chemists as they wish, market the product with whatever advertising campaign they wish, and develop the product in house or on a subcontract basis. Our point is that corporate managers would not likely feel threatened by normative beliefs institutionalized in their environment if any or all of these actions became public knowledge.

Likewise, in the example of governance disputes between managers and shareholders or stakeholders, the threshold of procedural norms does not hold corporate managers to a particularly lofty standard. Corporate managers are free to act in any way that they wish in their efforts to maximize either growth or dividends. However, when shareholders or stakeholders challenge them for acting unilaterally in their own positional interests—rather than in the best interests of the corporate entity—managers have to be able to convince the courts of two things: first, that the board of directors had been kept informed about management's actions and, second, that the board had acted fairly or disinterestedly rather than as the pawn of a self-aggrandizing management team.[28] That is, they have to convince the courts that the corporation's governance structure affords shareholders and stakeholders some opportunity to protect their own positional interests.

Most important, as we shall establish in the interior chapters of this study, the U.S. corporate judiciary does in fact impose *norms* of behavior on sitting management teams with an eye to protecting more than the positional interests of particular shareholders and stakeholders. It imposes norms on corporate management *on a public law ground,* namely that of maintaining the institutional design of a democratic social order.[29] Social scientists must thus not only describe and explain managers' actual behavior, as organization agents, but must also describe and explain the corporate judiciary's actual behavior, *as an environmental agent.*

We propose that changes in the governance of corporations (one set of organizations) and changes in the behavior of the corporate judiciary (an environmental agent) can go far toward accounting for differences in the direction of institutional change in advanced societies. More specifically, changes in the behavior of corporations and courts (or, in Europe and Japan, administrative agencies) can lead toward the formation of a more imposed social order or, conversely, toward the evolution of a more fully institutionalized democracy. We are proposing that particular advanced societies can undergo a transition toward an imposed social order even as they remain formal democracies. After all, all advanced societies today are likely to hold elections and otherwise qualify as formal democracies *even when their directions of institutional change diverge dramatically—from each other and from their own past practices.* Indeed, it is likely that the last step taken as an advanced society steadily loses the institutional design of a democratic social order will be to suspend the formalities of democratic government. Thus, social scientists should be able to draw distinctions among advanced societies well before the fate of democratic formalities becomes an issue.[30] They should be able to identify how these distinctions are manifested in the behavior of corporations in each particular sector of a society.

The first step in undertaking such a comparative study of organizational change and institutional change is to identify whether courts (or administrative agencies) intervene or fail to intervene into corporate governance disputes on the public law ground noted above. We will see in this volume that identifying these judicial interventions is central to describing and explaining the behavior of the U.S. corporate judiciary. Equally important, we will also see that this brings into view an ongoing, foreboding shift in the direction of institutional change in the United States today.

Organizations and Institutional Change: Two Distinctions

As we saw in Chapter 1, institutionalists acknowledge that they cannot identify when particular changes in organizations either anticipate or reflect institutional change. In summarizing our discussion thus far, we can now propose that they run into this obstacle only in part because they fail to distinguish the problem of democratic social order in a global economy from the classics' more general approach to social order as such. They are also hampered because they fail to distinguish (1) between intermediary associations and the larger category of organizations,[31] and (2) between institutionalized substantive norms, or "myths," and institutionalized procedural norms. Only intermediary associations have governance structures, with procedural norms, that can either support or challenge the institutional design of a democratic social order. Changes in other organizations do not carry such grand, that is, institutional, consequences.

From Organizations to Intermediary Associations

Intermediary associations bear their name because, unlike other organizations, they simultaneously mediate the state's power and broaden individuals' loyalties beyond their families and primary groups.[32] Restaurants, retail stores, and small businesses typically do not have either effect. Thus, they rarely qualify as intermediary associations.[33] By contrast, corporations and organizational sites of professional practice (such as hospitals, universities, museums, research and consulting facilities, and some governmental agencies) often qualify as intermediary associations. On the one hand, they are sites of individuals' employment and of self-interested behavior, as in other organizations. On the other hand, we also find at these sites three manifestations of private governance structures in civil society. A brief discussion of these structures—common to both professional and corporate settings—follows.

First, the positions of dependence occupied by corporate constituents and the clients of professional services contrast sharply with the more fluid commercial exchanges in which patrons and even most employees engage in restaurants and retail stores. Corporate agents (board members and top managers) and practicing professionals alike exercise power over individuals who occupy positions of dependence in ongoing *structured* situations. Only courts or administrative agencies can monitor the structure of the relationship between positions of unequal power. It is not possible for contractual guarantees of any kind (nor, certainly, for market forces alone) to reduce entirely the power differential that obtains between top managers and other corporate constituents. The same is true of the power differential that inheres in the relationship between professionals and their clients.[34]

Second, top managers and professionals potentially develop shared beliefs and ways of life, as "corporate cultures" and "professional cultures," that broaden their loyalties beyond their families and primary groups.[35] As with the ways that power is exercised, these loyalties can also encourage managers and professionals either to challenge or to support the institutionalized norms that distinguish democratic social orders from more imposed social orders. Finally, top managers and the administrators of organizational sites of professional practice both exercise their entities' collective power in civil society.

In short, intermediary associations are an identifiable subset of organizations in that they (1) contain governance structures and "cultures," both of which mediate how managers and professionals define and then act upon their own interests (personal and positional); (2) contain structured situations in which managers and professionals exercise positional power over dependents; and (3) are corporate entities that exercise collective power in the larger social order. Any organizations in civil society, and any independent governmental agencies, that exhibit these three qualities of governance qualify as intermediary associations.

This distinction between organizations generally and intermediary associations particularly opens the way for students of organizations to account for institutional change in both historical and crossnational perspective. Our first orienting hypothesis for crossnational and historical research is: *The governance of intermediary associations in democratic social orders differs empirically from the governance of intermediary associations in formal democracies and imposed social orders.* By contrast, the behavior of restaurants, retail stores, and other organizations is not likely to vary from one context to another in ways that tell us much about the direction of institutional change.

The governance of intermediary associations can either broadly support or broadly challenge the procedural norms institutionalized uniquely in democratic social orders. In turn, when the courts uphold these norms, this judicial behavior mediates short of arbitrariness (1) the state's exercise of collective power; (2) intermediary associations' own exercise of collective power; and (3) managers' and professionals' exercise of positional power in structured situations. We can thus propose a second orienting hypothesis for crossnational and historical research: *The procedural normative mediations just noted (1) will be found in a large and increasing number of sectors within institutionalized democracies; (2) will be found in a small and decreasing number of sectors within formal democracies; and (3) will be in even more rapid decline in more imposed social orders, those undergoing a transition toward an "iron cage."*

From Idiosyncratic "Myths" to a Fixed Threshold

In order to account for institutional change, in addition to distinguishing intermediary associations from the larger category of organizations, institutionalists must also sharpen considerably the concepts that they employ when describing the norms, routines, and practices institutionalized in organizations' environments. They must identify the types of norms, routines, and practices uniquely institutionalized in democratic social orders as opposed to formal democracies and more imposed orders. One way for them to accomplish this is to draw the following distinction: On the one hand, all social orders, whether institutionalized democracies, formal democracies, or more imposed orders, institutionalize substantive norms of one kind or another. All social orders mediate the economizing behavior of corporations and other intermediary associations short of disruptiveness.

This captures one part of what the classic social theorists were talking about when they accounted for social order as such. Institutionalists today are grounded in that approach when they refer to organizations' fidelity to "myths" institutionalized in their environments. All societies, after all, maintain orderly relations of economic and social exchange, and no society does so by relying exclusively on coercion or material incentives. All rely to some extent on institutionalized substantive norms of one kind or another. John Finley Scott puts the matter well: "The sociological mind reels at the cost of social controls which would have to cope with the unrestrained exercise of amoral human intelligence."[36]

On the other hand, and more important for present purposes, the threshold of procedural norms institutionalized uniquely in democratic social orders does more than simply maintain orderly relations of economic and social exchange. It anchors an institutional design, spanning the state and civil society, that distinguishes democratic social orders from formal democracies and more imposed orders. Concomitantly, an identifiable threshold of procedural norms is institutionalized uniquely in the environments of the intermediary associations of democratic social orders. This quality in these environments does not come into view when one studies the behavior of other organizations and is, moreover, obscured by institutionalists' general references to myths in organizations' environments.

When upheld by the courts, the threshold of procedural norms uniquely mediates the governance of intermediary associations short of arbitrariness. Furthermore, the threshold has this effect irrespective of whether corporate and professional behavior is otherwise economizing *or ritualistic.* Here we identify even more precisely what institutionalists have neglected in their efforts to distinguish their approach from neoclassical economics: In democratic societies even the ritualistic behavior of managers and professionals is normatively mediated short of arbitrariness when that behavior bears on the governance of intermediary associations.

Notes

1. I see institutionalists sharpening considerably the general theoretical points made earlier by Anthony Giddens and Pierre Bourdieu in linking social order to individuals' practical mastery of everyday activities.

2. When push comes to shove, both the French theorist Bourdieu and U.S. theorist Amitai Etzioni place too much emphasis on socialization and on systemic

factors. They downplay the significance of an institutional level of analysis. For Etzioni, see my book manuscript *Critical Functionalism: Etzioni's Social Theory.*

3. Powell's recent question is: How do biotechnology companies "learn" or develop new lines of research? This question is too narrow to orient social theory beyond the concerns of economists, namely, to account for corporate growth and profitability.

4. Put into historical context, the new problem of social order updates the tradition of moral philosophy that classical economics and the other social sciences once shared, and that institutional economics endeavored to retain against Marshall's neoclassical revolution.

5. DiMaggio and Powell (1991:27–30); Scott (1991:165); DiMaggio and Powell (1983:156–157).

6. Meyer's work revolves around this second issue. See Frank, Meyer, and Miyahara (1995), and Kamens, Meyer, and Benavot (1996).

7. Amy Gutmann (1995:155, citing Kateb).

8. Elkin (1993:128).

9. See Streeck and Schmitter (1985:11–14) on "caprice and arbitrariness" in European neocorporatism.

10. Perez-Diaz (1993:3–4).

11. See Seligman (1992:203–204) for a listing of characteristics of democratic government taken from Dahl (1971) and Lijphart (1984).

12. Perez-Diaz (1993:40–41).

13. See Cicourel (1993:101) for a clear statement of the problems involved in longitudinal studies of socialization processes.

14. See Braithwaite (1984, 1985) on how common such behavior is.

15. See the quotation from David Knoke in Chapter 1 (at page 15), along with note 8.

16. And, of course, each top manager endeavors to maintain and increase the power of his or her position vis-à-vis that of other top managers. See Morrill (1995) for a rich account of how positional struggles among top managers differ across three general types of corporations, namely those organized bureaucratically, those in which divisions are more insulated from each other ("atomistic management"), and those in which lines of authority overlap ("matrix management").

17. See Sciulli (1997a) for an extended discussion of positional interests in corporate governance structures.

18. Eisenberg (1989:1472).

19. Eisenberg (1989:1474).

20. Shareholders received a 50 percent premium over the earlier market value of their shares.

21. See Palmiter (1989:1354–1357) on Smith v. Van Gorkum (488 A.2d 858 Del. 1985).

22. See Morrill (1995) for a rich description of the local cultures of managers in thirteen corporations in Arizona.

23. Or, as Bourdieu would put it, it is a matter of the habitus in which they are currently operating.

24. Fuller (1964/1969:46–84).

25. See note 9 on Europe.

26. Offe (1983:710–711).

27. Correspondence from anonymous reviewer for Lynne Rienner Publishers, December 10, 1997.

28. See Palmiter (1989) on corporate boards' "fiduciary duty of independence" from management.

29. I address later (Chapter 3, pages 67–68) the difference between the courts' private law grounds for intervening into corporate affairs and their public law grounds for doing so.

30. Institutionalists follow Schmitter and other comparativists in distinguishing between pluralist, corporatist, and statist social orders (e.g., Jepperson and Meyer 1991). However, this distinction, as it stands, tells us little about whether either the state or private organizations exercise collective power in arbitrary ways as opposed to the normatively mediated ways that distinguish democratic social orders from more imposed social orders. See Chapter 3, page 58, note 32.

31. Sociologist Keith Hart (1990:157) laments the "invisibility" of intermediary associations in contemporary social theory, as opposed to their centrality in the works of Tocqueville and Hegel. He sees modern theorists focusing too exclusively on conceptualizing either the individual or the state. This is a bit of an overstatement, given Durkheim's work, Parsons's work on what he called the societal community, and Habermas's early study of the bourgeois public realm. The anonymous reviewer for Lynne Rienner questioned my effort to distinguish intermediary associations from other organizations, corporations from either large retail stores or restaurant chains. I endeavor to address his or her concerns in this subsection.

32. See Putnam (1993), Gans (1986), Bellah et al. (1985), and Banfield (1958) on the problems that privatism and familism pose for democratic societies.

33. It is not coincidental that the first private businesses that the Cuban state has permitted are restaurants.

34. The prospective clients of professional services, including the wealthiest and most powerful clients, are like other consumers *until they successfully secure these services*. Then, no matter how they conduct themselves, they enter a position of dependence in a structured situation. Ultimately, they have no alternative other than to trust the professional. This is why the courts extend norms of fiduciary law, the law of trusts, to professional services. See Sciulli (1997d).

35. See Ouchi and Wilkins (1985), and Morrill (1995).

36. Quoted by Hechter (1987:59).

3

A Conceptual Framework for the Empirical Study of Institutional Change

We proposed in the previous chapter that we could identify the direction of social change by altering the institutional approach to organizations in three ways. First, we shifted the focus of study from the classics' problem of social order to what we called the problem of democratic social order in a global economy. Second, we shifted the unit of analysis from organizations as such to intermediary associations, to corporate entities in civil society that mediate the state's power and individuals' privatism and familism. Third, in our effort to link the study of intermediary associations to the study of institutional change, we shifted our attention away from the issue of organizational homogeneity or heterogeneity. We focused instead on the issue of association governance and whether private arbitrariness is increasing or decreasing in structured situations in civil society.

Now we can explore some of the implications of these alterations for the empirical study of institutional change. For example, by monitoring the increase or decrease of arbitrariness across sectors of civil society, we can distinguish between when social order rests on individuals' possible integration and when it rests on their demonstrable control. This distinction overcomes institutionalism's relativism by bringing a baseline or fixed standard of comparison to the study of institutional change. Second, by focusing our attention on the problem of democratic social order in a global economy, we can identify the types of intermediary associations found uniquely in democratic social orders. Third, we can broaden institutionalism's scope of application by bringing into its purview corporate governance, the corporate judiciary as "an environmental agent," and a distinction that I will later draw between institutional externalities and immediate externalities of corporate power.

A Baseline and the Origins of Institutionalism's Relativism

Social Control and Social Integration

In Chapter 2 the procedural norms institutionalized uniquely in democratic social orders were distinguished from substantive norms or "myths." Substantive norms typically vary crossnationally. A few may be more general, as products of a global economy, but all simply maintain orderly relations of economic and social exchange; in themselves, they do not distinguish democratic social orders from others. The distinction between the procedural norms that span democratic social orders and the substantive norms that vary across social orders can inform the empirical study of institutional change. This distinction allows us to identify two very different bases of orderly behavior within and around intermediary associations. First, orderly behavior may rest exclusively on demonstrable control of subordinates. Subordinates are controlled when association governance encroaches against the threshold of procedural norms. This basis of orderly behavior may characterize intermediary associations across differing social orders. The second basis of orderly behavior is found uniquely within and around the intermediary associations of democratic societies, that is, when orderly behavior rests in some part on subordinates' possible integration. This becomes a possibility, in practice, only when association governance exhibits fidelity to the threshold.

We can visualize this distinction by considering it from the perspective of corporate constituents. When managers' positional power is mediated short of arbitrariness by a corporation's governance structure, it is at least possible for corporate constituents to recognize and understand prospectively what managers expect of them. Constituents are then able to adjust their behavior consistently with protections afforded them by the corporation's governance structure. When this condition holds, we can say that constituents' orderly behavior in corporations cannot be reduced analytically to control by superiors. The governance structure treats them as reasoning adults who, on the one hand, can understand rules and duties and, on the other hand, can be held accountable for their actions. We propose that this marks the most minimal condition for the *possibility* of constituents' integration in any corporation in today's global economy. When this minimal condition holds, constituents are in positions to affiliate themselves positively with a corporation or intermediary association, beyond their taste for pecuniary incentives and their tolerance for sanctions or restrictions.[1] More generally, we propose that this condition holds across sectors only in democratic civil societies, and, moreover, that it accounts for the possibility of citizen integration—and in turn collective vigilance—in these societies.

When the condition is not met, the implications are entirely different. When a sitting management team does not bother to establish a relatively clear pattern (an accessible governance structure) for its exercises of positional power, it has already failed to treat stakeholders as reasoning adults who can be held accountable for their actions. It relates to them instead as unruly children who, being incapable of following rules or fulfilling duties, cannot act responsibly. Like such children, the stakeholders in organizations whose governance structure is permitted to encroach against the threshold receive the message that they understand only two things: coercion and material incentives. This message is precisely what distinguishes the behavior of authorities in imposed social orders from the behavior of authorities in democratic social orders. Should constituents at some particular place and time nonetheless feel integrated (or wish to affiliate themselves positively), we can fairly say that their feeling (and construction of meaning) has been manipulated.[2]

On this minimal ground, by distinguishing between the demonstrable control of constituents and the possibility of their integration, we have found a fixed standard for describing and evaluating corporate governance structures. We have also found a baseline for the comparative study of the relationship between association governance and institutional change. When individuals in structured situations in civil society are not in a position to recognize and understand prospectively what authorities expect of them, we can fairly say that (1) the rules and duties that are sanctioned are arbitrary, and (2) these individuals' orderly behavior, or compliance, is reducible to their demonstrable control. With this baseline in view, but appreciating also that the courts' monitoring of corporate governance does not extend to relationships between constituents occupying the same position (here, of management), consider Calvin Morrill's account of *top managers'* supplication to those holding positions over them:

> Eighty of the 90 (80%) executives interviewed in the mechanistic firms experienced difficulty specifically articulating the formal criteria for performance evaluations beyond very general levels. . . . Less ambiguous . . . are the informal criteria for performance. Sixty-two (69%) of the executives interviewed (24 of whom occupied positions higher than vice president) in these four organizations identified the ability *to keep in line* and keep current with the plans and strategies, *and sometimes the whims,* of superiors as crucial to positive personal evaluations.[3]

Would we alter Morrill's wording substantially if we were describing the outlook of copyholders on a baron's manor?

> The old cliche "It's lonely at the top" captures yet another theme that emerged among executives. Executive loneliness is associated with one of two factors. In some organizations, there is simply little contact of any kind between top managers . . . and the social insularity and long working hours militate against social contacts outside of work. In other executive contexts, loneliness results more from the feeling, as one executive said, "that anything can and will be used against you."[4]

The situation can only be worse for stakeholders whose very positions are exposed to arbitrariness by management, the corporation's agent.

Our minimal condition, the possibility of subordinates' integration in structured situations, marks a baseline even in the face of radical skepticism regarding whether any fixed standards of comparison exist in human affairs. For instance, David Hume, the philosopher most skeptical about the possibility of finding any generalizable substantive standard of justice, acknowledged that arbitrariness defeats the essential purpose of justice— irrespective of how the latter is defined in substance.[5] We can fairly say that where individuals are subject to the "whims" of superiors, their compliance is always and everywhere reducible analytically to control. They are responding either to pecuniary rewards or to force; they are not in a position to be integrated. If they affiliate themselves more positively with the enterprise, they are being successfully manipulated.

> Such glimpses at executive life undoubtedly leave the impression of rather bleak personal existences amid material splendor and ostensible power. . . . Indeed, executives expressed little outward happiness about their work during the times I interviewed and observed them. . . . [One] speaker attempts to "self-rationalize" his own career beyond instrumental careerism.[6]

Again, the situation can only be worse for vulnerable stakeholders, whose positions lack comparable "material splendor and ostensible power."

Whenever we find a modern society (or sector of society) in which sitting management teams endeavor to establish and then maintain a relatively clear pattern for their sanctions, it is likely that managers are oriented *cognitively* to do so by norms *institutionalized* in their environment and upheld by the courts. It is hardly likely that managers act in this way more immediately, or affectively, on the basis of subjective beliefs that they somehow have internalized in common. It is also hardly likely that each manager has decided independently, on the basis of his or her own calculations of self-interest (or positional interest) alone, that this essentially normative (and likely costly) activity is a responsibility that he or she cannot shirk. Finally, it also is not likely that such managerial restraint is a product exclusively of a "negotiated order" established and then maintained on site by ongoing interactions between managers and constituents.[7] If this were the case, since such interactions occur everywhere, managers would exhibit restraint with relatively equal, or random, frequency across advanced societies, in both democratic social orders and in more imposed social orders. It is likely that advanced societies differ in this respect. They must differ also, then, in the measure to which they contain institutionalized norms, either substantive or procedural, that are capable of making the issue of "self-restraint" salient to managers.

Furthermore, whenever the rules and duties enforced through a corporation's governance structure remain understandable to stakeholders *over time,* the norms institutionalized in its environment will include the threshold of procedural norms. After all, managers' exercises of positional power are mediated short of arbitrariness even as managers presumably endeavor to maximize either growth or profits. In addition, if this particular mediation of managers' behavior is ongoing, is indeed institutionalized, managers' fidelity to the threshold of procedural norms is likely to be monitored and sanctioned in one way or another.[8] It is not likely that managers discipline themselves on an honor system (or, again, simply in negotiation with stakeholders on site). Rather, it is more likely that corporations' governance structures are organized in a particular way, in a particular form (which we shall later identify as the collegial form). Before proceeding to this question of form, however, we can consider how our effort to establish a fixed standard for historical and crossnational research contrasts with the new institutionalism's relativism.

Origins of Institutionalism's Relativism

It is ironic that when the new institutionalists introduced a cognitive dimension in salvaging a normativist response to the problem of social order they lost the possibility of distinguishing integration from control. They lost this possibility in part because they failed to distinguish procedural norms institutionalized in organizations' environments from substantive norms. They also lost it, however, because they studied organizational homogeneity or heterogeneity instead of identifying intermediary associations and the significance of association governance. Even today they remain oriented by the classics' problem of social order instead of accounting for the presence of democratic social order in particular.

The new institutionalists have held fast to their assertions that there is some identifiable relationship between (1) *organizations* as open systems (otherwise differentiated by sector and by for-profit or nonprofit status) and (2) *modern* social orders as such (otherwise differentiated by patterns of interest group competition, whether statist, corporatist, or pluralist).[9] Working with these two broad units of analysis, and with their admittedly vague references to the cultural pressures of isomorphism in organizations' environments, institutionalists ask: Are the environmental norms that constrain organizational behavior "based on recognized *sources* of authority"?[10]

This question aptly illustrates how far today's institutionalists have distanced themselves from a more critical stance taken by an earlier generation of institutionalists, Philip Selznick in particular. Selznick had the problem of *democratic* social order in view at least implicitly and, therefore, made room implicitly for the particular relationship between intermediary associations and a democratic social order.[11] Once we bring this problem and relationship explicitly into view, we ask a quite different question about the extra-economic pressures on associations: Do association agents whose positions are recognized or subjectively legitimate (both externally and internally) exercise their positional power in ways that are demonstrably controlling or in ways that are possibly integrative?

DiMaggio and Powell acknowledge that "something has been lost in the shift from old to new institutionalism."[12] Failing to distinguish intermediary associations from the larger category of "organizations," and failing to distinguish democratic societies from the larger category of "modern social orders," they characterize the loss in vague terms.[13] Their broad units of analysis are precisely what prevent them from distinguishing their approach to environmental pressures, and organization governance, from that of neoclassical economics. As we have seen, their units of analysis also undermine their efforts to account methodically for organizational and institutional change in both historical and crossnational perspective.

In contrast, earlier institutionalists were concerned in the 1950s about democratic societies regressing to "mass societies." This concern, even baldly stated, was sufficient to help distinguish their approach to environmental pressures from the more one-dimensional approach of neoclassical economics (focused on whether corporations are either growing or profitable). Indeed, the old institutionalists' fear of democracy's decline connected their approach not only to institutional economics but even more grandly to earlier traditions of political economy and moral philosophy shared by Scottish Enlightenment theorists (including Adam Smith) and the American Founders and Framers.[14] A concern about the contingency of democratic society would encourage crossnational and historical comparisons of successful and failed moments of transition, from imposed social orders to formal democracies, and then to more stable or firmly institutionalized democracies.

DiMaggio and Powell acknowledge at least indirectly this aspect of what has been lost when they review eight differences between "new" and "old" institutionalism.[15] Three of these differences are relevant to our discussion of control and integration, as is a fourth that can be inferred from an earlier point in their commentary.[16] We will discuss each of these four and their implications.

Conflict and governance.   Whereas earlier institutionalists studied the relationship between group conflict and organizational behavior, institutionalists today, much like neoclassical economists, downplay the significance of conflicts of interest both within and between organizations. They therefore downplay the significance of differences in organizations' governance structures, occluding from view the contingency of the corporate judiciary's efforts to resolve corporate governance disputes in ways that broadly support the institutional design of a democratic social order. Rather than ever being guaranteed or predetermined by "isomorphic pressures," the success of these efforts remains contingent with each generation.

Conflict and consensus. The old institutionalists emphasized that organizations contain divisive vested interests (which legal scholars and network analysts today call positional interests). In contrast, institutionalists today emphasize that organization constituents share often unarticulated common understandings. Whereas earlier institutionalists took note of the relationship between constituents' challenges to organization agents and ongoing changes in organization governance, new institutionalists follow Parsons and other "culturalists." They portray organization governance implicitly in terms of an overriding consensus and stability. As Powell puts it, institutionalists today have "a static, constrained, oversocialized view of organizations."[17] As DiMaggio puts it, institutional theory obscures the role that interest and agency play in organization governance and behavior. Instead, institutionalists emphasize the "preconscious understandings that organizational actors share, independent of their interests."[18]

Still, institutionalists clearly depart from Parsons when they say that isomorphic pressures result in organizational stability and a constructed consensus by preventing constituents from recognizing and then acting on their own (potentially divisive) interests.[19] Thus, when Meyer and Rowan held in 1977 that organization leaders take their cues from institutionalized "myths," they implied that the actions of such leaders are less reasoned, less publicly defensible, than actions that advanced more directly either their own or their organizations' "real interests." DiMaggio is explicit about this. He notes in criticism that organization theorists' efforts to explain either stability or change in "organizational forms" rests on the same presumption of knowing actors' "real interests" that informed Marxists' efforts to explain either stability or change in workers' false consciousness.[20]

Parsons's reason for refusing to account for contemporary social stability and normative consensus in this way remains compelling: He appreciated that a theorist who takes this step has to identify what individuals' or groups' "real interests" are. The theorist must therefore also account for how he or she came to divine these interests even as the individuals or groups said to hold them fail to recognize and act on them. In all such cases, a theorist is relying on an ontology as a grounding, a fixed concept of either "basic needs" or "objective interests" (whether of individuals, organizations, or classes). Only against such a baseline can the theorist identify when and how isomorphic pressures "distort" individuals' or organization agents' "real interests," or their understandings of them. When institutionalists take this tack today, their concepts offer them no better access—ontologically—to the substance of an agent's or organization's "real interests" than do the concepts of growth and profitability from neoclassical economists or the concepts of objective interests and basic needs from Marxism. Economists founder when attempting to identify the utilities that individuals "really" value most, and Marxists founder when attempting to identify either the working class's objective interests or individuals' basic needs.

Institutionalists try to get around this problem by asserting simply that organization agents act on two interests universally, namely on an interest in increasing certainty or predictability and on an interest in survival.[21] They contend that as organization agents respond to "coercive isomorphic processes" in particular,[22] they convert these two universal interests into concrete organizational practices. All of this talk of universal interests and coercive pressures, however, is vague and problematic. More important for present purposes, it is indistinguishable at a conceptual level from the neoclassical economists' explanation for organizational behavior, in terms of growth and profitability.

Even worse, institutionalists admit that they introduce into their analyses "all other non-universal interests *ad hoc.*"[23] Thus, they acknowledge that the "metaphysical pathos of institutional theory" stems from their inability to identify "who has institutionalized myths" in the first place. DiMaggio asks: "Who has the power to 'legitimate' a structural element?" Or "Do ceremonial rules arise from the mist?"[24] These questions point clearly to difficulty in identifying the "recognized authorities" in organizations' environments that establish and uphold the normative or ritualistic behavior institutionalized in particular sectors. They also reveal that DiMaggio has no idea whether "coercive isomorphic pressures" orient organization agents toward exercising positional power in ways that are demonstrably controlling or possibly integrative, and, worse, why this matters. This same combination of uncertainty about and indifference to issues of private governance is a hallmark of neoclassical economics.[25]

Personal values and institutional values. DiMaggio and Powell note that their predecessors held that organizations can become institutionalized themselves, can become "infused with value" and thereby ends in themselves.[26] As one example of this view, doctors at Massachusetts General or Boston City may attribute sacred or value-laden qualities to these hospitals or even to particular wards (for example, surgery or emergency), rather than treating them strictly instrumentally, that is, as the work site where they happen to pick up a paycheck. By contrast, today's institutionalists argue that the routinization or institutionalization of doctors' behavior can be understood independently of any "affect or cathexis" directed toward either organizations or institutionalized norms and practices.[27] They see the routinization or institutionalization of doctors' behavior as "fundamentally a cognitive process." Our Boston doctors provide their professional services reliably because they see that, given the norms or expectations institutionalized in their environment as well as their superiors' monitoring, it is in their best positional interests to do so. Thus, "normative obligations . . .

enter into social life primarily as facts" that organization constituents believe they cannot ignore.[28]

The problem here is twofold. First, the new institutionalists reduce the purported "value" of organizations and institutionalized norms to social psychological qualities, to the affect or cathexis that constituents may or may not share as they perform their duties. With this reduction, they fail immediately at a conceptual level to leave room for any other "value" that corporate entities or institutionalized norms might contribute, *including to the institutional design of a democratic social order.* The second problem is that the new institutionalists' social psychological turn obscures another issue: The normative obligations unique to democratic social orders never become this firmly institutionalized—that is, "as facts"—in any advanced society, including the United States. They never become this firmly institutionalized regardless of whether organization agents apprehend them affectively or cognitively.[29]

We saw in Chapter 2 that courts may intervene when organization agents disregard or encroach against the threshold of procedural norms as they advance their own positional interests. Even in democratic social orders the courts and the governance structures of intermediary associations endeavor ceaselessly both to identify such breaches and to punish or prevent them. When corporate managers exhibit fidelity to the threshold of procedural norms, their behavior is in fact being mediated by externally sanctioned—that is, institutionalized—norms distinctive to democratic social orders. Only then are their exercises of positional power being mediated short of arbitrariness by standards of behavior that are unambiguously normative, not strictly economizing or market mimicking. Our point is that this quality of corporate governance structures is a historical and crossnational variable. It is not a constant across "modern societies," like organizations' purported responses to putatively invariant "coercive isomorphic pressures." Here Perez-Diaz is instructive: "To the extent that [certain] formal, universalistic rules do not apply *fully* to the institutions of a given polity and society, we may observe that the rules of the game of democratic pluralism and the due process of law, open markets, and meritocratic competition may be systematically distorted."[30]

Constants and variables. Both old and new institutionalists view institutionalization as ultimately a state-dependent process, and one that typically limits the options organization leaders can pursue. Both sets of institutionalists believe that one result of the state's interventions into organizational affairs is that organizations become less instrumentally rational than they would in the absence of state interference. This is an important insight, but one clearly consistent with basic tenets of neoclassical economics. Economists tell us endlessly that the state only adds unnecessary paper work and transaction costs to business.

This convergence ends, however, when social scientists add another factor to the mix: The states of democratic social orders intervene into organizational affairs at times *on a public law ground.* At least at times, they normatively mediate organizations' strictly instrumental behavior *in order to maintain the institutional design of a democratic social order.* To be sure, this type of state intervention may well increase business costs. But if it truly serves a public law interest, who would claim to "value" greater economic efficiency over democratic stability? From this perspective, the questions posed by earlier institutionalists are pertinent: What kind of institutional design spanning the state and civil society are state officials endeavoring to maintain? Are the costs to business both necessary and acceptable in this light? And on what basis can we identify whether state officials are succeeding?

The new institutionalists treat the institutional design of the larger social order as a fact rather than a variable. They begin their studies of "organizational behavior" with a putative universalism of means, both instrumental *and symbolic.* They believe organization agents employ these means in response to equally universal isomorphic pressures that span all "modern social orders" as such.[31] They neglect at a conceptual level the historical and crossnational variable of ends: What kind of institutional design does a particular modern social order have? As a result, and more important for present purposes, they also neglect *how this variable normatively mediates how organization agents identify, select, and then use means:* Does the governance and behavior of organizations support or challenge the institutional design of a *democratic* social order?[32]

If state officials have in view the end of institutionalizing democracy more fully in civil society, courts will have a public law rationale for intervening into the governance of intermediary associations. Aside from the private law ground of upholding constituents' contractual arrangements with management, the courts will also intervene by, at the very least, normatively mediating association governance short of arbitrariness. In turn, this qualitative end in view will be reflected in identifiable ways in the forms in which association governance structures and some divisions are organized. As Streeck and Schmitter observe more generally: "The same [trade] associations that negotiate the terms of regulation of their members' behavior are charged as private governments with the responsibility to enforce them."[33]

The Intermediary Associations Distinctive to Democratic Societies

From Social Psychology to the Issue of Institutional Change

We noted earlier that institutionalists today are broadening their research agenda. Whereas earlier they turned their attention from rational factors institutionalized in social sectors to cultural factors ("myths"), they now consider the relationship between cognitive, cathectic, and evaluative elements of culture. They no longer wish to privilege the cognitive elements.[34] In making this turn, they combine very broad units of analysis—organizations and modern social orders—with a lower level of analysis. They move from studying the behavior of organizations as entities to endeavoring to identify the motivations of organization agents and constituents. This social psychological turn is consistent with institutionalists' ongoing effort to distinguish their approach from neoclassical economics. They wish to describe and explain how organizations and institutions alike normatively mediate individuals' self-interested behavior.

Still, their original research agenda revolved around another, grander line of inquiry, namely, to describe, explain, and possibly predict how organizations and institutions change and to identify the direction of change.[35] In studying the cathectic and evaluative factors bearing on the social psychology of organization agents and constituents,[36] they do not ask questions such as: Are the norms uniquely institutionalized in democratic social orders currently mediating managers' positional power within corporate governance structures and the collective power of corporate entities in the larger society? Are corporations and other intermediary associations instead being "rationalized" by putatively universal isomorphic pressures? Are corporations and other intermediary associations economizing under the "coercive isomorphic pressures" of a global economy and a market-mimicking state so that they increasingly challenge, not support, institutionalized norms that had once mediated their governance and behavior? These questions may be addressed in part through empirical historical and crossnational comparisons of each sector of each advanced society.

Four Forms of Organization

In addressing such questions, it is necessary to draw our (now familiar) conceptual distinction between organizations that are examples of the types of intermediary associations found uniquely in sectors of democratic social orders and organizations that either are not intermediary associations or are not of the kind found uniquely in democratic social orders. We identified in Chapter 2 some differences between intermediary associations and other organizations.[37] We may now consider the significance of collegial formations in corporate governance structures, which make possible managers' ongoing fidelity to the threshold of procedural norms. The collegial form uniquely institutionalizes deliberation and, more generally, disinterested behavior within corporations and other intermediary associations.[38] Put more technically:

Collegial formations are deliberative (and professional) bodies in which even competing constituents (or heterogeneous individuals) exhibit fidelity to the threshold of procedural norms as they establish and maintain shared understandings of those qualities in their environments (or in their clients' lives) that carry consequences for their performance and, ultimately, for their position.[39]

When managers truly deliberate—over the meaning of subordinates' behavior, or over the meaning of qualitative changes in their industry—they offer each other reasons for their interpretations and proposed lines of action as formal equals. They do not substitute threats, material incentives, or even appeals to substantive normative beliefs ("team loyalty") for a more or less public, more or less disinterested, give-and-take of reasons.

Unlike the collegial form, all other forms of organization are oriented toward the substitution of threats, material incentives, or peer pressure for this deliberative give-and-take of reasons. (Consider again the failure of the Trans Union Corporation board to maintain its integrity in the face of pressures from their CEO, Van Gorkum.[40]) We are proposing that by virtue of the collegial formations in their governance structures, intermediary associations in institutionalized democracies, or at least some of their divisions, can be distinguished from intermediary associations found in the civil societies of formal democracies and more imposed social orders. The divisions pertinent to this discussion are those in which professionals are expected by the public, and by managers in their public statements, to act like professionals, not like controlled (cowed or bribed) constituents. Correlatively, we are proposing that when intermediary associations lack collegial formations and instead contain one or more of three alternative formations, they fail automatically to support the institutional design of a democratic social order. The three alternative formations in question are the bureaucratic, the formally democratic or majoritarian, and the patron-client.[41] Each is incapable in itself of supporting managers' ongoing deliberation, managers' fidelity to the threshold of procedural norms, or managers' disinterested behavior more generally. We will consider each alternative in turn.

First, the major responsibility of managers who are organized bureaucratically is to exhibit fidelity to a top-down chain of command, not to the threshold of procedural norms. Thus, managers may enforce a retroactive rule because a CEO or director orders it. In doing so, they exhibit fidelity to the bureaucratic form but they also encroach against the threshold. Second, the majoritarian form, which is rarely present in practice in association governance, subordinates deliberation to a majority's vote or opinion. The major responsibility of managers organized only in this form is to exhibit fidelity to the majority, not to the threshold of procedural norms. This means that managers can enforce a retroactive rule acclaimed by majority vote, and thereby exhibit fidelity to this form of organization even as they act arbitrarily. Finally, the major responsibility of managers organized only in a patron-client form is to maintain their strictly personal relationships of trust and dependence. When managers enforce a retroactive rule out of personal indebtedness to their patrons (including the board), they exhibit fidelity to this form but also act arbitrarily.[42]

These three formations thus fail to institutionalize deliberation or disinterested behavior. As such, none of them is *distinctively* present in the corporations and intermediary associations of institutionalized democracies. Rather, all three are found in corporations and intermediary associations in all advanced societies, including the most repressive.

Because these three formations subordinate deliberation and disinterested behavior to commands, votes, or personal allegiances, all three challenge the institutional design of a democratic social order. These challenges are stemmed, in practice, only when the courts (or, in Europe and Japan, administrative agencies) impose normative restrictions on the governance of corporations and other intermediary associations. The courts can be said to perform this mediating role when their interventions into corporate governance disputes have two characteristics: (1) when their rulings exhibit all eight qualities of the procedural normative threshold discussed in Chapter 2; and (2) when they purposefully and persistently endeavor on a public law ground to extend legal protection to collegial formations, to sites of deliberation and disinterested behavior in civil society. When judicial interventions into private governance structures are marked by these two characteristics, the courts do more than enforce procedural norms upon everyone who exercises positional power in structured situations. They simultaneously instruct citizens generally, in everyday life, about which exercises of collective power are acceptable in a democratic social order. They instruct citizens about the actual meaning of vigilance in a democratic society, even as corporations and other intermediary associations endeavor to compete effectively in a global economy.

From Formal Democracy to Democratic Society

Social scientists can fairly well identify two conditions under which the integration of corporate constituents is possible. These are (1) when managers are themselves organized in the collegial form (and publicize their directives); and, (2) more essentially, when managers organized in some other form nonetheless respect the integrity of collegial formations found in divisions where professional conduct is expected—by the public and by managers in their public statements. When collegial formations are not present either in corporations' governance structures or in selected divisions, then the advanced society in question lacks the institutional design of a democratic social order. It is, at best, a formal democracy. Formal democracies typically mediate the state's power over individuals; they lack, however, the institutional design unique to democratic social orders, namely collegial formations and the threshold of procedural norms that together mediate private power in structured situations.

Historically, Western democracies typically institutionalized normative mediations on state power first. They generally did so by institutionalizing federalism or other divisions of governmental powers in substance—not necessarily by mediating government's exercises of collective power procedurally.[43] Because of this historical precedent and also because all democracies since World War II have tended to adopt these formalities of government, comparativists frequently treat these formalities as the sine qua non of democratic social orders.[44] This is a faulty reductionism, however, since the collective power exercised in everyday life by corporations, professions, and other intermediary associations has increased considerably since the 1920s. It has yet to be empirically determined whether, and to what extent, these private bodies support or challenge institutionalized procedural norms that mediate arbitrariness. That is, does corporate power lend a lived, everyday reality to democratic norms or does it confirm their status as formalities? It has also still to be determined whether the intermediary associations of any formal democracy help to socialize their own constituents to recognize arbitrariness in common and then to react collectively against it. If the concept of a vigilant citizenry means anything today, it means at the very least that educated, middle-class and upper-middle-class individuals are not being subjected to—and thereby socialized to accept—arbitrariness and abuse in their everyday lives, as the constituents of intermediary associations.[45] That is, does corporate power buttress or enervate citizen vigilance in civil society?

Unlike today's comparativists, the founders of the U.S. government were quite aware of the importance to institutional design of normatively mediating private power, and not only of limiting government. To this end, the first U.S. state legislatures and state courts developed corporate law doctrine from England's fiduciary or equity law tradition. They did so explicitly with an eye to normatively mediating corporate power (see Chapters 4 and 5). In fact, in the republic's first century, state courts placed absolute substantive limits on the longevity of corporations as commercial enterprises, the amount of capital that private corporations could accumulate, and the investment practices of corporate owners.

Why Managers Maintain the Collegial Form

When managers maintain the collegial form in corporate boards and other governance structures, their exercises of positional power are mediated short of arbitrariness.[46] When the collegial form is absent, even managers' normative appeals and ritualistic behavior can be manifestations of arbitrariness. Moreover, management's fidelity to the threshold of procedural norms certainly mediates as well their strictly economizing behavior. It increases, not decreases, a corporation's transaction costs. After all, managers' fidelity to norms of any kind is never the most efficient means to maximize the production of *quantities* of utilities, of priced goods and services; rather, such behavior at best contributes *qualities* to everyday life in civil society.

Why would corporate managers adopt the collegial form and thereby institutionalize their own fidelity to procedural norms? Why wouldn't they instead adopt one or more of the three alternative formations that permit them to act more directly in market-mimicking (and, presumably, self-interested) ways? There are two reasons.

First, in addition to organizing professionals such as scientists in corporate research divisions, the collegial form often institutionalizes managers' deliberations over qualitative changes in their environment that can affect their corporation's performance and, therefore, their own positions. These qualitative changes might include the corporation's legal environment, the intentions or plans of competitors, and the preferences or expectations of major clients or customers. As qualitative matters, managers cannot divine the meaning of these changes from quarterly reports, fluctuations in the stock market, or techniques of rational accounting. It may nonetheless be critically important for them to come to some shared understanding about their meaning. Responding to such changes in only uncoordinated, ad hoc ways can jeopardize their positions. Deliberation in corporate decision-making is not, however, easily established nor easily maintained, as the experience of the Trans Union Corporation board demonstrates. The practices and outcomes of deliberation are not likely to survive in the face of top managers' decrees, votes of shareholder or board majorities, or top managers' personal allegiances—unless the courts extend legal protection to directors' and managers' disinterested behavior and, therefore, to the collegial form.

This leads us to the other reason why managers adopt the collegial form, one more important for present purposes. The corporate judiciary helps to institutionalize the threshold of procedural norms in corporations' environments by monitoring corporate governance structures with an eye to limiting managerial caprice. What is unique about a democratic social order is that the courts (or equivalent administrative agencies) maintain its institutional design by ultimately trumping more unilateral efforts by managers to ensure the survival and then profitability or growth of their corporations. The success of these "constitutional" efforts by the corporate judiciary, however, is always and everywhere contingent. It is never automatic. It is never somehow guaranteed by the formalities of democratic government.

And it is certainly never guaranteed by systemic pressures originating from a global economy and market-mimicking state, pressures of "coercive iso-morphism" that span all advanced societies.

In line with institutionalists' "cognitive turn," we are proposing that managers' fidelity to corporate collegial formations is a product of the procedural norms institutionalized in their environments and of the corporate judiciary's monitoring of corporate governance in light of those norms. We are not proposing that managers' fidelity to corporate collegial formations is, somehow, a product of their having internalized the same substantive normative beliefs during primary socialization, or a product of environmental pressures that everyone occupying their positions experiences more or less uniformly.

To illustrate our point, consider what is necessary for corporate scientists to be able to deliberate over the meaning of professional integrity in given instances and to act in disinterested ways for any extended period of time. The possibility of their acting in these ways hinges on whether the courts and the governance structures of corporations and other intermediary associations insulate or "buffer" such qualitative ("ritualistic") practices from managers' exercises of positional power over research divisions. Deliberation over the meaning of professional integrity in a particular case is not possible, is not available as a mode of decisionmaking, when managers command or induce scientists to arrive at a specific understanding of this or any other qualitative practice. It is not possible when managers *reduce* the qualitative meaning and value of professional integrity or any other "ritualistic" behavior to the *quantitative* issue of whether it helps directly to maximize profits or growth.

Only when deliberation is successfully "buffered" from both arbitrariness and economic reductionism can corporate constituents actually deliberate over what professional integrity and other rituals require of them in particular situations. Only then can everyone involved—constituents, managers, judges—exhibit fidelity to the threshold of procedural norms. The collegial form, in turn, is what institutionalizes such qualities of ritualistic behavior within and around corporate and association divisions.[47] We propose that this holds true regardless of the economizing activities to which these divisions are otherwise dedicated; regardless of the substantive norms of behavior that corporate and association constituents have otherwise internalized during their primary socialization; and regardless, too, of the substantive norms of behavior that corporations and associations otherwise institutionalize as their organizational "cultures." The same principle should therefore hold true crossnationally. It should apply equally as well to structured situations in Iran or the People's Republic of China as to structured situations in the United States and France. It should hold true across most sectors of any particular society. It should hold as well, therefore, for the governance of U.S. corporations and universities as it does for the workings of the U.S. Congress and agencies of U.S. state governments.

Finally, we also propose that *collegial formations (1) will be found in great and increasing numbers within the corporate and association divisions and sectors of institutionalized democracies; (2) will be found in far fewer and decreasing numbers within the divisions and sectors of formal democracies; and (3) will be in even more rapid decline within the divisions and sectors of more imposed social orders.*[48] To the extent that this hypothesis holds up in crossnational and historical study, it provides us with a generalizable standard by which to identify shifts in the direction of institutional change in any advanced society. The presence of collegial formations within corporations and other intermediary associations and the degree to which courts or administrative agencies extend legal protection to these formations bear directly on the issues of institutional design and institutional change.

Broadening Institutionalism in Substance

Institutionalists have been slow to study corporations, let alone the contingency of the corporate judiciary's efforts to normatively mediate corporate power. When sociologists assume, in referring to social order as such, that *all* changes in corporate governance and behavior automatically help to institutionalize democracy in civil society—as if guided by a hidden hand—they cannot account empirically for the behavior of the U.S. corporate judiciary from the Founding to today. The corporate judiciary endeavors to mediate what I call the institutional externalities of corporate power, and not only the more immediate externalities—those exercises of corporate power that harm employees, suppliers, bondholders, or local communities.

Corporations as Intermediary Associations

Although corporations are private, profit-seeking enterprises, corporate managers do more than oversee investment and production.[49] They hold positions of relative power in organizations whose norms and practices can either support or enervate those in the larger social order. In the first place, corporations are chartered by state legislatures as "legal persons," as entities in society recognized by law. As corporate managers advance these "persons'" interests, they at times exercise collective power in the larger social order. In the second place, corporations are sites of adult employees' ongoing secondary socialization into norms of behavior. The very term "corporate culture" conveys this. In the third place, the governance of corporations is related in at least two ways to norms institutionalized in the larger social order. Corporate governance is likely to reflect in some basic respects a social order's institutional design, as opposed to baldly challenging or disregarding it. This means that how corporations perform their dual role as agents of state power and as agents of adult socialization can carry externalities or consequences not only for individuals but also for a social order's institutional design. As a result, changes in corporate governance can reflect, anticipate, or even initiate challenges to the institutional design of a democratic social order.

Whether managers acknowledge it or not, corporations mediate the state's power, including its enforcement of formal social controls. They also mediate their own constituents' social constructions of meaning, including the importance they attach to particular norms institutionalized in the environment. This is so whether or not managers perceive their own behavior to be reasoned, responsible, and legitimate. Corporate managers' exercises of positional power through governance structures and their exercises of the corporate entity's collective power in the larger social order can alter these constructed meanings.

Sociologist Melvin Kohn's extensive research—over a period of two decades—on the relationship between work and personality bears this out. Kohn is confident that his research "resolves" two issues.[50] First, "work does affect adult personality."[51] Second, "job conditions affect adult personality mainly through a direct process of learning and generalization— learning from the job *and generalizing what has been learned to other realms of life. . . . In short, the lessons of work are directly carried over to nonoccupational realms.*"[52] Sociologist Cynthia Fuchs Epstein makes a similar assessment:

> Jobs have mystiques, auras—and, sometimes, stigmas—attached to them that go well beyond the content of their tasks. Jobs bring their occupants prestige or dishonor, a sense of being manly or womanly, and sometimes of being sacred or profane. . . . The wider culture establishes rules that specify how people ought to think and act about their work, and consequently about themselves.[53]

Likewise, legal scholar Mark Barenberg summarizes the labor law literature in this way: "Workers' preferences, interests, and emotional bonds are not exogenously fixed but rather created, transformed and chosen."[54]

In short, changes in corporate governance can change how employees and other constituents publicly define, and then publicly act upon, their own self-interests and positional interests.[55] Once institutionalists acknowledge at a conceptual level that corporations are indeed intermediary associations, they then come face to face with two central questions of corporate governance familiar to legal scholars, namely the questions of corporate agency and corporate purpose. First, which managers or constituents make corporate decisions in any particular instance, and thereby exercise the corporation's collective power? That is, who is the agent of the corporate behavior in question? Second, and more important for present purposes, how, if at all, do changes in the governance of corporations affect other intermediary associations and thereby affect the institutional design of the larger social order? That is, what are the limits, if any, of the corporation's place and purpose in a democratic social order?[56]

The Corporate Judiciary's Normative Interventions into Corporate Governance

Contrary to generally held sociological expectations, the behavior of the corporate judiciary is at times unambiguously normative, not more narrowly rational or "market mimicking." More specifically, the Delaware courts and other state courts normatively mediate how corporate managers may endeavor to maximize either shareholders' dividends or corporate growth. One example familiar to legal scholars but not to institutionalists and other sociologists is sufficient to illustrate this point.

In 1989 the management of Time Inc. announced a friendly merger with Warner Communications. In short order, Paramount Communications countered by offering Time shareholders a far more lucrative deal in a hostile bid. That is, Paramount went over Time management's head by offering the deal directly to Time shareholders. The Time-Warner merger favored *Warner* stockholders, promising them $70 a share; but Paramount was guaranteeing *Time* shareholders $200 a share. On strictly rational grounds, the courts should have allowed Time shareholders to accept the hostile bid. Yet, Chancellor William Allen of Delaware's Chancery Court permitted Time management to block this more lucrative deal for its own company's shareholders, the corporation's *owners*. He accepted Time management's argument that it not only has a contractual obligation to shareholders but also a fiduciary or moral obligation to maintain the integrity of "Time culture" and its unique place in U.S. society.

With this ruling, Chancellor Allen continued a long line of such decisions, a line that may be traced not only to the American Founding but as far back as fourteenth-century England. He held that a corporate entity itself can have a legally cognizable interest that, under some circumstances, overrides the private property interests of its shareholders or owners. In the case of Time Inc., he held that this corporate entity carries some *qualitative* significance for the larger social order, beyond whatever its divisible material assets might be. In the language of the judiciary and of legal scholarship, Chancellor Allen held that a corporate entity can advance a public law interest, as opposed only to fulfilling contractual or private law obligations to shareholders and other corporate constituents.

Since the Founding, U.S. state courts have distinguished between "private law" and "public law" grounds for intervening into the governance of corporations and other intermediary associations. They continue to draw this distinction today. Citing "private law grounds," the courts endeavor to correct harms that corporations cause to discrete corporate constituents as a result of breaches of contract. Citing "public law grounds," the courts endeavor to correct harms that corporations cause more generally, as a result of what can be called breaches of social order. As far back as the fourteenth century, English chancellors imposed norms of "equitable" or "fair" behavior on barons. They believed that barons' behavior on their own manors could carry institutional externalities, harmful consequences for the institutional design of the kingdom. Thus, English chancellors intervened into barons' private affairs on a "public law ground." U.S. corporate law is directly descended from this fourteenth-century principle.

U.S. state legislatures have a long history of imposing absolute substantive limitations on corporations' behavior by statute. These are called public law norms because, presumably, they help to maintain the institutional design of the larger social order. We will begin to explore the rise and fall of these public law norms in Chapter 4. It is safe to say, however, that the secular trend of change has generally been for state legislatures steadily to remove public law norms from corporate law's core of "mandatory rules" with each generation.[57] As a result, the only truly resilient set of norms in corporate law's core of mandatory rules today is a set that originated in the courts' own fiduciary law tradition, not in legislative statutes. U.S. state courts continue to impose fiduciary or moral duties on corporate managers, controlling shareholders, and all other corporate agents *independently of state statutes and independently of private law contracts*. We will briefly review the history of the fiduciary law tradition in Chapter 5.

By the 1980s, even the Delaware courts became uncertain about when and why they should continue to enforce management's fiduciary duties. This is why Chancery's Time-Warner decision strikes many legal scholars and judges as both inscrutable and controversial. Legal scholars have difficulty identifying the public law interest served by this decision, and Chancellor Allen has backed away from opportunities to identify it himself.[58] Indeed, in the wake of the hostile takeovers and leveraged buyouts of the 1980s, Chancellor Allen acknowledged that the corporate judiciary in general suffers from "institutional angst."[59] As an institution, the corporate judiciary is uncertain about why it should continue normatively to mediate management's business judgment in an effort to uphold the "integrity" of any corporate entity.

Institutional Externalities and Immediate Externalities

A process of institutional change is under way in the United States today, a process involving both the corporate judiciary and the governance of corporations and other intermediary associations. This would seem to offer institutionalists an ideal opportunity to plumb the promise and identify the limits of their approach. To do so, however, they clearly would need to appreciate that a process of institutional change is indeed under way in the United States. Such a recognition would entail moving away from the issues of whether organizations are becoming more or less homogeneous and more or less amenable to "learning" and exploring instead a more specific way of identifying the relationship between organizational change and institutional change. Certain changes in private governance structures carry *institutional* externalities for the larger social order, aside from whatever *immediate* externalities they may—or may not—carry for particular individuals and groups. This distinction may be found implicitly in the writings of major economic theorists from Adam Smith to Milton Friedman and Friedrich Hayek. It may also be found, again implicitly, in the works of major social theorists from Marx, Durkheim, and Weber to Arendt, Habermas, and Parsons. However, economic theorists and social theorists have yet to draw this distinction explicitly. As a result, they have yet to apply it methodically to the governance of corporations and other intermediary associations.

The concept "immediate externalities" refers to substantive decisions made in private governance structures *that cause immediate harm to discrete, readily identifiable constituents.*[60] When a corporation pollutes a stream, this is an immediate externality for residents of local communities who, taken together, constitute a readily identifiable corporate constituent. All organizations, not just intermediary associations, are capable of generating immediate externalities. By contrast, the concept "institutional externalities" refers to a qualitatively different set of consequences, that is, to changes in private governance structures *that broaden the scope and increase the frequency of arbitrary exercises of collective power in the larger social order.* Only corporations and other intermediary associations can bring institutional externalities into the larger social order.

Our example earlier of managers' treatment of chemists in a research division illustrates how institutional externalities differ from immediate externalities. In that example managers instruct chemists to falsify product test results or else to say that they tested a product even though they did not. We propose that this behavior by managers carries institutional externalities for the larger social order even if the product in question is not hazardous or harmful in any way—that is, even if it does not carry any immediate externalities for anyone. The product may satisfy some consumers, and the chemists directly involved may receive promotions, pay raises, or bonuses for exhibiting "team loyalty." Nonetheless, because this managerial behavior in essence socializes corporate employees to tolerate arbitrariness in their everyday lives, it carries institutional externalities for the larger social order: Such behavior helps to broaden the scope and to increase the frequency of arbitrary exercises of collective power in civil society.

The threshold of procedural norms presented in Chapter 2 offers social scientists a "grounding," a fixed standard, upon which to identify the institutional externalities of corporate power. (In our example, one indicator of the managers' arbitrariness is the likelihood that they would not be willing to announce publicly their treatment of corporate biologists and chemists.) From this discussion we may draw a general principle, an additional orienting hypothesis for the empirical study of institutional change: *When anyone who holds a position of power within an intermediary association socializes constituents to tolerate and accommodate arbitrariness, this carries institutional externalities for any existing democracy, whether formal or institutionalized.*

In this way sociologists may move beyond economists' allusions to encroachments and arbitrariness by government. For Milton Friedman, who calls externalities "neighborhood effects":

> The use of government to overcome neighborhood effects itself has an extremely important neighborhood effect which is unrelated to the particular occasion for government action. Every act of government intervention limits the area of individual freedom directly and threatens the preservation of freedom indirectly . . .[61]

This passage reveals that Friedman has the concept of "*institutional* externalities" in mind, albeit implicitly. It also reveals, however, that he follows other neoclassicists in recognizing only those institutional externalities that government brings into the larger social order. Sociologists can go further. We can expose to empirical study encroachments and arbitrariness by corporations and other intermediary associations. We can establish in historical and crossnational perspective that certain changes in private governance structures do indeed broaden the scope and increase the frequency of arbitrary exercises of collective power, even as most changes do not. Thus, we can establish empirically that these changes threaten democracy in the United States just as surely as does an encroaching state.[62] Finally, we can use this approach to explain behavior by the corporate judiciary that economists cannot explain. We can identify when the corporate judiciary intervenes into corporate governance disputes on public law grounds, in cases where there are no shareholders or stakeholders suffering any immediate harm.[63]

Our distinction between immediate externalities and institutional externalities is thus more than a heuristic device. It can shed light on historical trends in U.S. corporate law doctrine and judicial behavior. It holds the key to our describing and explaining value-neutrally the current behavior of the U.S. corporate judiciary and the institutional change currently under way in the United States.

Notes

1. Our distinction between control and integration cuts across Etzioni's (1961) well-known bases of "compliance" within organizations, namely coercion, pecuniary incentives, and normative appeals.

2. See Sciulli (1992:30). Whether subordinates agree subjectively with what agents are doing (or expecting) is also a substantive issue, subject to manipulation, not a procedural issue, capable of being resolved independently using our baseline.

3. Morrill (1995:47, my emphases).

4. Morrill (1995:40–41).

5. Hayek (1973–1979) is similarly skeptical, and similarly acknowledges the importance of keeping a market society framed by procedural norms that mediate arbitrariness. Anthropologist Mary Douglas captures the universal importance of mediating arbitrariness when she says, citing Hume, that the tests of "coherence and non-arbitrariness" are not subjective preferences but rather a "straightforward [way] to study human systems of justice objectively" (1986:120–121). Douglas begins her account of *How Institutions Think* by discussing Lon Fuller's 1949 allegory of the relativism of subjective accounts of events, "The Case of the Speluncean Explorers" (1986:6–8).

6. Morrill (1995:44–45).

7. See Anselm Strauss (1978) on the negotiated order perspective in the interactionist study of organizations, and then Fine (1996) for an application. Fine reports comments by kitchen workers that reveal their sense of being oppressed by corporations (1996:174–175). It is clear from his account that these employees lack protections that a governance structure can extend to at least some stakeholders.

8. Rational choice theorist Michael Hechter (1987) accounts for group solidarity on the basis of members' control and dependence. He does not consider whether control mechanisms are kept consistent with norms uniquely institutionalized in democratic social orders. Yet, as Jack Gibbs puts the matter (1981:53ff), a concept of control should allow us to distinguish a British bobby from a Gestapo agent.

9. On the three interest group patterns, see Jepperson and Meyer (1991) and the literature they cite; see also note 32 below.

10. This question is consistent with the relativism of positivist legal theorists Kelsen and Hart. Fuller developed his "procedural morality" of law in reaction to positivists' relativism in treating law as whatever duties a subjectively recognized or legitimate state enforces.

11. Even today, when commenting on the new institutionalism, Selznick (1996) is not explicit about either part of this relationship.

12. DiMaggio and Powell (1991:27). In addition, they also acknowledge (1991:23) that their cognitive turn, a reaction against Parsons's focus on internalized norms, carries a price. This, it seems to me, is a concession that need not be made so readily.

13. They say that a one-sidedly cognitive theory has replaced a more multidimensional theory. It is unclear, though, why the latter is inherently better able to orient empirical study, including historical and crossnational comparisons.

14. See Chapter 6 of this volume, as well as Soltan (1993:8–12) on connections between the "new constitutionalism" in political science and the tradition of political economy.

15. DiMaggio and Powell (1991:12–15, and table 1.1).

16. DiMaggio and Powell (1991:11).

17. Powell (1991:183). Zucker (1988:xiv) and Friedland and Alford (1991) are endeavoring most strenuously to bring conflict back into the institutionalist approach, but they do not attempt first to identify qualities of intermediary associations that are unique to democratic social orders.

18. DiMaggio (1988:3–4).

19. For examples, see DiMaggio and Powell (1983), DiMaggio (1988:4–5), and Zucker (1977/1991).

20. DiMaggio (1988:16).

21. DiMaggio (1988:7).

22. See Chapter 1, page 17.

23. DiMaggio (1988:8).

24. DiMaggio (1988:9).

25. See neoclassicists' five assumptions about organizations and environments in Chapter 6, at pages 141–144.

26. See Scott (1987:493).

27. DiMaggio and Powell (1991:15), quoting Zucker (1983:25).

28. DiMaggio and Powell (1991:15), quoting Meyer and Rowan (1977).

29. We will see later in this chapter that the same is true of the normative obligations unique to professional integrity and also to the integrity of any deliberative body.

30. Perez-Diaz (1993:51, my emphasis).

31. Friedland and Alford (1991:257).

32. This approach cuts across Schmitter's distinction (1974) between pluralist and corporatist social orders. Schmitter (with Streeck, 1985:28, note 1) distinguishes "corporate associations" from "voluntary associations." Corporative associations—whether based on class, sector, or profession—contribute to social and political order because (1) they are limited in number, (2) they are monopolistic in representing the interests of their respective functional sectors, and (3) they mutually recognize the legitimacy of others' monopoly within their sectors. Thus, they share a positional interest in arriving at relatively stable compromises—"pacts"—as they advance their own function-based interests (1985:10–11; also 1983:896). The problem is that Schmitter lacks the concepts with which to identify when intermediary associations of any kind help to institutionalize norms that mediate arbitrariness. This same problem runs through Schmitter's earlier effort (1983) to identify when "neocorporatism" contributes to democracy. This is why he and Streeck focus on how corporative associations contribute to social and political order, or in their words to "organizational concertation."

Schmitter comes closest to addressing the relationship between intermediary associations and institutionalized norms when he says (1983:899–900) that "the most democratic standard one can apply" to *governments* is the extent to which citizens hold rulers accountable through some process of regular consultation "and nonarbitrary deliberation." The problem is that he does not offer social scientists concepts with which to identify such deliberation in historical and crossnational perspective. This is why he alludes (1983:895) to neocorporatism possibly being compatible "with the prevailing 'procedural minimum'" of democracy, and yet fails to offer social scientists any standard with which to identify when this minimum is being upheld and when it is being encroached against. Indeed, he says at various points (1) that "neocorporatism is intrinsically undemocratic" (1983:904), (2) that he cannot really evaluate neocorporatism's positive or negative consequences for democracy (1983:906), and (3) that neocorporatism may deprive citizens of resources to hold representatives accountable (1983:913–914, also 918–925). Elsewhere (1981:296) Schmitter acknowledges that his approach to corporative associations is "generally not applicable to the organization of . . . the professions that seem to have quite distinctive patterns of associability."

33. Streeck and Schmitter (1985:22).

34. Powell and DiMaggio (1991:24).

35. Powell and DiMaggio (1991:30–33).

36. See Etzioni (1988) and Wolfe (1989) for similar efforts in socioeconomics and communitarianism.

37. See Chapter 2, pages 43–44.

38. See Sciulli (1992:80). Wolfe sees well the problem posed by self-interested or economizing behavior that is unmediated by norms: "The market leaves us with no way to appreciate disinterest" (1989:102).

39. This definition slightly modifies the wording in Sciulli (1992:80) to fit our discussion of corporations and intermediary associations.

40. See Chapter 2, page 36.

41. I believe that the four forms of organization presented here, the collegial included, are exhaustive. I remain open, however, to considering other forms that are not simply combinations of two or more of the four. As examples of combinations, a majority vote may hinge on deliberation (organized in the collegial form), political party divisions (organized in the bureaucratic form), or pork-barrel considerations (organized in the patron-client form). Relatedly, a bureaucracy may be headed by a collegial leadership, or it may be riddled from top to bottom by patron-client networks.

42. Sciulli (1992:162–164). Morrill's case of "matrix management" seems to illustrate the patron-client form, not the collegial form (1995:chap. 6).

43. The United States is a partial exception to this rule. Habermas (1962) chronicles the decline in the 1830s and 1840s of the "public sphere" in Europe, an arena comprised of coffee houses, salons, and other sites at which the bourgeoisie informally deliberated over politics and the arts. Tocqueville documented the presence of voluntary associations in the United States at this time. In addition, U.S. state legislatures and state courts imposed *substantive* norms of behavior on corporate owners and managers until the 1920s (see Chapters 4 and 6 of this volume).

44. For example, Lipset (1994).

45. Encroachments by corporate managers against the integrity of the professional practice of research divisions are in every respect as serious a threat to the institutional design of a democratic social order as the activities that Lipset (1960) attributed a quarter of a century ago to "working class authoritarianism." Indeed, in a great many respects the encroachments of middle-class and upper-middle-class managers against the integrity of corporate research divisions and other deliberative bodies pose a far more serious challenge to the institutional design of a democratic social order than ethnic, racial, or religious intolerance by the working class. The literature in comparative politics devoted to regime changes in Latin America, for instance, is clear that regardless of which groups in society initiate social and political changes, the interests and the ethos of the middle class determines whether change actually occurs or not. Even coup d'états hinge upon whether the ethos of the middle class tolerates military government—thus, Alfred Stepan's phrase "the middle-class coup."

46. See Useem (1984) on corporate boards in particular, and see Sciulli (1997a) on corporate governance structures in general.

47. See Sciulli (1992) for an extended discussion of the relationship between Fuller's threshold, the collegial form of organization, and Habermas's communication theory.

48. The *Fuhrerprinzip* is an institutionalization of arbitrariness, not of deliber-

ation and the collegial form. For studies of how the institutionalized arbitrariness of Nazism affected the professions, see Geoffrey Cocks (1985) on psychotherapy in the Third Reich and Ingo Muller (1987) on courts in the Third Reich. See Ringer (1969) for a now classic account of the cultural and organizational antecedents of arbitrariness in the Third Reich.

49. Easterbrook and Fischel offer legal contractarians' narrower view (1991:10): "Corporations are a subset of firms. The corporation is a financing device and is not otherwise distinctive." Sociologist James Coleman sounds similar, at least at times: "Slowly or rapidly, the Weberian form of rational organization [that is, the bureaucracy] is being replaced by a form which acts largely as an investor, facilitator, and guide to the successful employment of the resources it invests" (1990:425, also 435–446, 449–450).

50. Actually, Kohn discusses six resolved issues (which may be found at 1990:40–43). See Demo (1992) for a review of the literature on "the self-concept over time."

51. Kohn (1990:40).

52. Kohn (1990:42), my emphasis.

53. Epstein (1990:91).

54. Barenberg (1994:795).

55. Perez-Diaz sees individuals' internalization of certain rules of work as unique to a "civilized" or "open" society (1993:50): "These rules require that work be carried out with professional honesty, eschewing fraud, sloppy standards, or cover-ups for technical incompetence . . ." My point, however, is to focus attention on the forms in which such work is organized, and whether these forms support a "civilized" society, not to turn more immediately, with Perez-Diaz, to the norms that individuals purportedly internalize when their work putatively supports a "civilized" society. See the second half of Keane's definition of civil society (Chapter 1, note 24) where he points out that individuals' activities within associations can "preserve *and transform* their identity" (my emphasis). Also see Offe (1981:146–149) on organizations not only aggregating power but also providing individuals with a "*qualitative* definition of ends to which power is to be applied" (my emphasis).

56. Easterbrook and Fischel acknowledge that their contractarian approach brackets the issue of corporate purpose (1991:35–36): "An approach that emphasizes the contractual nature of a corporation removes from the field of interesting questions one that has plagued many writers: what is the goal of the corporation? . . . Our response to such questions is: who cares?" Unlike Easterbrook and Fischel, rational choice theorist James Coleman does not dismiss the issue of corporate purpose and "social responsibility" (1990:553–578). However, he reduces it to balancing corporate constituents' rights and interests, a position that I discuss elsewhere.

57. Corporate law doctrine continues to revolve today around two distinct sets of rules (Eisenberg 1989:1461; see also Orts 1993:1578–1587). One set is a core of mandatory rules. The core contains all of the norms of behavior that state legislatures and state courts continue to impose on corporate agents that mediate contracting. These rules are mandatory and thus literally nonnegotiable. The other set is suppletory rules and enabling rules. These are the rules that facilitate contracting. Shareholders, suppliers, middle managers, and all other corporate constituents are free to negotiate and renegotiate these rules with top management in their own interests. Thus, when management brings suppliers or middle managers into a corporation's governance structure (under the conditions that I discuss in Chapter 7, pages 164–166), it does so through suppletory or enabling rules. Neoclassical economists and contractarians want corporate law doctrine to contain only suppletory

and enabling rules whereas "legal traditionalists" want at least some existing mandatory rules to remain at the core.

58. See Chancellor Allen (1993).

59. See Chancellor Allen (1992a).

60. See Ullmann (1983) for a collection of essays that traces the "social costs" or immediate externalities of health policy, electric generation, industrial pollution, occupational disability, unemployment, old age, slums and poverty, duplication of capital facilities, drugs, transportation, food production, general government, and the military. Ullmann sees that assessing these costs is largely qualitative (1983:3), and he has difficulty establishing that reform is either desirable or practicable (e.g., 1983:253). Instead, he concedes (1983:7) that the whole debate has "an ideological cast." Bruyn (1991:228) offers two intriguing measures of "the capacity of [trade associations] to cooperate both for self-regulation and for competition in the public interest. . . . One important measure would be the ability of associations to control the conduct of their members while respecting their rights to freedom, individuality, and fair competition, since such a capacity would help a market sector remain independent of government regulation. Another key measure is the ability of associations to influence members to become organizationally viable, that is, to help them meet the welfare needs of their own constituencies while developing effectively within the framework of their democratic organization."

61. Friedman (1962:32).

62. I confine the substantive focus of this volume to U.S. corporations and U.S. courts, but the concepts I propose here are designed to allow social scientists to monitor the institutional externalities of corporate power in crossnational and historical perspective.

63. In this light, it is not clear that Chancellor Allen's Time-Warner decision does advance a public law interest. Demonstrating this is beyond the scope of this volume, but see Sciulli (1997a).

PART 2

U.S. Corporate Law: From Vigilance to Complacency

4

The Quest for Doctrinal Coherence: Initial Approaches to the Corporation

Chancellor William Allen candidly reports that judicial and scholarly approaches to the corporation have become "schizophrenic."[1] Even radical legal scholars, contributors to the critical legal studies movement, acknowledge that corporate law doctrine fails to conform to the way radicals typically portray "elite ideology."

> Critical legal studies critiques often suggest that mainstream doctrine tends to induce complacency about or confidence in institutions by lending a false sense of coherence and completeness to the doctrines that describe them [and Gerald Frug is cited]. [But] this point applies less strongly to corporations than other subjects. Corporation doctrine is distinctively contentious and relatively openly chaotic.[2]

To say that U.S. corporate law doctrine is more schizophrenic and chaotic than coherent and consistent is to say that judges today do not approach the corporation with settled principles.[3] It is also to say that judges do not approach the corporation with any widely accepted framework of concepts. Rather, judges approach the corporation with different "social visions"—with different views of the corporation's place and purpose in U.S. society and, for that matter, with different views of U.S. society itself.[4] In addition, all judges without exception have particular difficulty today conceptualizing, and thereby identifying at a doctrinal level, the respects in which a corporation is an intermediary association that exercises collective power in U.S. society.

One set of judges and legal scholars, legal contractarians, define the terms of today's debate over corporate governance and corporate law.[5] They do so, however, by default of any compelling alternative theory, not by the self-evident merits of their own approach.[6] Their central proposition is that "corporate law has an economic structure, that it increases the wealth of all by supplying the rules that investors would select if it were easy to contract more fully."[7] However, legal contractarians acknowledge that this proposition holds true only to the extent that corporate power does not adversely affect third parties, "strangers to the contract." That is, they acknowledge that they legitimately reduce corporate law to its "economic structure" only to the extent that corporate power does not carry *any* immediate externalities for third parties, let alone institutional externalities for the larger social order. "Contracts maximize private value. Whether they also maximize social welfare depends on whether the contracting parties bear the costs of their deals at the same time as they reap the benefits. Throughout this book [that is, through chapter 7 of Easterbrook and Fischel's *The Economic Structure of Corporate Law*] we have treated the corporate contract as one without third-party effects."[8]

Like social theorists, legal scholars pride themselves on value-neutrally describing and explaining their subject of study, in this case existing corporate law doctrine and current judicial behavior. However, we will see beginning in this chapter that value neutrality is possible only if the concepts that legal scholars employ also adequately describe and explain the evolution of corporate law, judicial behavior, and corporate governance over time. This is the case because from the Founding to today, state courts have been concerned about corporations' immediate externalities for discrete third parties *and also about their institutional externalities for the larger social order.* Only recently have some sitting judges (including Frank Easterbrook) *advocated* that the courts narrow their sights to the "economic structure" of corporate law in and of itself. The problem is that Easterbrook and other contractarians present this proposal as a value-neutral description and explanation even as their concepts clearly fail to account for U.S. judicial behavior over time.[9] Moreover, at times they acknowledge that their concepts also fail to account for certain aspects of existing corporate law and current judicial behavior.[10]

Legal contractarians are certainly correct in one important respect, however. They are correct that U.S. courts have been evolving steadily as an institution from normatively mediating corporate governance on public law grounds to instrumentally facilitating private contracting. That is, the courts have been evolving from a position of *republican vigilance* to one of *liberal complacency.* A historical perspective likewise reveals that legal contractarians just as clearly err in a different but equally important respect. They wrongly suppose that the externalities of corporate power that once concerned U.S. courts have themselves somehow disappeared from the economy and the larger social order: "The corporation's choice of governance mechanism does not create substantial third-party effects—that is, does not injure persons who are not voluntary participants in the venture."[11] Legal contractarians thus cannot explain a major fact of existing corporate law and current judicial practice: U.S. state courts continue to resist adopting a position of liberal complacency outright, even as they have clearly abandoned their earlier position of republic vigilance. Legal contractarians cannot account at a conceptual level for this resistance, for judges' continuing reluctance to permit their institution to drift toward liberal complacency. The Time-Warner case presented in Chapter 3 illustrates this reluctance, as does the Van Gorkum decision presented in Chapter 2.

One purpose of this volume is to provide such an accounting and thus to make possible value-neutral descriptions and explanations of existing corporate law and current judicial behavior. To this end, a short, theoretically informed history of U.S. corporate law doctrine and judicial practice is offered to sociologists here. The success of this theoretical approach (or of any competing theoretical approach, including legal contractarianism) may be gauged by two criteria. First, can it successfully describe and explain judicial behavior, corporate law, and corporate governance both historically and today? Second, can it successfully predict what the courts will do in the future and whether (and if so, how) this judicial behavior will affect corporations, other intermediary associations, and the institutional design of the larger social order?

Republican Vigilance and the Artificial Entity Theory

U.S. courts' first sustained effort to grapple with the issue of corporate agency, the issue of who bears legal responsibility for a corporation's behavior, began during the colonial period and extended to the 1820s. During this early period, it was settled conclusively that state lawmakers, not federal lawmakers, would take the lead in normatively framing commercial activity. As historian Kent Newmyer puts the matter, the general corporate form had to be created by U.S. lawmakers, and most of this creative process occurred at the state level. The Supreme Court could only broadly influence state law, in particular by defining the relationship between the corporation and the state legislature that incorporated it.[12] Even today U.S. corporate law must still be understood in this historical context. The Founders and Framers were extraordinarily reluctant to grant broad legal support to private commercial activity, let alone to grant it at a federal level. Their reluctance followed logically from their rebellion against the aristocratic privileges and "mercantile monopolies" of English society.[13]

England's lawmakers had granted private corporations monopolies over sectors of their economy, and U.S. lawmakers, already highly critical of the "decadence" of English society, were loath to follow this practice. The Framers' wish to avoid England's "excesses" also helps to explain why they refused to federalize the power of incorporation, to centralize it either in Congress or in the executive branch.[14] Because they preferred to decentralize this power, they continued colonial practice insofar as permitting each state legislature (which earlier were state assemblies) to incorporate the businesses within its jurisdiction. In turn, each of the original thirteen state legislatures continued colonial practice in this area—refusing to assume, as a matter of general legal principle, that private commercial enterprises have any inherently legitimate place and purpose within its jurisdiction.[15]

Vigilance in the New Republic

The colonists' early concerns about commercial activity may be placed in the context of the basic proposition that informed their rebellion against England's monarchy and "excesses": "All power . . . is of an encroaching nature."[16] For the Founders and Framers, a republic meant not simply that they would replace the English monarchy with an elected legislature and elected executive. It also meant that they would limit the popularly elected government's power; that is, they would keep its power constitutionally framed. In their efforts to restrain government from succumbing to its "encroaching nature," they institutionalized federalism or the sovereignty of state legislatures as well as the division of governmental powers at federal, state, and local levels. To this same end, they institutionalized citizens' equal rights before the law, including their right to own and sell private property. We will see momentarily that this latter right did not yet include any license to accumulate private property without restriction. Finally, the Founders and Framers expected citizens' elected representatives to deliberate over the issues of the day with the goal in mind of keeping government limited. They did not want elected officials simply to mirror their constituents' immediate interests or sentiments nor, certainly, did they want them to use their public positions to advance either their own or others' strictly private interests.[17]

Because the framers of the U.S. republic saw all power as encroaching by nature, as tending naturally toward abuse and arbitrariness, they insisted that rules of fair play govern any team activity or joint enterprise, including any private commercial enterprise. Thus, they refused to permit those who held positions of power within private commercial enterprises to bend the latter's rules to their own personal advantage.[18] This is also why they were reluctant to grant broad legal rights to private commercial enterprises: They believed that the law's accommodation of citizens' strictly self-interested behavior carries two *institutional* externalities for the larger social order, and they feared those effects.[19] First, it weakens citizens' respect for rules of fair play and good governance more generally. Second, it discourages them from developing their capacities and powers in well-rounded ways, as citizens of a republic, and thereby erodes their ongoing vigilance in monitoring government's limits.

The Founders' and Framers' sense of "republican virtue" was consistent with the ancient Greek ethic of encouraging excellence in a public realm. It was quite *in*consistent with laissez faire, a then nascent liberal ethic of maximizing wealth in the *oikos,* the household or private realm.[20] "Republican virtue" rested on the proposition that citizens' first responsibility is to keep government's power limited because an abusive state destroys the public realm, the only site at which the pursuit of excellence remains a possibility. Thus, the most important goal of these New World republicans after the revolution was to establish institutions that supported both limited government and citizens' vigilance in monitoring government's limits. In this endeavor they faced a very practical issue: What kinds of institutional arrangements can help citizens to recognize in common when the state's exercises of power become abusive or arbitrary, when the state is succumbing to its "encroaching nature"?[21]

Given the Framers' basic distrust of concentrated power, they were convinced that the best way to support citizen vigilance was to decentralize state power wherever practicable. After all, if citizens are to recognize in common what abusive government is, then they must also be able to recognize in common what limited government is. Confronting the problem of maintaining in practice citizens' shared recognition and collective vigilance, the Framers retained the thirteen colonial legislatures and adopted Montesquieu's idea of dividing state powers. These two institutional devices supported citizen vigilance in three ways. First, both devices decentralized and limited government's exercise of collective power. Second, federalism and the division of powers provided citizens with "trip wires" by which they might recognize *in common* when the state succumbs to its "encroaching nature." An encroaching state will at the very least collapse the division of powers and replace federalism with a more centralized administration. Third, both devices also slowed down all state actions, thereby giving citizens valuable time during which they might organize popular resistance, before the state became too powerful to resist.[22]

Thus, "republican virtue" had everything to do with maintaining an "ordered liberty," a "constitutional liberty."[23] It had little to do with laissez faire. Indeed, "the doctrine of laissez faire was hardly known to the framers of the Constitution."[24] To be sure, "republican virtue" included a strong defense of private property. Ironically, however, this defense was at odds with a social order characterized by laissez faire: The qualities of citizen vigilance and limited government they saw as necessary to a republic rested on a social order marked (1) by a proliferation of yeoman farmers, small shopkeepers, and craft laborers, and (2) by an absence of wealthy merchants and impoverished laborers. Their defense of private property was not synonymous with supporting the free and unfettered pursuit of wealth. The Founders and Framers were so reluctant to grant broad legal support to private commercial activity in part because they were loath to countenance "imbalances" of private wealth. They feared that a widening gap between rich and poor would disrupt social order, erode citizen vigilance, and thereby threaten the republic.[25] Indeed, they saw this gap as one mark of England's decadence. England's "mercantile monopolists" used the power of government to secure private economic privileges at others' expense. The framers of the U.S. republic were convinced that when businessmen are permitted to use government's power in this way, only private disorder and public abuse can result.[26]

The radical nature of this early view of private commercial activity may be appreciated by putting it into the terminology of contemporary corporate law: Whenever private contracts *that are otherwise legal—and otherwise profitable*—make it more difficult for citizens to recognize in common when concentrated wealth or collective power is being used in abusive or arbitrary ways, the courts may legitimately nullify these contracts *on this public law ground.* The point of the Framers' republicanism was precisely that an overriding public law interest, an interest in reducing the institutional externalities of private power, legitimately assumes a higher legal status than otherwise lawful and profitable private contracts. Thus, like other political economists of their day, including Mandeville and Smith, the Framers were concerned first and foremost about the institutional externalities of private commercial activity, not the immediate externalities, the more direct harms done to discrete individuals.[27] By contrast, a century later neoclassical economists would be concerned first and foremost with whether corporations maximize their owners' private wealth and with how corporations perform their "production function" (see Chapter 6).[28]

Our updated wording of the Framers' position sounds hopelessly impracticable in the context of today's intensifying international economic competition. The extremity of the wording to contemporary ears sheds light on why basic principles of contemporary corporate law doctrine—mandatory rules—are so exposed to challenge by economists and legal contractarians. The corporate judiciary and bar has had increasing difficulty since the 1970s retaining any concepts that integrate into contemporary practice the Framers' belief that private commercial enterprises also perform a governance function, one that in some part must serve a public law interest (see Chapter 7). It has difficulty identifying at a conceptual and doctrinal level the institutional externalities that changes in corporate governance can bring into the larger social order today—the respects in which arbitrary exercises of collective power may originate within enormously wealthy and powerful intermediary associations rather than exclusively within government.

Why the Corporation Is an "Artificial" Person

Precisely because student editors of *Yale Law Journal* appreciate how radical the Framers' view of private commercial activity was, as compared to our view today, they label the courts' first doctrinal approach to the corporation "Hobbesian."[29] This is an apt characterization only at one level of analysis, however. It correctly conveys the Framers' belief, with Hobbes, that individuals populated the allegorical state of nature, not corporations. Like Hobbes, they rejected the idea that corporations have "inalienable rights" originating in a state of nature. Whatever "rights" corporations may have are conferred by the state. Since the very presence of corporations within a society already presupposes the legal protections that only a state can provide, the framers of the new republic thought of corporations as "artificial" beings, not "natural" beings. Unlike Hobbes, however, they clearly distrusted state power.

Still, this first approach to the corporation was clearly consistent with Hobbes's social contract theory, and other legal scholars label it the *artificial* entity theory and the state action approach.[30] By this doctrinal approach, when a state legislature grants a corporate charter to a private commercial enterprise, it essentially recognizes a new "person" in society, one who otherwise would not exist with any rights in the eyes of the law. As historian Newmyer puts it, state legislatures retained the power to regulate the companies they incorporated by reserving this power in their charters.[31]

The exemplar of this first doctrinal approach to the corporation is Justice Marshall's opinion in Dartmouth College v. Woodward (in 1819), in which he borrowed heavily from Edward Coke's position (in 1702) and William Blackstone's (in 1765):[32]

> A corporation is an artificial being, invisible, intangible, and existing only in the contemplation of the law. Being the mere creature of the law, it possesses only those properties which the charter of its creation confers on it, either expressly, or as incidental to its very existence. These are such as are supposed best calculated to effect the object for which it was created. Among the most important are immortality, and . . . individuality. . . . It is chiefly for the purpose of clothing bodies of men, in succession with these qualities and these capacities, that corporations were invented and are in use.[33]

In the early decades of the republic, only a state legislature could grant corporations legal rights, including the legal right to accumulate private property without restriction. No state legislature granted corporations this legal right *until 1875.* Indeed, *until 1888,* every act of incorporation in the United States was more like an elaborate naturalization ceremony than like the formality of recognizing a citizen's birth.[34] Each request for incorporation was subjected to the same lobbying and debate as any other item on a state legislature's agenda. This meant, of course, that each request was subjected to the same power plays, personal intrigues, and local favoritism as any other piece of legislation.[35] Only upon such a rite of passage, however, did any private business assume any "rights" at all.[36] There was no such thing as the natural birth of a corporate person, codified in general articles of incorporation.

The Demand for State Charters

The demand for corporate charters was not great at first, and this explains why colonial law lacked any "separate policy or rules on business corporations."[37] Even after the Founding, U.S. state legislatures chartered a total of only 317 business corporations from 1780 to 1801. Of these, only eight were manufacturing firms; over 60 percent were public transportation enterprises; 20 percent were banks or insurance companies; and 10 percent were local public services such as water supply.[38] After this slow start, however, demand for corporate charters picked up steadily. By 1815 Massachusetts alone had incorporated 128 manufacturing firms (mostly in textiles), and by 1830 it had incorporated another 300.[39] From 1791 to 1875, New Jersey granted 2,318 charters, and other states granted just as many if not more.[40]

Still, state legislatures acted on republican principles by keeping their "artificial persons" on a short leash. In incorporating each private business on a case-by-case basis, the charters often mandated that the business contribute to the general welfare—and republicans' sense of what this meant was expansive. It included not only the obligation that corporations contribute to general economic growth but also that they conform to extra-economic, decidedly normative, standards of behavior:

1. State legislatures considered whether a corporation contributed to community services.
2. They prohibited the owners of one corporation from owning stock in another.
3. They placed limits on the amount of capital a corporation could accumulate as well as on its duration as an enterprise.[41]
4. They protected constituencies vulnerable to the corporation's power, including shareholders, creditors, and even employees.

This last item followed from judges imposing fiduciary duties, duties of fair play, on corporate agents. All four items reflected the republican vigilance of state legislatures and state courts over private exercises of collective power.

Relatedly, state legislatures often placed "self-destruction" clauses in their special charters. If an incorporated business failed to complete its legally mandated public works projects within the time period specified, for instance, it could forfeit its charter and legal rights.[42] In short, state legislatures used their special charters to control private commercial activity on a public law ground, namely to maintain the institutional design of the larger social order as they understood it, one capable of supporting limited government and citizen vigilance.

Given the extra-economic restrictions that state legislatures placed on corporate activity, why did business owners and merchants seek state charters rather than retain their unchartered partnerships? First, they valued state charters because they carried prestige. It was widely believed in the early republic that incorporated enterprises "represent[ed] the main type of the most ambitious and sophisticated business associations of the time."[43] Thus, a corporate charter "implied a high value [was being] put upon [its] organizational vitality."[44]

In addition, state charters afforded an enterprise's owners at least some legal protections.[45] First, incorporation meant that a state legislature formally acknowledged that their private business had *some* legitimate place and purpose within U.S. society. The legislature might limit its capitalization and otherwise normatively restrict its commercial activities, but their private business nonetheless had "rights" now as a "person" independently of their own natural rights as property owners. Once chartered, a corporation itself could sue and be sued, contract, acquire and dispose of real and personal property, transfer shares and ownership, and change its membership or constituents.[46] All of these "rights" could be legally enforced not only against the state but also against the enterprise's natural-person founders and owners.

Second, incorporation through state charter meant that a private business's legal identity, its formal recognition as a "person" within U.S. society, could survive its owners' lives as well as the lives of its other founding constituents.[47] Third, incorporation eventually came to mean as well that owners could be exposed only to limited liability for their business's losses.[48] Like everything else about the corporation, limited liability is a "right" granted by the state, not an inalienable right that may be traced allegorically to a state of nature. "The universal adoption of limited liability in the legal systems of the industrialized world rests on relatively modern legislative enactments reflecting politico-economic values, not on fundamental jurisprudential concepts of the nature of the corporation as a legal unit."[49]

Strengths of the First Doctrinal Approach

Until the late nineteenth century, all U.S. state legislatures kept in mind, however implicitly, republicans' dual concern: In granting a charter to one corporation, they might deny opportunities to other citizens as well as undermine the "balance of economic power in American society" that supports limited government and citizen vigilance.[50] The first concern speaks to corporations' immediate externalities, but the second speaks to their possible institutional externalities. This second concern is what distinguishes republican vigilance over the corporation, consistent with the courts' fiduciary law tradition, from today's liberal complacency in treating the corporation as a power-neutral site of private contracting. Given state courts' two concerns, and particularly the second, they read their legislatures' special charters narrowly. They read them as granting to each corporation a specific, delimited set of privileges designed to prevent it (1) from becoming a monopoly that denies opportunities to others and (2) from adding unnecessary imbalances of wealth and power to U.S. society.[51]

One benefit of state courts' narrow reading of special charters was that they could for a time readily answer both of the central questions of corporate law doctrine. First, they could readily identify the corporate agent: Ultimately, the corporate agent was the state legislature that granted the corporation a special charter, not the corporation's owners. Second, state courts could also readily identify the corporation's place and purpose within society: A corporation's activities could not legitimately exceed or contradict the "public law interest" codified explicitly in its special charter. Historian Seavoy puts this well: "[Each charter] assumed that corporations were legally privileged organizations that had to be closely scrutinized by the legislature because their purposes had to be made consistent with public welfare."[52]

Each corporate "person" was a state legislature's creation, and each state legislature treated its "artificial persons" accordingly, that is, paternalistically. It treated them as if they were children in need of constant supervision rather than adults who could be trusted to advance their own interests and aspirations in socially acceptable ways. Even today, many analogies may still be drawn between the workings of the family judiciary and the workings of the corporate judiciary.[53]

Relatedly, state courts could also for a time readily oversee corporations' internal governance. This was not because state legislatures codified explicitly in their special charters how each corporation was to be governed. Rather, corporate decisionmaking was framed by a practical factor and a legal structure that together kept corporate governance from varying significantly. The practical factor was that a corporation's owners (or partners) typically managed its daily operations. The legal factor was that state corporate law typically required unanimous shareholder (or partner) approval of any major corporate transaction (such as a merger or acquisition). Indeed, as late as 1927, only twenty state legislatures permitted a shareholder majority to sanction a merger; all others still required unanimous shareholder approval.[54]

The Rise of a New Doctrinal Approach

Initial Moves Toward Liberal Complacency

We have seen that U.S. corporate law was originally more analogous to the public law norms that protect children and other dependents from harming themselves and others than to the private law contracts that facilitate adults' self-interested behavior. This began to change in the 1830s with a depression and stock market crash in 1837 and widespread reporting in the popular press of the poor performance of publicly owned canals. Public opinion began to question the existing relationship between public law norms and private law contracts. By midcentury, the public was far more inclined than the Founders and Framers had been to tolerate private commercial enterprises that were clearly dedicated more or less exclusively to increasing their owners' wealth. For the first time in the new nation, proponents of laissez faire were able successfully to blame government and state investments for an economic downturn. Another depression and stock market crash twenty years later, in 1857, only enhanced their position.[55] Thus, by midcentury the substantive normative restrictions placed on corporations during the republican era no longer posed insurmountable obstacles to those who wished to maximize their private wealth in U.S. society.[56]

In this context of changing popular beliefs amidst the country's metamorphosis from a yeoman republic to a commercial society, state courts began to develop a second doctrinal approach to the corporation at least somewhat independently of state legislatures. Their new "Lockean" approach would orient the judiciary from the 1830s and 1840s, through the early stages of industrialization and urbanization, to the 1920s.[57] *Yale Law Journal* editors label this second approach "Lockean" because state courts increasingly conceded that private commercial enterprises had a "natural right" to accumulate private wealth.[58] Eventually they held at a doctrinal level that this was indeed consistent with corporations' place and purpose in U.S. society. Many other legal scholars label this second approach the natural entity theory and the private action approach.[59]

Still, we have moved the discussion too far by begging the question: *Why* were substantive norms changing in the civil society of the United States? Why were state legislatures conceding an inherent right to accumulate private wealth, thereby laying the groundwork for general charters of incorporation that would loosen their hold on private commercial activity and leave the monitoring of corporate governance to state courts? The widely reported scandals surrounding public canals contributed to a broader change in public sentiment but also reflected the change. State legislatures were responding in some significant part to the public's growing suspicion that the traditional incorporation ceremony for private businesses was more riddled by local favoritism and corruption than informed by any identifiable public law interest.[60] Moreover, two developments that began in the 1840s and 1850s were steadily exposing general limitations in the republican approach to corporate law doctrine. The exposure of these limitations helped to shift public opinion toward favoring the removal of many existing normative restraints on corporate behavior.

First, even the earliest corporations proved to be far more dynamic commercial enterprises than state legislatures had ever anticipated.[61] More and more of them came before the courts (or were brought before the courts) to determine whether their activities exceeded the mandate of their special articles of incorporation.[62] This alone exposed limitations in existing corporate law doctrine.

Second, more and more owners of corporations began delegating control over their companies' daily operations to others, to full-time managers.[63] As early as the 1850s and 1860s, the founding owners of U.S. (and European) railroad and telegraph companies delegated corporate control to sitting management teams.[64] This separation of ownership and control greatly complicated corporate governance, one result of which was an increase in the kind and number of disputes requiring resolution in the state legislatures and state courts. By the end of the century, state legislatures finally drafted standard corporate charters, effectively transferring these disputes as well as the enforcement of corporate law generally to a specialized judiciary and bar.[65] When they took this step, belatedly codifying what had been taking place in practice since midcentury—the rise of the management corporation—they actually initiated yet a third doctrinal approach to the corporation. (We will explore this in greater detail later in this chapter and in Chapters 6 and 7.)

Even during their interim second approach to the corporation, sitting judges already had to find new answers for the questions of corporate agency and corporate purpose. Judges had particular difficulty answering the question of corporate purpose because they were not prepared to abandon the Founders' concerns about the institutional externalities of corporate power, and yet the United States was now a commercial society, no longer a yeoman republic. On the one hand, they were not prepared to declare outright that the corporation's sole purpose is to maximize its owners' wealth and to perform a production function (see note 28, this chapter). On the other hand, exacerbating their difficulties, their answer to the question of corporate agency—that the corporation's owners are *the* corporate agent—could not keep pace with events. Active owners began passing control over daily operations to management teams, thereby becoming absentee owners, passive investors.

The Rise of the Standard Charter

The new social order in the United States was particularly distinguished from its predecessor by the presence of rich and poor, namely the presence of owners of large and rapidly growing businesses and the presence of manual laborers who were propertyless, unskilled, and often unemployed.[66] Indeed, U.S. citizens did not really accept even the existence of a wage-earning class until the mid-nineteenth century. Prior to this, everyone "pretend[ed] that every wage earner was a potential artisan, shopkeeper, or capitalist." It did not fully strike Americans until the 1880s and 1890s that some of their fellow citizens might have "to occupy the condition of a wage earner indefinitely."[67] Government's dealings with the two new categorical groups in civil society, a rich business class and wage earners, expanded far beyond what the Framers had ever anticipated. Given that by midcentury state legislatures had already permitted significant imbalances of private wealth,[68] by the end of the nineteenth century they also found that they could no longer adequately monitor corporate behavior. In addition, and to an even greater extent, they lost their earlier sense of control over the economy's direction of change and that of the larger social order.[69] As we have seen, the republican approach to the corporation that state legislatures had inherited from the Founders hinged on such monitoring and such a sense of control. This was reflected in corporate law's *quo warranto* procedures and *ultra vires* acts. State legislatures used *quo warranto* procedures against corporations that violated their charters or otherwise acted illegally. In turn, dissatisfied stockholders could use *ultra vires* acts to charge corporations or corporate officers with overstepping their statutory authority. "In the nineteenth century, judges often treated corporate actions such as charitable contributions and expenditures on behalf of employees as beyond the power of the corporation, or *ultra vires*."[70] And, again, state legislatures' ordinary remedy for either type of abuse was to dissolve the offending corporation's charter.[71]

The anachronism of these procedures and acts may be appreciated by considering how legislatures and shareholders could abuse them if they wished. From 1839 *to 1910,* commercial activity in the United States was formally intrastate, not interstate. Corporations were formally prohibited by provisions in all special charters from entering into interstate contracts even with unanimous shareholder approval.[72] And again, through midcentury, "the idea persisted that the state conferred privileges of incorporation not simply for the private benefit of incorporators, but also to further the general welfare."[73] Thus, a corporation's legitimate activities could not at this time exceed or contradict those that a particular state legislature explicitly mandated in its charter. State legislatures, however, were steadily losing their capacity—and willingness—as institutions to enforce these extra-economic limits on private commercial activity.

When state legislatures finally acceded to the changes taking place all around them by drafting their first general charters and standard articles of incorporation, they created the distinctively American body of law called corporate law doctrine. This process began, however, with state legislatures' drafting such articles for nonprofit associations (both religious and philanthropic). They then extended general charters to banks, beginning with Michigan's free banking law of 1837 and New York's a year later.[74] By 1867, Congress had extended bankruptcy law to corporations.[75] In 1875, New Jersey took the lead in abolishing limitations on corporate capital accumulation.[76] Still, a state as sophisticated as New York continued to limit capitalization, in 1881 to $2 million and, as late as 1890, to $5 million.[77] Finally, in 1888 New Jersey became the first state to develop standard articles of incorporation for private businesses.[78]

Delaware followed New Jersey's lead a year later, offering even lower franchise tax rates in an effort to attract takers for its corporate charters.[79] It took some time, however, for Delaware to cut into New Jersey's dominant position. Ninety-five percent of all major U.S. corporations were at that time incorporated in New Jersey.[80] In fact, in 1889 Lincoln Steffens identified New Jersey as a "traitor state" that had "sold out the United States" by amendeding its general charter to permit the owners or shareholders of one corporation to purchase shares of stock in other corporations.[81] Unruffled by reformers and journalists, New York followed suit a year later.[82] This opened the way for the holding company, a major turning point in the history of U.S. business.[83]

Along with the stock-transfer trust and the asset-transfer combine, the holding company exposed huge gaps in U.S. corporate law doctrine. It thereby fostered another distinctively American invention: antitrust law.[84] "Back of the generous powers which New Jersey and Delaware were willing to confer on corporate entrepreneurs were the pressures of a relatively small force of financial ventures [particularly J.P. Morgan's] and their lawyers."[85]

In short, by 1900 nearly all incorporations in the United States were by general charter, and state competition for charters intensified considerably. West Virginia, for example, charged $6 for incorporation and its annual corporate tax was $50.[86] One legal scholar at the time called West Virginia the "Mecca of irresponsible corporations."[87] To complete our chronology, we can note that in 1909 Congress made corporations' interest payments tax deductible, but not their dividends on common stock.[88] A year later, the Supreme Court finally nullified "the traditional rule [of 1839] that denied corporations the power to act beyond the borders of the states that chartered them."[89] This nullification, along with general incorporation acts, ended the *ultra vires* doctrine and inaugurated the era of "great corporations."[90]

Corporate Agency and the Courts

With the rise of general charters and the decline of state legislatures' active monitoring of corporate behavior, corporate law doctrine became the handiwork of an increasingly specialized corporate judiciary and bar. U.S. state courts continued to enforce whatever public law norms remained in their state legislatures' general charters, but they also enforced corporate agents' private law contracts. In addition, the state courts broke new legal ground by imposing a set of *normative* duties on corporate owners and corporate managers *independently of the public law norms in their states' standard charters*. These were norms of behavior codified in English and U.S.

courts' own fiduciary law tradition. Indeed, it was the U.S. state courts rather than England's courts of equity and common law courts that transferred these extracontractual norms from the law of trusts or fiduciary relationships to the law of corporations. They accomplished this by imposing two broad "regimes" of normative duties on corporate agents, whether stockholder-owners or sitting management teams.[91] First, the courts held all corporate agents responsible to a "fiduciary duty of care": This normative duty prohibits corporate agents from stealing or self-dealing and otherwise wasting the corporate entity's assets. Second, the courts also held corporate agents responsible to a "fiduciary duty of loyalty": This normative duty compels corporate agents to exhibit fidelity to the corporate entity itself, to advance *its* interests "fairly" or "disinterestedly."[92]

Fiduciary law's two "regimes"—the duties of care and loyalty—are essentially court-enforced relational norms of behavior. That is, when judges impose these duties on corporate agents, they normatively frame *relationships between* intracorporate *positions.*[93] They provide a normative frame for corporate agents' self-interested behavior, that is, for their advancement of what legal scholars call their *positional interests* and for their exercise of what legal scholars call their *positional power.* It is through the competition of corporate constituents for positional power that their everyday conflicts of interest may escalate into what legal scholars call *positional conflicts.*[94] This is the point at which one or more constituents—particularly minority shareholders—appeal to a state court to intervene. The result is a full-blown *corporate governance dispute:* Corporate constituents essentially present a state court with competing claims to corporate agency. In imposing relational norms on corporate positions, therefore, the courts endeavor to mediate constituents' everyday conflicts of interest or divergences of performance so that they do not escalate into positional conflicts and outright governance disputes. To this end, that of normatively mediating private exercises of collective power for the purposes of maintaining social order, U.S. state courts traditionally have enforced fiduciary law's relational norms by delimiting the types of contracts into which corporate constituents may legally enter in their own positional interests.

In response to the rise of the management corporation—the increasing separation of investors' ownership of the corporation from management's control over its daily operations—U.S. state courts imposed two levels of relational norms on management in particular. At one level, they imposed relational norms on how management could legally advance its own positional interests within the corporation. At the other level, they imposed relational norms on how management could legally invest the corporation's concentrated wealth and legally exercise its collective power within civil society.[95] As state legislatures drafted general charters, and as many republican-inspired public law norms such as *ultra vires* fell out of favor, U.S.

state courts used fiduciary law's relational norms to keep corporate power broadly consistent with the institutional design of the larger social order, as they interpreted it.

In sum, then as now, U.S. state courts held corporate agents to two quite different sets of legal duties. First, they held them to their contractual obligations and statutory obligations. Second, they held corporate agents to extracontractual and extrastatutory obligations, namely their fiduciary obligations to act "fairly" or "disinterestedly" in advancing the corporate entity's "own" interests as an independent "person" within society. England's Chancery Court and other courts of equity had developed these extracontractual duties not only independently of Parliament but also independently of common law courts (see Chapter 5). Again, however, it was U.S. state courts that brought these fundamental normative duties into the law of corporations.

Consider what is at stake whenever judges enforce either the public law norms that state legislatures place in their standard charters or else the relational norms of the courts' own fiduciary law tradition. On the one hand, when judges hold corporate agents to any extra-economic norms of behavior, they hold them to a burden of proof in any cases where they are charged with abusing or misusing their positional power. Judges do not concede that corporate agents' behavior is strictly a private matter, governed exclusively by contract law. Rather, they expect corporate agents to demonstrate that their behavior is sufficiently benign *in its institutional consequences for the larger social order* that the courts may safely treat it as a private matter, one properly left to contract law. On the other hand, when judges no longer believe that existing public law norms or fiduciary duties advance any public law interest, the burden shifts. Now they are conceding that a corporate agent's behavior is essentially a private matter. They expect a state legislature or another court to prove—to the satisfaction of other law-making institutions—that some public law interest is at stake in imposing any extra-economic norms of behavior on corporate agents. To this end, a state legislature or sitting judge must: (1) identify the institutional externalities that these norms of behavior mediate, (2) reconcile legislative or judicial restrictions on commercial activity with existing social norms and public opinion, and (3) keep their enforcement of these restrictions at least broadly consistent.

The courts' second or Lockean approach to the corporation still revolved around rather stringent public law norms, including the absolute limits that state legislatures placed on corporate capitalization. In retrospect, however, an important trend was already under way. The United States was in the midst of a century-long process whereby judges would move corporate law doctrine steadily away from public law norms and even fiduciary duties and move it toward facilitating (and enforcing) corporate agents' private law contracts. This meant that judges were moving corporate law doctrine away from republicans' concerns about limiting corporate power and supporting citizen vigilance and instead moving it toward accommodating and facilitating the corporation's more one-dimensional production function. Put differently, the courts no longer treated the corporation as a child likely to harm itself or others if released from all external supervision. They instead now viewed the corporation as an adult capable of advancing its "own" interests without necessarily harming either itself or others. The evolution of this perspective rested on the assumption that management's efforts to advance its corporation's "own" interests *are more likely to support the institutional design of the larger social order than to foster either private disorder or public abuse.* Thus, state courts shifted their attention from the institutional externalities of corporate governance and behavior to the immediate harms that corporate production and investment might cause to shareholders and other discrete corporate constituents.[96]

The shift from republican vigilance to liberal complacency, in short, is marked by state courts' treatment of the corporation as a private commercial enterprise that performs a production function more or less exclusively. State courts operate on a working assumption that efficient corporate production automatically advances a public law interest—without carrying any significant externalities, immediate or institutional. Today, legal contractarians Frank Easterbrook and Daniel Fischel articulate liberal complacency quite directly: "The firms and managers that make the choices investors prefer will prosper relative to others. *Because the choices do not impose costs on strangers to the contract,* what is optimal for the firms and investors is optimal for society."[97] The pervasiveness of this working assumption today explains in part why judges rarely have republicans' fear of "imbalances" in mind even when they enforce existing public law norms and fiduciary duties.

By the 1920s and the end of the courts' second doctrinal approach to the corporation, state legislatures and state courts alike were routinely conceding as institutions that the corporation is essentially a for-profit commercial enterprise. They also were conceding as institutions that the corporation is such a dynamic entity that its governance and behavior are neither easily nor fruitfully restricted by public law norms or even court-enforced fiduciary duties. They appreciated that the corporation's agents respond in the corporation's "own" interests to the competitive pressures of self-regulating markets. They also appreciated that the outcomes of economic competition are often beyond the powers of government to mediate, let alone to control.[98]

Corporate Purpose and the Courts

As noted earlier, judges nonetheless continued to impose the fiduciary duties of care and loyalty on corporate agents; even at the end of the nineteenth century corporate agents continued to be shareholder-owners rather than management teams. For that matter, state legislatures continued to impose some republican-inspired public law norms on corporate agents. The more important pattern, however, was that many of the absolute normative restrictions that state legislatures had once imposed on corporate agents "suddenly disappeared" in the wake of New Jersey's and Delaware's general charters.[99] With their disappearance, state legislatures and state courts faced a crisis at a conceptual and doctrinal level. They had largely put the Founders' and Framers' republican concerns behind them. The principles and concepts that they had inherited, however, from the common law tradition (the private law of contracts) and from the U.S. constitutional system (the division of powers and federalism) had all been designed to mediate conflicts between individual citizens, between individual citizens and the state, or between state agencies.[100] None had been designed explicitly to address the place and purpose of large intermediary associations within society, whether for-profit commercial enterprises or nonprofit associations. Thus, for better or worse, New Jersey and Delaware now took the lead in fashioning *in practice* what essentially would become U.S. constitutional law for intermediary associations, for corporate persons.[101]

With the demise of republican vigilance and the rise of liberal complacency, neither state courts nor state legislatures were comfortable identifying explicitly, at a conceptual and doctrinal level, any unambiguous corporate purpose other than that of performing a production function efficiently.[102] Sitting judges and state legislators alike began pulling back from their earlier activism in monitoring corporate power. They began deferring to all corporate agents under what became known as the *business judgment rule:* "[Agents'] business judgments are immune from judicial review if [they] had no conflict of interest with respect to the decision in question, acted in good faith and on an informed basis, and rationally believed that their action was in the best interest of the corporation."[103] By deferring to corporate agents regardless of whether they are shareholder-owners or management teams, the courts in particular withdrew from monitoring the details of corporate governance and behavior. They essentially left the issues of corporate agency and corporate purpose "open."

With their reduced monitoring, however, state courts also left "open" a doctrinal question that they would soon have to face in one way or another as an institution: What public law interest do judges serve when they impose any extra-economic norms of behavior on corporate agents, as opposed simply to enforcing contracts and thereby instrumentally facilitating the corporation's production function? Put more specifically: What public law interest do judges serve when they normatively frame how corporate agents exercise their business judgment within self-regulating markets? The courts' second doctrinal approach to the corporation already complicated this issue considerably by conceptualizing the corporation as a

Lockean individual in a state of nature. When state legislatures began drafting general charters, after all, they were acknowledging formally that this Lockean individual is often physically present within society well before its formal recognition at incorporation. They were acknowledging this by converting the incorporation ceremony into a formality, much like the formality of certifying any natural person's citizenship at birth. State legislatures were also acknowledging that the corporate natural person has interests "of its own," and that the corporate agent has the discretion to interpret and advance these interests on "its" behalf.

The Transition to a Third Doctrinal Approach

State courts began developing a third doctrinal approach to corporate agency during the 1920s and 1930s as the United States underwent another metamorphosis, this time from a commercial society to an industrialized, urbanized society. As we have seen, this doctrinal development actually began earlier in the century, with New Jersey's and Delaware's general charters. The courts moved to this new approach when they finally acknowledged at a doctrinal level that corporate agents were no longer likely to be shareholder-owners but rather elected boards and appointed management teams.[104] During the period of transition, from the 1890s to the 1920s, state courts began treating the corporation's owners collectively *as the principal.* They saw that the principal typically permits its elected agent, a board of directors, to appoint and oversee the "real" corporate agent, a management team.[105] This third doctrinal approach would orient the corporate judiciary through the 1970s into the early 1980s, until a new market emerged for control over the corporation itself in the form of hostile takeovers and leveraged buyouts.

By withdrawing from monitoring corporate power, state courts began treating relationships between corporate agents as strictly private or contractual matters. They did not see the rise of boards and management teams as posing any greater challenge to the state's sovereignty—or, for that matter, to the integrity of the social order—than the challenge posed by the institution of private property itself. After all, once a state legislature concedes on Lockean grounds that property is a private thing that individuals may sell *or accumulate* like any other private thing, it follows as a corollary that most contractual arrangements surrounding the sale, *if not the use,* of this thing are also strictly private matters.[106] When a state legislature drafted a standard charter, it was in effect acknowledging that the management corporation as an organizational form has a legitimate place and purpose within U.S. society.[107] The standard charter legitimated an intermediary association whose agents were dedicated more or less exclusively to efficient production, and either to maximizing the owners' private wealth or else to maximizing the corporation's "own" growth. State legislatures nonetheless treated the management corporation like they treated any other incorporated intermediary association or "natural person." They treated it as simultaneously (1) independent of and yet ultimately subordinate to the state, and (2) independent of and yet ultimately superordinate to all of its constituent parts, including its dispersed shareholder-owners.[108] In accepting a state legislature's new standard charter, a corporation's dispersed owners in effect acknowledged that management could act as their agent, as overseen by their elected board.[109]

We must keep in mind that state legislatures' removal of normative restrictions on the corporate natural person's governance and behavior was a century-long process. Moreover, certain normative restrictions remained, and remain today. Putting this point differently, the courts have never embraced liberal complacency outright, whether during their third doctrinal approach or today. The corporate judiciary has never declared explicitly, at a doctrinal level, that it no longer expects corporations to advance any public law interest whatsoever. To the contrary, judges continue to intervene into corporate governance disputes on public law grounds whenever they believe that management or any other corporate agent exercises its positional power "unfairly" or "inequitably." By the late nineteenth century, however, they intervened less often by citing the public law norms that remained in states' standard charters. Rather, they intervened more often by citing the relational norms unique to the courts' own fiduciary law tradition.

This shift in judges' rationale for intervening into corporate governance disputes is significant. As long as the courts continue to impose fiduciary law's relational norms on corporate agents, they endeavor still to delimit the corporation's place and purpose in U.S. society, and they do so independently of state legislatures' standard charters. Thus, as long as the courts continue to enforce management's fiduciary duties of care and loyalty, their decisions continue to recognize, however implicitly, two distinct types of corporate behavior: that which is consistent with the institutional design of the larger social order, even if it contributes to greater imbalances of wealth and power, and that which challenges the institutional design of the larger social order, by increasing the frequency and broadening the scope of arbitrary exercises of collective power. Of course the courts do not conceptualize the distinction in this manner. It is in danger of being lost from the courts' institutional memory, even as it remains codified in the fiduciary law tradition.

Today legal scholars and judges alike ask openly what public law interest corporations can possibly be expected to serve in a global economy, other than to maximize profits or corporate growth in their "own" interests. They have great difficulty identifying institutional externalities in any changes in corporate governance and behavior. They correctly appreciate that intensifying international competition has closed off any possibility that the courts might again enforce traditional republican restrictions on private commercial activity. Even as the corporate judiciary correctly concedes this, though, it nonetheless faces numerous conceptual or doctrinal problems as an institution: Can judges update traditional republican restrictions at a conceptual level so as to convert them into doctrinal options that are both economically practicable and legally enforceable? Can judges impose any norms of behavior on corporate agents without jeopardizing U.S. corporations' domestic profitability and international competitiveness? Why exactly should they enforce such norms in any case? Again, what unambiguous public law interest can this possibly serve? All of these questions speak to the contemporary problem of social order as we conceptualized it in Chapter 1, the problem of *democratic* social order in a global economy.

Notes

1. Chancellor Allen (1992b).
2. Simon (1990:394).
3. Easterbrook and Fischel, for instance, contest the centrality of corporate investors' limited liability as well as the corporation's legal identity as a "person," including its "perpetual existence" beyond the lives of its founding constituents (1991:11–13).
4. For example, see Easterbrook and Fischel (1991:4).
5. See Chapter 7, pages 178–186. Contractarians do not always dominate today's debate, but they raise issues for debate far more frequently than do legal traditionalists.
6. For example, see Chancellor Allen (1993:1404–1407). Similarly, sociologist Michael Hechter often offers a default defense of rational choice theory. He argues that irrespective of the many conceptual problems riddling this social theory, it nonetheless holds greater promise for orienting methodical empirical study than any alternative. See Hechter (1983:158; 1987:31–33, 183–186); see also Friedman and Hechter (1988:211–213).
7. Easterbrook and Fischel (1991:vii).
8. Easterbrook and Fischel (1991:170).
9. Eisenberg (1989).
10. For example, Easterbrook and Fischel (1991:136, 205–209).
11. Easterbrook and Fischel (1991:17).
12. Newmyer (1985:128–129).
13. Bourgin (1945/1989:44).
14. Blumberg (1993:6).
15. Hovenkamp (1991:11–12); also Roy (1997:41–77). Even today, with our very different outlook about the "rights" of private commercial enterprises, every corporate charter in the United States is still granted by one or another state legislature. Moreover, the United States Supreme Court routinely reaffirms the states' primary authority over corporate governance and behavior in no uncertain terms. For instance, in CTS Corps v. Dynamics Corp. of America, 481 U.S. 69 (1987), it asserted that "no principle of corporation law and practice is more firmly estab-

lished than a State's authority to regulate domestic corporations" (quoted by Orts 1992:50). Still, it must also be noted that the republic's founders and the Constitution's framers held a quite different position regarding large *public* works and their *national* funding. In their view, "powers such as those over roads and canals, *granting charters of incorporation* [to public improvement projects], encouraging agriculture and manufactures, and establishing seminaries and schools were well within the scope of *federal* authority" (Bourgin 1945/1989:45, my emphasis). Thus, Thomas Jefferson, for instance, easily combined a staunch belief in democratic rule with a great willingness to finance *public* improvements with federal funds. He was willing to amend the Constitution, if necessary, to bring these programs into effect (Bourgin 1945/1989:107–147). The point is that he saw that the Constitution would have to be amended to this end.

16. McDowell (1988:7).

17. This view did not hold in the colonies. Rather it sprang rather suddenly from constitutional principles developed by the new republican state governments during the spring of 1776. See Hoffer (1992:113–121).

18. Sellers (1991:31).

19. Roy concedes that "the law played an autonomous role in shaping the social relations institutionalized in the new corporate organization of property" (1997:144; see also his chaps. 3 and 6). Nowhere, however, does he identify what state legislatures and state courts were trying to accomplish in restraining corporate growth. We propose that the corporate judiciary has always been concerned about the institutional externalities of private power, and that it approaches corporate governance with an eye to maintaining the institutional design of a democratic social order.

20. Lasch (1990:175); compare to Daniel Bell's neologism the "public household" (1976:220–282).

21. This is the issue that begins to identify law's "autonomy," which Roy (1997) fails to bring into his "power theory" explaining the rise and consolidation of the corporate form.

22. See Sciulli (1992:68–69, 202–239) on the allegory of the constituent force that ultimately protects the Constitution.

23. McDowell (1988:65–66).

24. Bourgin (1945/1989:37, 47). Whether or not Adam Smith's ideas were well known to the Founders and Framers is a controversial issue among historians. On the one hand, Bourgin points out (1945/1989:24) that although *The Wealth of Nations* first appeared in 1776, it was not published in North America until 1789. He is convinced that Smith's ideas were neither well known nor influential. On the other hand, Gary McDowell finds (1982:52) that "the exact influence of the Scottish moralists on American thought is impossible to measure, but we do know that, during the American Founding, such Scottish authors as Adam Smith and Adam Ferguson were widely read and discussed and frequently invoked by the proponents of the 'new science of politics.' In particular, James Wilson was responsible for introducing many Scottish Enlightenment theories into American political thinking." Wilson was a signer of the Declaration from Pennsylvania and, McDowell notes, second only to James Madison in his theoretical contributions to the Constitution. He later served as a justice on the U.S. Supreme Court (1982:52–53); see also McCoy (1980:13–47). Herbert Hovenkamp (1991:21–23) argues that Jeffersonians were influenced by Smith's writings, but he is not as clear about Jefferson himself.

25. See Reich (1991) for this same concern today. Even early American liberals who were otherwise critical of republicans' zeal in condemning private commerce nonetheless accepted republicans' view of the social order supporting citizen

vigilance and limited government (Lasch 1990:195–202). Legal scholars and historians continue to debate the relationship between liberalism and republicanism; see, for example, Banning (1978); McCoy (1980); Appleby (1984); Diggins (1984); Kammen (1986); Bourgin (1945/1989); *Yale Law Journal* symposium (1988); and Sunstein (1990:chap. 1). The same is true about the relationship between democracy and republicanism; see, for example, Kammen (1986) and McDowell (1988:34). Historian Charles Sellers notes that until the Jacksonian period, Americans preferred the term "republican" to the term "democrat" (1991:31–32).

26. Sellers (1991:chap. 2); Mark (1987); McDowell (1982:chaps. 1–3); McCoy (1980).

27. "Of course I do not believe in literal 'laisser-faire'; I know of no reputable economist who ever did. Certainly neither Smith and Ricardo nor Cobden and Bright would have restricted the state entirely to the negative functions of policing individual liberty and defense against outside attack. No one denies that 'man is a social animal'; and in fact society makes men far more than men make society, meaning by deliberate thinking and action" (Knight 1921/1948:lii).

28. The corporation's production function is "the physical relationship between [its] output and various inputs, [and it] tells us how much output we can hope to get if we have so much labor, so much capital, so much land, etc." (Samuelson 1948:521).

29. Note (1982).

30. For example, Millon (1990) and Blumberg (1993).

31. Newmyer (1985:150).

32. Blumberg (1993:3–4).

33. Quoted by Buchanan (1958:6).

34. Millon (1990:206) citing Friedman (1973/1985:188–191). See Roy (1997:57–70) for comparisons of corporate law in Pennsylvania, Ohio, and New Jersey.

35. Roy focuses his attention on manueverings by urban merchants, finance capitalists, state officials, and farmers (1997:55).

36. Actually, the situation has always been more complicated. Only in the 1970s (with Bellotti) did the Supreme Court find that the corporate "person" enjoyed First Amendment rights of free speech. To this day the corporate "person" lacks Fifth Amendment rights against self-incrimination. See, for example, Coffee (1981:429–433) citing Bellis v. U.S., 417 U.S. 85 (1974). Christopher Stone notes (1982:1489) that the corporate person's claim to freedom of speech is strongest in the law whereas all of its other rights are "cloudy."

37. Hurst (1970:7); also Friedman (1973/1985:198).

38. Hurst (1970:17).

39. Blumberg (1993:10).

40. Hurst (1970:17–18). Pennsylvania chartered 2,333 corporations from 1790 to 1860, nearly two-thirds of which were for transportation and only 8 percent for manufacturing (Roy 1997:57).

41. Millon (1990:208–210) citing Hurst (1970:44–45).

42. Hovenkamp (1991:56–67).

43. Hurst (1970:14).

44. Hurst (1970:25, also 28). This fits well with institutionalists' notion of organizations seeking legitimation from "environmental" norms.

45. Samuelson (1948:120–121).

46. Blumberg (1993:4–5). Roy (1997) refers to this as the "socializing of capital," as converting a once private or family-centered enterprise into a social enterprise, one more widely owned and managed.

47. Millon (1990:205–206); Alchian and Allen (1964/1972:284).

102   *U.S. Corporate Law*

48. Hovenkamp (1991:49–55). See Blumberg (1993:10–12) on the delay in limited liability, and Easterbrook and Fischel (1991:40–62) for a discussion of its deficiencies. Roy (1997:158–164) sees limited liability as one of three sine qua non characteristics of the corporate form after the 1870s, which is true for this later time period. The other two characteristics are intercorporate stock ownership and an independent board of directors.

49. Blumberg (1993:7).

50. Hovenkamp (1991:4, 37).

51. Millon (1990:207–208).

52. Quoted by Roy (1997:48).

53. I explore some of these analogies later in this chapter (at pages 94–95). See also Chapter 5, pages 113–114; and Chapter 7, pages 183–185.

54. Millon (1990:215).

55. See Goodrich (1960) on canals and Roy (1997:71–75) on the stock market crash and depression.

56. Mark (1987:1446–1447). As early as 1811, Justice Joseph Story feared that U.S. citizens were losing their shared understanding of arbitrariness. By 1832, he felt the situation was "truly alarming" (McDowell 1982:71–72). This period coincides with the demise of what Habermas (1962) calls the "public realm" in Europe.

57. This second approach was anticipated by the Supreme Court as early as 1809 (Blumberg 1993:27). Bratton (1989a) sees two periods here instead of one, the first from the 1850s to the 1880s, and the second from the 1880s into the twentieth century. Hovenkamp (1991:14–15) does the same. It is unclear, however, what the legal threshold or principle is that separates the two periods.

58. Note (1982).

59. For examples, see Bratton (1989a:1474, 1485–1489); Millon (1990); Blumberg (1993:27).

60. Samuelson (1948:119); see also Millon (1990:208) citing Hurst (1970:33–36). This factor eludes Roy's account (1997:71–77).

61. Hovenkamp (1991:48).

62. Mark (1987:1451).

63. Hovenkamp (1991:16).

64. See Friedman (1973/1985:181); Chandler (1977:70–205; 1990:1–2, 54–59); Haar and Fessler (1986:109–140); Williamson (1985:274–278); and Roy (1997:78–114). In England, the Railroad Clauses Consolidation Act of 1845 both concentrated power in the hands of railroad magnates and also imposed on them a common law duty to serve (rather than to abuse) the public. This duty extended to the railroads' rate structure; by comparison, railroad rate discrimination was not a concern for U.S. courts until the 1880s (Haar and Fessler 1986:106, 119). Frank Norris popularized the problem in 1901 with his novel *The Octopus* (see Kennedy 1991:138–181 for history and analysis). Public regulation of private economic activity in the United States began with the states' regulation of railroads, grain elevators, and other monopolies. Eventually the limitations of state regulation became evident, particularly with regard to railroads' interstate operations. This led in 1887 to the formation of the Interstate Commerce Commission, the first great federal agency (Breyer and Stewart 1985:26; Friedman 1973/1985:445–453).

65. Hurst (1970:82–83). The state Courts that hear corporate governance disputes, including Delaware's Supreme Court, are general courts that hear all kinds of cases. But Delaware's Chancery Court specializes in corporate law and the law of trusts, and its increasing influence across the corporate judiciary originates during this period. Moreover, a case can be made that "corporate law" in the United States

is essentially a product of courts in four states: Delaware, New York, New Jersey, and California.

66. See Melanie Archer and Judith Blau (1993) for a review of the literature on the U.S. middle class in the nineteenth century.

67. Christopher Lasch (1990:206).

68. "Between 1833 and 1848, the percentage of wealth owned by the 1 percent wealthiest Bostonians climbed from 33 to 37 percent. Between 1826 and 1845, the corresponding figures went from 29 to 40 percent in New York and from 22 to 42 percent in Brooklyn. . . . Today, *Forbes* magazine suggests that no less than 59 percent of the richest Americans owe their wealth to their ascendants . . ." (Clignet 1992:41–42).

69. Hovenkamp (1991:48).

70. Easterbrook and Fischel (1991:102).

71. Hovenkamp (1991:56–59); see also Newmyer (1985:150).

72. Millon (1990:209).

73. Millon (1990:207); see also Hovenkamp (1991:56–57). Often in passing sociologists of organizations assert that a much closer relationship existed between the U.S. government and "the creation of the private corporation"; see, for example, Powell (1990:306). But this flies in the face of all of the republican restrictions that U.S. state governments routinely placed on for-profit businesses. Lasch offers a fine overview of historians' and social scientists' "rediscovery" of the importance of these limitations (1990:168–225). The legal historians cited in this section and the next never forgot them.

74. Friedman (1973/1985:180).

75. This Bankruptcy Act was repealed in 1878; in 1898 Congress passed a new act that would last for eighty years (Delaney 1992:21). In 1938, the Chandler Act's Chapters X, XI, and XII were added to business bankruptcies in particular (Delaney 1992:22). Under Chapter X bankruptcy management could be replaced by a court-appointed trustee, but under Chapter XI bankruptcy management typically stayed in place (Delaney 1992:24). The Bankruptcy Code was revised again in 1978, with the three chapters above consolidated into Chapter 11 (and Arabic numbers replaced Roman numerals). Chapter 11 addressed reorganization under existing management, whereas Chapter 7 addressed liquidation (Delaney 1992:30).

76. Hurst (1970:147).

77. Friedman (1973/1985:523).

78. Actually, New Jersey passed three acts, in 1888, 1889, and 1893; the latter two were more important in allowing industrial combinations (Blumberg 1993:56; see also Roy 1997:152–153). In the early republic, the New Jersey legislature pushed hard (albeit unsuccessfully) in 1778 and then again in 1781 to enlarge the federal government's commerce power (Bourgin 1945/1989:46–47). New Jersey's legislature also formally chartered Alexander Hamilton's grand plan to spearhead U.S. industrialization, which he called the Society of Useful Manufactures. On November 21, 1791, the SUM was authorized to secure $1 million in capital, a huge figure for the day: If it had gone forward as planned, it would have been as large as the fifty largest manufacturing firms in Europe. But, once again, the New Jersey legislature was too far ahead of its time or, better put, unlucky. After the SUM had selected its site, in Paterson, a speculative debacle in 1792 wiped out the wealth of some of its leading promoters, and Hamilton's plan fell apart (Bourgin 1945/1989:103–104).

79. Hurst (1970:147–148); Friedman (1973/1985:520).

80. Blumberg (1993:57). Roy is more specific (1997:152): "By 1901, 66 percent of U.S. firms with $10 million in capital or more and 71 percent of those with

$25 million or more were incorporated in New Jersey." Today the situation is quite different. Delaware incorporates over half of the *Fortune* 500 companies, and over 40 percent of all companies listed on the New York Stock Exchange (Orts 1992:28). Moreover, Delaware's share of the pie is growing: "Approximately 80 percent of firms that change their state of incorporation move to Delaware" (Easterbrook and Fischel 1991:212–213). However, it must be kept in mind that California incorporates the most companies by far overall: "California has many more incorporations than Delaware, even though Delaware has the lion's share of the largest firms" (Easterbrook and Fischel 1991:215).

81. Steffens was famous (or infamous) for announcing "I have seen the future and it works," upon returning from Moscow and marveling at the changes Leninism had wrought (McWilliams 1973:514). Name calling seems to be New Jersey's lot. Contractarian legal scholar Bernard Black calls New Jersey the "first chartermongering state" (1990:548).

82. Hovenkamp (1991:257); Blumberg (1993:57). See Roy (1997:233–235) on holding companies in the tobacco industry. James Burk points out (1988:71–74) that as state legislatures passed the first general incorporation statutes, they were simultaneously prohibiting the trustees of estates, mutual savings banks, and life insurance companies from investing in the stock market. They compelled them to seek "safe investments," those that the legislatures formally listed as such, including: local, state, and federal bonds; bonds of public utilities and transportation companies; and government bank annuities. By 1980–1981, many states followed the Carter and Reagan administrations in changing their laws to permit public employee pension funds to invest in leveraged buyouts.

83. Chandler (1962); Blumberg (1993:58).

84. Hovenkamp (1991:249–267). I do not have much to say about antitrust law in this volume and the reason is somewhat ironic: Antitrust law has little to do with corporate governance. Antitrust law affects the size of corporations, and how corporations may legitimately grow. But once a corporation of any size is then present within U.S. society, antitrust law has little to say about how it or any other intermediary association is to be governed. It has little to say about how this corporation or any other intermediary association may otherwise use its concentrated wealth and exercise its collective power within civil society.

85. Hurst (1970:72).

86. Hurst (1970:135); Friedman (1973/1985:524). Today, reincorporation in Delaware costs between $40,000 and $80,000, far less than any top manager's annual salary (Black 1990:587–588). These monies nonetheless add up, and particularly in a small state like Delaware: In 1987, 184,000 corporations paid Delaware state franchise fees totaling $170 million; this was 17 percent of the state's total revenues (Yago 1991:192). Looking back, New Jersey paid off its entire public debt by 1902 using corporate fees and taxes. Moreover, its entire state budget for that year was covered simply by the corporate fees and taxes gained from the New York firms that incorporated in New Jersey (Blumberg 1993:57).

87. Cook in 1894, quoted by Orts (1992:38).

88. Anders (1992:21). Eighty years later, with memories of the Depression forgotten, economist Michael Jensen (1988) would propose that debt replace equity in financing corporate growth. This would provide the backdrop in economic theory for the turbulence of the 1980s (see Chapter 6).

89. Millon (1990:212–213).

90. This doctrine was already in decline, in practice, by the 1890s. See Hurst (1970:65–69, 127, 157–158); Friedman (1973/1985:518–519); Millon (1990:212–213); Hovenkamp (1991:60); and Roy (1997:144–175). Robert Sobel begins his

history of "Corporate America" in 1914, the year following the opening of North America's tallest building (the Woolworth Building, at 793 feet), the Grand Central Terminal, the Panama Canal, and the first Ford assembly line (1984:ix).

91. The term in quotation marks is Palmiter's (1989).

92. See Chapter 7, pages 172–174.

93. See Coleman (1990:450, 542–547) on the importance of corporate positions.

94. Eisenberg (1989:1471–1472); see Easterbrook and Fischel (1991:9–10) on "divergences" in performance.

95. Mitchell (1990:1171–1172).

96. Millon (1990:208–210).

97. Easterbrook and Fischel (1991:6–7, my emphasis).

98. Millon (1990:211); Mark (1987:1441–1442).

99. Bratton (1989a:1489); Mark (1987:1455); Hovenkamp (1991:62–63).

100. Mark (1987:1447). This is in contrast to the broader legal doctrines of equity or fairness that had been developed independently in fiduciary law (see Chapter 5).

101. See Gordon (1991) on the Delaware courts' "constitutional" powers today, and Blumberg (1993:30–44) for background; also see Orts (1993:1578).

102. Hurst (1970:57–62). Roy uses Hurst in discussing the rise of an "efficiency ethic" and decline of the earlier "responsibility ethic" (1997:75).

103. Loewenstein (1989:70); see also Easterbrook and Fischel (1981:1195–1197) and Fischel (1982:1288).

104. Butler (1989:101).

105. Dent points out that the legal requirement that shareholders select a board to "direct" the firm was by no means inevitable (1989:883, note 4). From 1862 to 1929 British law, for example, did not require corporations to have a board. Even today in the United States many states (including Delaware) permit close corporations to eliminate their boards. Close corporations do not trade their stock publicly on the exchanges.

106. We will see in Chapter 5 that fiduciary law emerged in fourteenth-century England as a law of property use, whereas contract law was the unquestioned law of property ownership and sale.

107. The courts' accommodation of the management corporation solved two very different problems at a conceptual or doctrinal level (see Hovenkamp 1991:247–248, 266). First, it solved the problem of how the courts might assign corporate agency, as the legally recognized positional power to exercise the corporate natural person's "rights" or constitutional claims. The courts now granted this positional power to directors, and then to managers. They flatly denied to the corporation's passive and absentee owners any legal authority to exercise the corporate natural person's rights or claims. Second, it also solved the problem of how the courts might reconcile their treatment of corporations with their treatment of private property generally. For the first time, the courts gave the corporation's shareholder-owners the same constitutional protections that they gave to individuals who owned other types of property in their own names. In both cases, property *ownership* was seen as a strictly private law matter, not a public law matter. In both cases, however, property *use* continued to be seen as a public law matter, not a strictly private law matter.

108. Mark (1987:1465); Hovenkamp (1991:62–63).

109. Mark (1987:1460); Millon (1990:214–215).

5

The Chancery of Old and the Problem of Social Order

Before resuming the chronology of U.S. judicial approaches to the corporation, it is worthwhile to backtrack a bit and briefly review the English fiduciary law tradition. In identifying corporate agency and corporate purpose,
U.S. state courts have until recently been oriented first and foremost by
corporate law doctrine's core of mandatory rules.[1] In turn, the parts of the
core that have been most resilient over the years, from the Founding to
today, are the relational norms that stem from the courts' fiduciary law tradition—not the public law norms that state legislatures codify more explicitly as statutes. We have already seen that many public law norms dating
from the republican period did not survive the rise of a commercial society
in the 1830s and 1840s. Many others "suddenly disappeared" when New
Jersey and Delaware developed general charters that, among other provisions, allowed corporate owners to buy and sell shares in other corporations. We will see in Chapter 6 that state legislatures themselves annulled
even more public law norms beginning in the late nineteenth century as the
United States urbanized and industrialized. What has survived, again until
recently, are mandatory rules that originated in England's fiduciary law tradition. This is a tradition of court-created law that predates not only the
American Revolution but Jamestown, England's first American colony.

The king's chancellors began creating fiduciary law in the fourteenth
century. They began by imposing norms of "equitable conduct" on local
barons that exceeded barons' legal obligations under common law contract
and later under legislative statute. U.S. state courts continue this practice
today despite the consolidation of equity law and common law in many
states in the 1850s and Congress's abolition of the distinction in 1938.
What began to change at the turn of the twentieth century, however, was
that U.S. state courts became less inclined as an institution to impose fiduciary law's norms of behavior on management and other corporate agents
as mandatory rules. By the mid-1970s, in turn, the courts began facing
strong pressures to permit shareholder majorities to "opt out" of all manda-

tory rules and instead to make whatever arrangements they wish with the management team handling daily operations. For the first time in U.S. history, they began to reduce corporate law, including the courts' longstanding relational norms, to contract law.

Let us examine more closely the parameters and uses of relational norms. U.S. judges enforce relational norms when they prohibit any corporate agent—whether directors, managers, or controlling shareholders—from so tampering with a corporation's governance structure that only its positional interests prevail.[2] It is important to see both the content and purpose of these judicial actions—the "what" and the "why" of them. When judges enforce relational norms, by definition they *normatively* mediate corporate agents' self-interested behavior. Moreover, they do so not as an end in itself but rather in order to prevent corporate agents from abusing the power of their positions, from using their positions to take unfair or inequitable advantage of other corporate constituents. *Judges enforce relational norms, then, in an effort to ensure that corporate agents' behavior within corporate governance structures—private structured situations, like barons' manors—is more disinterested than self-interested.*

This initial characterization of fiduciary law's relevance today reveals a general principle at the center of the fiduciary law tradition as a whole. Within structured situations, we can identify on the one hand certain positions of power and discretion and, on the other hand, positions of dependence and trust. Any relationship between these positions, therefore, is intrinsically unequal, irrespective of who fills them, why they fill them, and how they fill them. Put differently, any individual who enters a position of dependence and trust within a structured situation has literally only two options, neither of which is costless: He or she may trust those who hold positions of power and discretion to act disinterestedly on his or her behalf rather than more strategically in their own interests. Alternatively, he or she can exit the structured situation and enter a more fluid site of self-interested contracting within competitive markets.[3]

Judges enforce relational norms whenever they re-establish disinterested behavior in the relationship between (1) corporate agents who occupy positions of power and discretion and (2) corporate constituents who occupy positions of dependence and trust. In enforcing relational norms they maintain the continuing "integrity" of a corporation's governance structure *as a structured situation.* They are not trying to insulate the corporate entity from competitive pressures in the marketplace, thereby trying to ensure its continuing survival *as a long-term economic enterprise.*[4] They are not treating particular corporate entities, after all, as if they are national landmarks, historical sites, or endangered species. They are not trying to establish that certain corporate enterprises contribute uniquely to the cultural patrimony of the country. Rather, again, they are treating corporations as powerful "persons" in civil society—like barons—who exercise positional power within their domains and collective power in civil society.

Thus, the distinction between seeing (1) a corporation's governance as a structured situation meriting judicial oversight and seeing (2) a particular corporate entity as a putatively treasured long-term economic enterprise meriting judicial protection is critical to the very future of the fiduciary law tradition today. However, the judges and legal scholars who defend this tradition, aptly labeled "legal traditionalists," have blurred this distinction for decades.[5] The erosion of the distinction has jeopardized the future of this legal tradition and helped to open the way for "legal contractarians" to pressure the courts to reduce corporate law to contract law. Judges properly hold corporate agents to fiduciary law's relational norms of behavior only when they believe, whether explicitly or implicitly, that a corporation contains structured situations of dependence and trust whose governance can carry externalities for the institutional design of the larger social order. Judges properly act in this way only when they are more concerned about the qualitative end of preventing corporate agents from abusing their positional power than about any quantitative end, whether that of maximizing shareholder dividends or that of maximizing corporate growth.

Nonetheless, the question remains: Why are U.S. state courts still oriented by this priority at the end of the twentieth century? Does it really serve any *unambiguous* public law interest? Or does this priority result in unnecessary judicial intervention into corporate affairs, in ways that are anachronistic and that jeopardize the domestic profitability and international competitiveness of U.S. corporations?

Rather than attempting here to answer these questions directly, we may examine the actual current behavior of U.S. state courts. For better or worse, these courts do in fact continue to impose relational norms on corporate agents. They continue to impose court-enforced norms on corporate agents that mediate (1) how corporate agents may legally advance their own positional interests, (2) how they may legally interpret the corporation's "real" interests as an entity, and (3) how they may legally exercise this entity's collective power in the larger social order. Increasingly, however, judges fail to clarify at a conceptual or doctrinal level their grounds for intervening into corporate governance. Perhaps they intervene because corporations are long-term enterprises, not fly-by-night operations, and it is important at times to insulate them from competitive pressures in a global economy. The problem here is that the public law interest at stake is not clear. On the other hand, perhaps they intervene because corporations contain sets of structured situations whose governance can either support or challenge the institutional design of the larger social order. The public law interest served here is clear, but there is still a problem. State courts as an institution have been losing sight of the importance of identifying those structured situations within corporations that qualify unambiguously as fiduciary relationships. Today, the corporate judiciary and bar is literally experiencing a breakdown of shared meaning over this issue—just as Max Weber would have predicted (see Chapter 7).[6]

Contemporary critics of the courts' fiduciary law tradition, the legal contractarians, gain points with state judges by posing a basic question: Why exactly are you still supporting any variation of extra-economic norms of behavior at the end of the twentieth century that originated in England in the fourteenth century? What *is* the point of the courts enforcing such norms *as mandatory rules?* What unambiguous public law interest can fiduciary law's relational norms possibly serve today?

Legal contractarians insist that whatever contribution inherited, court-enforced norms may (or may not) have made to American (or English) society in the distant past, this same contribution can be made today more simply by enforcing the contractual obligations into which individuals enter in their own self-interests. To state the matter succinctly, they propose that all of corporate law's existing mandatory rules may be replaced by optional rules—called suppletory rules and enabling rules. They hold to this absolutist position quite irrespective of whether particular mandatory rules originated historically as legislatures' public law norms or as courts' fiduciary duties. Once critics of the fiduciary law tradition gain judges' attention with their initial challenge, they then push them even further into a corner by posing three additional questions:

1. First they ask: When *exactly* does a particular corporate governance structure or corporate division qualify as a structured situation that falls unambiguously within fiduciary law's scope of application?
2. Then they ask: What *unambiguous* public law interest is served by imposing any norms of behavior on managers and shareholder majorities, given that this not only constricts shareholders' contractual freedom but also likely distorts management's interpretations of the corporate entity's "real" interests?
3. Finally they ask: What *possible* harms can befall U.S. society if judges confine themselves to enforcing managers' contractual obligations to shareholders and stakeholders, and drop all efforts to enforce managers' putative fiduciary obligations of duty and loyalty to the corporate entity?

In order to convey what is at stake in these questions for organizations, for social sectors, and for the larger social order, we may review when, how, and why fiduciary law originated in England. Then in the next two chapters we can explore why the intersubjective meaning and institutional significance of this legal tradition have become increasingly uncertain in the twentieth century.

A Short History of Chancery's Rise and Fall

England's first courts, its system of local common law courts, originated during the rise of the medieval system and reign of Henry II (1154–1189). This rise was marked by two events in particular: first, the Constitutions of Clarendon in 1164, when barons recognized a list of customs as the practice of the realm; and second, the first treatise on the common law, written by the king's justiciar Ranulf de Glanvill in 1187.[7] Over a century later, in 1328, common law courts formally secured their independence from the Crown in the Statute of Northampton. Edward III accepted that royal commands could not challenge the judicial system's chain of legal precedents. In return, common law judges agreed to restrict their jurisdiction largely to criminal cases and, as a reflection of their strong interrelationship with the existing medieval system, to disputes over land *ownership*. In these two areas, therefore, common law courts operated independently of the king's prerogative.

Fiduciary law originated during this same period of time, the mid-fourteenth century, as an instrument of the king's prerogative over land *use* law. Common law courts might well settle disputes over who owned the land independently of the king's prerogative. But the king would retain his longstanding right to hear complaints about how *legally owned* land was being used. To this end, the king controlled a separate system of courts as part of his staff (dispersed across the kingdom) and his council (his immediate advisors). Staff and council, taken together, were the king's parliament and court (*Curia Regis*). Into the fourteenth century, England's parliament was not yet an independent political institution; it was rather the king's legislative body and highest court.[8] Throughout the thirteenth century, the king periodically summoned his entire staff of officials from across the kingdom to answer questions posed by his council's permanent staff. This special event became known as a colloquy, a parliament. Thus, the term "parliament" did not refer originally to a distinct institution of government but rather to this periodic gathering of officials around the Crown.[9]

The institutional significance of land use law was that all land in the kingdom was technically held in trust as part of the king's domain. Thus, the king and his judges exercised prerogative in preserving this public trust as they interpreted it. When they heard complaints that land was being wasted or used without care, they acted on their own, independently of the common law system. They also dispensed with the rigor, the concern for precedent, that already marked early common law proceedings over land ownership cases. Moreover, instead of restricting themselves to the sorts of facts that could then be properly pleaded before common law courts, the king's courts deliberated over any and all evidence that they could find that bore on reported breaches of trust.[10] Thus, the king's courts originated what we now call "discovery" in judicial proceedings. Using this new judicial power, the king himself as well as his personal representatives on his court, the justiciars, literally traveled the kingdom in an ongoing effort to stem barons' corruption of local law enforcement.[11] From the start, therefore, the Crown's courts of prerogative established their own jurisdiction as well as their own institutional practices.

Meanwhile, the common law courts turned inward after they gained independence from the Crown. Within their delimited jurisdiction, they adhered more and more strictly to their own precedents and procedures. What this meant, in practice, was that they developed ever more elaborate defenses of the medieval system and of landed barons' privileges within it. As England's commercial economy steadily outgrew the medieval system, common law courts remained dedicated to examining property records. These courts were therefore neither willing nor able as an institution to respond to "laborers'" grievances. The term "laborer" at this time referred to anyone outside the medieval system. Thus, a "laborer" was neither peasant nor baron. He was either a free farmer, which included the largest independent landowners, or a trader, which included the wealthiest merchants.

Even the wealthiest and most influential laborers were convinced that they could not get a fair hearing before common law courts, and they and many other laborers often petitioned the king for redress from these courts' rulings. Their willingness to petition the King's Council directly was more structural than social psychological: Their transactions could not be facilitated by existing law, and their disputes could not be resolved by existing law. They needed a court that was willing to "discover" new evidence, beyond that which common law judges typically heard in ownership cases. Moreover, this court would also have to be willing to develop and codify new rules of business behavior, as well as new procedures for handling laborers' disputes effectively, with consistency over time. The common law courts were so rigid in their ways, so tied to the medieval system, that no one expected them to develop these new practices and procedures on their own. On the contrary, common law judges refused even to recognize laborers' customary property rights in land that they worked for generations. Thus, even customary tenants, "copyholders," had no alternative within the existing judicial system other than to appeal directly to the King's Council for protection and redress.[12]

As England's commercial economy exceeded the limits of the medieval system, so many laborers petitioned the King's Council for redress that his entire staff—parliament—could not keep pace. In its attempt to handle these cases, the King's Council soon developed functional divisions. For instance, the King's Bench emerged within Council to handle routine requests for redress, and it eventually became known as the Court of Common Pleas. At first this court concentrated more or less exclusively on resolving disputes among the king's own tenants over their feudal rights and duties. But as it handled other matters, as its caseload both multi-plied and diversified, it developed its own functional divisions or special-ized bodies: All finance matters went to the Exchequer, all routine land ownership cases and criminal matters were still left, as agreed, to common law courts, and all administrative or executive duties, including laborers' petitions for redress from common law rulings, went to the King's Council.[13]

By the end of the thirteenth century, these appeals were increasing so rapidly that Edward I insisted that all complaints against common law courts be submitted in writing, as formal petitions. This technicality, how-ever, did not stem the sheer numbers involved. The petitions so drained the council's time that it could no longer perform its original function, namely advising the king more generally. By the middle of the fourteenth century, at the same time that common law courts were gaining their independence from the Crown, parliament came under the control of barons and secured its independence too from the Crown. One of the new Parliament's duties, in fact, was to oversee, and to restrain as best it could, the corruption and excesses of common law courts.

Council continued to exercise the king's prerogative, but the situation had become terribly confusing. Laborers were sending their petitions for redress to the king, to Council, and still to Parliament—and now, for that matter, to Council's own permanent staff advisor, the chancellor. Eventually, Council would call upon this Chancery office to carry out most of its judicial business, and yet Council still did not return to its original role of advising the king. Instead, it turned to criminal cases that involved barons and, more generally, to monitoring whether legal contracts, legisla-tive statutes, and royal decrees were actually being enforced (as opposed to being corrupted by barons).[14]

Why did Council turn to Chancery at all, given that the chancellor was merely an informal delegate to Council? Like Parliament, Chancery was not originally a distinct body but rather a part of Council. It was part of the permanent staff that posed questions at the colloquy gathering. The chan-cellor himself was a bishop or archbishop whose original role was to advise the king on matters of church and state. Eventually his advisory role expanded to include other political matters. In this advisory capacity, the chancellor controlled a staff of clerks that, in time, became specialized in copying Crown documents, including all official correspondence between the Crown and common law courts.[15] Thus, by the time Council turned to Chancery for help on laborers' petitions, Chancery had already developed a well-organized staff familiar with judicial business. In addition, the chan-cellor also happened to be the one official who most constantly attended Council meetings.[16]

Eventually, Chancery took over Council's equity cases in civil law matters, but not in criminal law matters involving barons. The latter went in time to Star Chamber, a court we shall discuss momentarily. Unlike Council, which distanced itself from common law judges, Chancery used its earlier connections with common law courts by calling upon judges for advice.[17] From the outset, however, Chancery operated independently of the common law system, and the chancellor had distinct advantages over common law judges. As a court wielding the king's prerogative, Chancery had the authority to discover new evidence, to consider all available evidence rather than restricting itself to matters properly pleaded at the common law. Moreover, Chancery's jurisdiction over civil law matters was far broader than that of any common law court. Chancery could hear not only complaints about land use but also complaints about the abuse of children, the mentally ill, and other family matters.[18] Chancery treated all of these complaints as matters of *public* trust, even as they took place within civil society, within seemingly *private* settings. It treated them as matters subject to the king's prerogative.

In short, Chancery was from the outset a unique judicial institution with broad powers. For example, even though all early chancellors were ecclesiastics, Chancery had sufficient power as an institution to turn against its own when clergy were accused of violating the public trust. During the fourteenth century, monks and friars at times decoyed children into monasteries. The courts overseeing their conduct, the church's own ecclesiastical courts, typically failed to provide parents with much remedy. In 1402, Chancery brought the king's prerogative to these cases by hearing parents' complaints of abduction.[19] As another example, at midcentury Chancery demonstrated its independence as a judicial institution during the civil war between the houses of York and Lancaster, the War of the Roses. Chancery brought the king's prerogative to cases in which propertied single women had been abducted to castles and forced to marry in order to surrender their estates and goods.[20]

As each succeeding chancellor addressed the complaints coming before him, he literally filled gaps of practice and procedure in the common law. Moreover, as each succeeding chancellor codified the obligations he was imposing on trustees and other agents of the king, Chancery slowly developed its own body of precedents. These precedents became codified as trustees' and agents' fiduciary duties, their duties of equitable conduct. Thus, the chancellors restricted property use, enforced specific performance of contracts, and protected women, children, and "idiots," all on the public law ground of upholding norms of basic fairness, of equity, across the kingdom.[21] Historian Karl Polanyi writes:

> [The Tudors' and early Stuarts'] chancelleries and courts of prerogative were anything but conservative in outlook; they represented the scientific spirit of the new statecraft, favoring the immigration of foreign craftsmen, eagerly implanting new techniques, adopting statistical methods and precise habits of reporting, flouting custom and tradition, opposing prescrip-

tive rights, curtailing ecclesiastical prerogatives, ignoring Common Law. If innovation makes the revolutionary, they were the revolutionaries of the age. Their commitment was to the welfare of the commonalty, glorified in the power and grandeur of the sovereign . . .[22]

In contrast to Chancery's reputation for innovative and swift rulings, common law courts were widely despised for their slowness, rigidity, expense, inefficiency, technicality, openness to abuse by local barons, antiquated methods of proof, opposition to volunteer witnesses, and unwillingness to compel parties to discover evidence useful to their adversaries:[23] "The undercurrent of grave discontent which never ceased from the Peasants' Revolt in 1381 down to the Pilgrimage of Grace in 1536 had a good deal of its origin in the inefficiency of legal enforcement and the inadequacy of the law itself . . ."[24]

Indeed, common law judges would not extend even basic legal protection to laborers for another two centuries.[25] As a result, during the enclosure movement that swept across England from the 1490s to the 1640s, the chancellors stood with the king virtually alone in defending the public trust as they saw it. England's commercial economy was blossoming into a nascent market society, and land that customarily had been left available for the use of all—the commons—was being "enclosed" by its formal owners for their own private use. Again, Polanyi captures the issues involved:

> Enclosures were an obvious improvement if no conversion to pasture took place [which threw peasants off the land, leaving them to become beggars or thieves]. Enclosed land was worth double and treble the unenclosed. Where tillage was maintained, employment did not fall off, and the food supply markedly increased. . . . [But] enclosures have appropriately been called a revolution of the rich against the poor. The lords and nobles were upsetting the social order, breaking down ancient law and custom, sometimes by means of violence, often by pressure and intimidation. They were literally robbing the poor of their share in the common, tearing down the houses which, by the hitherto unbreakable force of custom, the poor had long regarded as theirs *and their heirs'*.[26] The fabric of society was being disrupted . . . turning [people] from decent husbandmen into a mob of beggars and thieves. *Though this happened only in patches, the black spots threatened to melt into a uniform catastrophe. The King and his Council, the Chancellors, and the Bishops were defending the welfare of the community and, indeed, the human and natural substance of society against this scourge.*[27]

No one questioned Chancery's authority and legitimacy to challenge enclosures in the sixteenth and seventeenth centuries. After all, it was widely accepted as early as the reign of Edward I in the late thirteenth century that the king's courts of equity properly imposed fiduciary duties or relational norms on barons who abused dependents on their own manors.[28] It was not problematic, therefore, for Chancery to apply the same fiduciary duties or relational norms during the enclosure movement to those lords and nobles who were abusing peasants and free laborers in England's emerging market society.[29] The problem, however, was that the chancellors continued to oppose enclosures for another century, and on the same public law ground, even as land was being freed for tillage rather than for sheep pasture. Thus, Chancery ended up obstructing England's market society well after its emergence had become a *fait accompli.* It thereby converted a once defensible concern—the enforcement of equitable conduct across the kingdom in order to preserve basic social order—into an increasingly indefensible restraint on modernity itself, on systemic social change. This is why Chief Justice Edward Coke could oppose Lord Chancellor Ellesmere (Thomas Egerton) in 1613–1614, in Courtney v. Glanville, by arguing that Chancery rested not on fundamental law but on the caprice of the Crown.[30]

As understood more analytically, the result of the chancellors' pattern of action was to hypostatize a particular substantive normative vision of social order that, as such, soon became anachronistic. The same thing happened a century later when republicans across the Atlantic hypostatized a particular substantive normative vision of social order at the Founding, namely one comprised only of yeoman farmers, local merchants, and artisans. Only a single generation later, with the rise of Jacksonian democracy and a commercial republic, this vision had become anachronistic.[31]

Resuming our discussion of the king's courts of equity, by the early sixteenth century the modern idea of fiduciary law or equity law was firmly institutionalized in England. The first modern chancellor, William Warham, Bishop of London, was appointed in 1502, and in 1530 Sir Thomas More became the first lay chancellor.[32] By this time Chancery's jurisdiction was quite broad indeed. It settled cases involving accidents, accounts, frauds, infants, trusts, and specific performances (of a contract, or of a land use restriction).[33] It must be kept in mind, moreover, that Chancery was not the only court exercising the king's prerogative. Aside from the Court of Exchequer, there was also the equity jurisdiction of the Scotch courts, *the colonial system of equity and appeal* (which brought this legal tradition to the North American colonies), the Court of Requests, and Star Chamber.[34]

The Court of Requests was another committee of Council that eventually secured a specialized jurisdiction of its own. Its jurisdiction was poor men's civil law petitions as well as petitions from the king's own servants.[35] The Star Chamber emerged because Council continued to receive petitions regarding crimes committed by barons after it assigned to Chancery all civil law cases. Council was particularly inundated with accusations that local barons and local magnates were committing crimes but escaping successful prosecution because they intimidated judges and juries.[36] Juries were widely distrusted at the time because packing and general corruption were so common.[37] Star Chamber was one of the many rooms that Council occupied during the fifteenth century as it considered these criminal petitions. As Council dedicated more and more of its time to hearing these cases, along with overseeing the enforcement of legislative statutes and royal proclamations, it became known as the Court of Star Chamber.[38]

Consider for a moment that these prerogative courts lacked both the consecration of time and the backing of parliamentary statutes. Moreover, all of them clearly sidestepped the solemnities of common law precedent and procedure.[39] Neither their authority nor their legitimacy, however, was seriously challenged until 1641. Even then, Chancery survived while Star Chamber was abolished for perceived abuses. Why? Even by this late date common law courts were still tied to a now rapidly declining medieval system. They were still unwilling as an institution to hear cases involving breaches of trust. "It [was] clear that equitable relief was necessary, and was valued. [Plus] there were rapidly increasing property interests whose protection rested solely in Chancery."[40] As a result, Chancery survived the abolition of Star Chamber in 1641, and then the turn to republican rule from 1649 to 1660. It also survived Charles II's restoration of the monarchy in 1660 and the Glorious Revolution of 1689. It survived all of these political changes because republicans and monarchists alike appreciated that equity rulings were indispensable to maintaining social order.

Around this time, however, the Crown began losing legitimacy, and sovereignty, to Parliament, and the common law system finally became more reform-minded.[41] Earlier in the century, common law judge Sir Edward Coke successfully challenged royal absolutism, at least in principle. Then, during the Civil War, Parliament abolished outright many of the Crown's prerogative courts. As we have seen, Chancery's authority and legitimacy as a distinct judicial institution withstood these challenges as well as those that would come for another two centuries.

Thus, in 1726 Chancellor Peter Lord King held in Keech v. Sandford that a fiduciary was responsible for renewing a lease he held in trust for an infant beneficiary.[42] In the same year, Richard Francis published *Maxims of Equity,* which would become "the most often cited summary for rules of equity in English Courts."[43] Over time English courts extended their enforcement of fiduciary law's relational norms from financial trusts to many other structured situations, both public and private. They extended fiduciary duties to the operators of public utilities and common carriers (barges and railroads),[44] and then to private partnerships and early corporations. Even as late as 1828, Joseph Parkes concluded his otherwise blistering critique of Chancery by calling for its reform, not its abolition.

From English Trusts to U.S. Corporations

The point of our historical overview is that Chancery enforced norms of equity in those structured situations that the chancellors and the Crown believed carried institutional externalities for the larger social order. These were situations in which individuals found themselves in positions where they had no alternative other than trusting those holding power over them to act equitably or disinterestedly on their behalf rather than more strategically in their own interests.[45] This is why the Crown granted its own courts the prerogative (1) to punish officials' excesses and any other unlawful public conduct and (2) to review and alter the rulings of common law courts in certain private law matters, including certain contracts.[46] "To the extent that all forms of public interventions seek to eliminate the contingencies attached to personal agreements, they remind private contractors that they are all *equally* subjected to the good will of the prince."[47]

Thus, England's courts of equity sanctioned any trustee, any individual exercising power in the public trust, who took unfair advantage of dependents. It did not matter if the structured situations in which dependents happened to find themselves were located in a medieval manor, an independent farm, or a commercial business. What mattered was that these situations were structured and, by definition, contained positions of trust and dependence. England's courts of equity operated on the assumption that self-interested exercises of positional power within structured situations violate the public trust as such. They operated on the assumption that self-interested exercises of positional power within structured situations violate the most basic norms—the most basic expectations—underpinning the public's trust in anyone holding a position of responsibility, whether public *or private*.[48] In short, they operated on the assumption that these exercises of positional power carry externalities for the institutional design of the larger social order. Once the public's trust in those holding positions of authority is disrupted, the only way social order can be maintained is by relying more and more exclusively on coercion, manipulation, material incentives, or other formal mechanisms of social control. Social order then becomes reducible to the demonstrable social control of individuals. It no longer rests in any part on individuals' possible social integration.

With this theoretical point in mind, let us return to our historical discussion. England's courts of equity were concerned first and foremost with monitoring changes in the *quality* of social order over time, not simply with maintaining social order as such. As their response to the enclosure movement indicates, they were quite willing to sacrifice possible *quantitative* gains in private wealth (Lockean contracts) and possible *quantitative* gains in social wealth (Pareto optimal outcomes) in order to secure a *qualitative* end, namely that of maintaining a relatively benign social order. Such a social order is one in which exercises of collective power are mediated short of abuse and arbitrariness, such that individuals might gain integration rather than require control. That is, from the very beginning fiduciary law's "jurisdiction" was comprised of the institutional externalities of trustees' self-interested behavior, not the immediate externalities for discrete beneficiaries and dependents. Indeed, whether trustees' self-interested behavior actually carries *any* immediate externalities for beneficiaries and dependents is not simply a secondary concern in the fiduciary law tradition. *It is ultimately an irrelevant concern.*[49]

This explains why Chancery and England's other courts of equity largely discounted the subjective interpretations of the individuals directly involved and instead endeavored to "discover" independent evidence of the abuse at issue. On the one hand, they discounted trustees' subjective motivations for behaving self-interestedly. On the other hand, they discounted as well dependents' subjective interpretations of whether trustees' behavior had actually caused them harm. Indeed, it did not matter to courts of equity whether any discrete dependent actually suffered immediate harm from trustees' self-interested behavior. It did not matter, in fact, if a *dependent* actually profited from a trustee's self-interested behavior in a particular instance, or if a trustee's self-interested behavior ended up redistributing wealth rather than concentrating it. What mattered was whether a trustee had acted in a self-interested way in a structured situation.

Thus, Richard Francis promulgated the thirteenth "maxim" of equity law, first published in England in 1726: "Equity regards not the circumstances, but the substance of the act."[50] This maxim was central because Chancery and England's other courts of equity were extending judicial protection to structured situations, to ongoing relationships between unequal positions, on a public law ground. Their public law ground was that these situations and relationships merit judicial protection, as islands of disinterested conduct and equitable behavior in a vast sea of otherwise self-interested conduct and strategic behavior. They merit judicial protection because the very presence of these islands in civil society normatively mediates what would otherwise be cumulative challenges to the institutional design of the larger social order. As legal historian Peter Charles Hoffer puts it, chancellors looked beyond both sides of a suit in an effort to identify principles of "communal justice" and to provide for "systemic, institutional relief."[51] In short, awarding damages to the parties involved in a particular breach of trust is not as important to courts of equity as rearranging social relations in order to protect any individuals who might find themselves in similar situations.[52]

Chancery steadily suffered as an institution because it remained essentially a one-judge court.[53] Only in the early nineteenth century did Parliament add other judges to it. By then, however, common law courts were compelling discovery and taking over other procedures that Chancery had developed. For example, common law courts extended their own equitable doctrine—common carriers' duty to serve the public at large—to private monopolies that provided public services. "The distribution of scarce goods that are public in nature—goods such as municipal services—need to be equitable and fair."[54] Given this convergence in judicial practice, Parliament formally fused common law and equity law jurisdictions into the same judicial bodies in 1881.[55]

Meanwhile, in England's North American colonies the colonial governors had greater power over their subjects in the seventeenth and eighteenth centuries than the king had over his in England.[56] Legally trained colonists breathed the air of the fiduciary law tradition; some were even aware that John Locke had been the secretary of Chancellor Shaftesbury and had "cited the concept of trust far more often than that of contract."[57] Thus, they used the language of trust to identify what they believed were their rulers' accountability to the governed. Jefferson, for instance, "was an equity specialist." Instead of characterizing the obligation of the Crown to colonists as a contract, he used the language of equity to develop a concept of public trusteeship capable of justifying the colonial rebellion against England.[58] Even legal scholars a generation later who were influenced by Adam Smith's writings nonetheless conceded that "the common law required certain firms such as common carriers to charge only reasonable rates."[59] The only issue of dispute was how to determine when rates are "reasonable." By the end of the nineteenth century, U.S. courts began to recognize that the common law duty to serve applied not only to common carriers but also to many other businesses whose activities carried consequences for the public at large.[60] Soon, however, the courts began narrowing the types of businesses that they held to this public law interest.[61]

Like the jurisdiction of fiduciary law's relational norms, the jurisdiction of the common law duty to serve has in the United States also been contested continually rather than ever being settled. The Constitution notes the equity power in Article III, Section 2, where the Supreme Court is given jurisdiction over all cases "in law and equity," but this power is not defined. Equity is also mentioned briefly in *Federalist Papers* (numbers 78 and 80) "as a judicial means of offering relief *to individuals* from 'hard bargains' in cases of fraud, accident, mistake, or trust, and as a means of confining [the harm done] by 'unjust and partial laws.'"[62] The social vision of U.S. courts was thus narrowed at the outset from the institutional externalities of exercises of positional power in structured situations to the immediate externalities.

In its Judiciary Act of 1789, Congress extended equity jurisdiction to all federal courts; it also established a firm rule as to when the courts could apply it.[63] By the 1820s and 1830s, Supreme Court Justice Joseph Story became so concerned that U.S. deliberative bodies were losing their integrity to the populism of Jacksonian democracy and to a rampant states' rights movement that he made it his life's mission to convert equity law into a science.[64] His *Commentaries on the Constitution of the United States,* published in 1833, articulated precedents for chancellors that were already well developed in practice.[65] "Story was . . . the last major [American] defender of the original understanding of equity."[66] By the 1850s, with the movement led by David Dudley Field to codify state law in statutes, New York and other states in the East merged common law and equity. Finally, in 1938 Congress formally abolished the distinction between equity procedures and common law procedures.

One outcome of amalgamating common law and equity law is that the Supreme Court and other appellate courts typically hear appeals using only the record created in trial courts. This is the common law procedure. At times, however, these courts sit in equity, seeking additional factual findings, as the Supreme Court did in its Brown decisions of 1954 and 1955. Federal judges exercise their powers of discovery in this fashion as well.[67] Courts sitting in equity thus employ an inquisitorial process, not the adversarial process of common law courts.[68]

In 1955 the United States Supreme Court, in its second Brown decision, transferred its concerns about the immediate externalities of inequitable conduct from individuals seeking relief in particular cases to groups claiming psychological deprivation as an ongoing condition.[69] Ironically, by expanding equity's scope of application from individuals' disadvantages in "hard bargains" to the ongoing condition of groups, the Court *severed fiduciary law's linkage to any specific, delimited set of structured situations.* That is, by permitting U.S. courts to apply "equity law" literally wherever judges find inequitable outcomes, the Court enervated the principle that some applications of fiduciary law's relational norms are beyond interest group lobbying or any negotiated settlement over outcomes. The Court thus formalized balancing or ongoing group competition over defining and remedying inequitable conduct. It did not continue the effort to identify a particular set of structured situations in civil society whose governance carries institutional externalities for the larger social order.[70] Hence, it was only a matter of time before the U.S. corporate judiciary would lose sight of when, and when not, to enforce relational norms within corporate governance structures and corporate divisions. It would lose sight of the public law interest served by this function.

This relatively recent development in corporate law is significant. It was U.S. state legislatures and state courts that took the lead from England in working fiduciary law's relational norms into corporate law doctrine. Delaware's Chancery Court, after all, remains an independent court of equity that specializes in resolving corporate governance disputes on a public law ground.[71] On occasion this court, as well as Delaware's Supreme Court, still treats corporate governance structures and corporate divisions as structured situations whose positions of dependence and trust carry institutional externalities for the larger social order. As such, it treats them as falling within fiduciary law's unique scope of application, as meriting judicial protection on a public law ground. Moreover, the Delaware Chancery's most important jurisdiction, much like that of England's Chancery three centuries ago, is trustee and guardianship proceedings where a plaintiff seeks an equitable remedy for a breach of trust. This jurisdiction may be contrasted to one of the common law courts' most important civil jurisdictions: a plaintiff who seeks performance of a contract when, for example, a defendant's payment of a scheduled fee is late or insufficient.[72]

Are the Social Relationships
Covered by Fiduciary Law Increasing Today?

Students of fiduciary law often say in passing that the earliest fiduciaries recognized by law were trustees, administrators, and bailees.[73] There is a certain disingenuousness here, however. The generalization supports legal contractarians' narrow view of this legal tradition by focusing the discussion of fiduciary law on the matter of the immediate externalities that exercises of positional power carry for discrete individuals (or groups). It focuses the discussion on how fiduciary law normatively mediates the actions that particular trustees take to advance the interests of particular beneficiaries. It thus neglects from the outset how fiduciary law normatively mediates institutional externalities and thereby supports the institutional design of a democratic social order.

   Clearly, the first fiduciaries were the king and his chancellors, followed eventually by England's common law judges. Certainly, these fiduciaries acted, in one way or another, with an eye to the institutional design of the larger social order. After all, aside from being fiduciaries to the particular claimants who came before them, they were also fiduciaries (1) to existing social arrangements as they interpreted them, and (2) to their own courts' institutional practices and organizational forms.[74] Indeed, we can say, following our discussion of the new institutionalism in Chapters 1–3, that England's chancellors were major environmental agents: They literally created the institutionalized environment for barons and early corporations. All later fiduciaries (and dependents) appealed to the chancellors for legal protection, and these later fiduciaries had far more limited effects on the larger social order. Compared to the chancellors, they were minor environmental agents. My point is that legal traditionalists today—defenders of the fiduciary law tradition—do not help matters by obscuring the earlier stages of the story of fiduciary law. Nor does it help that they neglect the contemporary importance of identifying those structured situations within corporations whose governance carries institutional externalities. Failing to identify such situations when they impose fiduciary duties on corporate agents, they appear to be treating corporations simply as long-term commercial enterprises that, in order to survive, need protection from competitors in the marketplace.

   For example, Tamar Frankel begins at the later stage of the story when she points out that two crosscutting developments have increased individuals' vulnerability to abuses of power today, one historical and the other more contemporary.[75] The historical moment was the entrance of former apprentices and members of households into England's new industrial labor market, which broke the medieval bonds of paternalism. In the initial period of England's transformation into a commercial society, the traditional social controls on master craftsmen and barons of medieval manors were not applied to the new structured situations emerging in civil society. At the same time, these traditional controls were losing their mediating power even in their original jurisdiction. Only much later, at the end of the eighteenth century, did the law catch up, when some former status or paternal relationships were reclassified as contract or agency relationships. Centuries also passed between the time when the chancellors treated trustees, administrators, and bailees as fiduciaries and the time when the chancellors and common law judges began treating some corporate agents as fiduciaries. By the early twentieth century, U.S. and English courts were both treating the controlling owner-shareholders of corporations as well as some labor union leaders not only as agents but as fiduciaries.

In sum, as more and more individuals moved outside of status or paternal relationships, *some of the new structured situations into which they entered were eventually classified as fiduciary relationships.* Nonetheless, the courts that oversee these relationships have shifted their focus toward the immediate externalities of exercises of positional power and away from the possible institutional externalities. "The reason that agents, trustees, partners, and directors are subjected to the fiduciary obligation is that they have a leeway for the exercise of discretion in dealings with third parties which can affect the legal position of their principals."[76] We can see in the narrowness of this statement that republican vigilance has given way to liberal complacency.

The more contemporary development to which Tamar Frankel refers is individuals' increasing vulnerability to abuses of power as a result of the professionalization of personal and social services. (The most recent fiduciaries recognized by law are physicians, psychiatrists, and other professionals.[77]) This kind of vulnerability can also be identified in the rise of large financial institutions that pool and invest capital. Few social scientists or legal scholars, however, treat the experts involved with this development as "professionals" who, as such, qualify as fiduciaries.[78] Thus, a critically important issue today is how to distinguish those experts who qualify as fiduciaries from those who do not. The rise of the specialist who "becomes the substitute for all those in society who seek his expertise" has steadily increased the range and types of structured situations that might eventually qualify as fiduciary relationships.

This contemporary development (classifying certain contractual relationships in civil society as fiduciary relationships) moves in the opposite direction of the historical development discussed previously (reclassifying certain traditional status relationships as contractual relationships in civil society). More and more individuals today are moving beyond contract or strictly agency relationships into what appear to be modern status or "paternal" relationships. The historical and contemporary developments taken together illustrate that the modern fiduciary relationship stands somewhere between strict contract relationships and strict status relationships. Frankel's thesis in pointing to both developments is that however contemporary fiduciary relationships emerge, they "give rise to the problem of abuse of power." This thesis begins to bring the problem of the institutional externalities of exercises of positional power back into the picture. For Frankel, "the purpose of fiduciary law should be to solve this problem, and . . . the differences in the rules applicable to various fiduciary relations stem from differences in the extent of the problem."[79]

One result of both the historical and contemporary developments is that more and more individuals today find themselves within structured situations wherein they cannot costlessly avoid trusting others' judgment and expertise. With this, they become vulnerable to others' opportunistic behavior and potential abuse of positional power. Even if individuals seeking professional services could somehow on their own design the structured situations into which they enter so as to reduce their vulnerability to abuse, the costs of doing so would likely far exceed whatever benefits they could expect to receive from the situation.[80] This is why Frankel believes that fiduciary law is still needed. Only court-enforced relational norms can counterbalance this secular trend of individuals' increasing vulnerability. This vulnerability, after all, is not a product of individuals' *initial* inequalities; it is not incurred as they *seek* professional and expert services. It is rather a product of individuals' *subsequent* inequalities, *after they have successfully secured these services*.[81] Frankel's point is that this trend cannot be counterbalanced entirely by developing more sophisticated contractual protections.

*   *   *

I close this chapter with the following description of Delaware's Chancery by a journalist who covered the Time-Warner case of 1989 (see Chapter 2):

> In Delaware's Chancery Court . . . judgments of fairness rather than strict rules of law govern the outcome. In the U.S., chancery courts as such are a rarity except in what some lawyers call the "Kingdom of Delaware." Chancery springs from the old British tradition of equity, correcting injustices more informally and swiftly than other courts can. "Equity," wrote a seventeenth century jurist, "is a roguish thing. For the law we have a measure and know what to trust; equity is according to the conscience of him

that is Chancellor. One Chancellor has a long foot, another a short foot, a third an indifferent foot. 'Tis the same thing in the Chancellor's conscience."[82]

Chancery does indeed have the capacity to act swiftly. The Time-Warner case was heard July 11, 1989, beginning at 10:10 A.M.; proceedings resumed after an hour-long lunch break and concluded at 3:24 P.M. A decision was rendered, in favor of the Time-Warner merger, three days later. The Delaware Supreme Court is no more dawdling.[83] It heard the appeal of Chancellor Jacobs's decision in another case, the Paramount-Viacom case, on December 9, 1993, giving each side one hour to present oral arguments. It upheld Chancellor Jacobs's ruling with an eleven-page preliminary decision "only hours after hearing the case."[84]

Notes

1. See Chapter 3, note 57.
2. See Kester (1991:62–75) on trust and implicit contracting in Japanese corporations, including informal safeguards against opportunism.
3. See Hirschman (1970) generally.
4. One of the controversies surrounding Chancellor Allen's decision in the Time-Warner case (see Chapter 3, at page 67) is precisely that he seemed to treat Time Inc. as a long-term economic enterprise worthy of preservation in itself—similar to a national landmark or endangered species. He did not focus his decision on the more generalizable issue: Had the managers of Time Inc., Warner Communications, or Paramount Communities exercised their positional power arbitrarily in a structured situation in civil society?
5. See Sciulli (1997a, 1997d).
6. See Hoffer (1990:247, note 17) on the "partial unraveling" over the past three decades of "the compromise" between courts of equity and legislative oversight, which compromise Hoffer traces to the American Revolution.
7. Plucknett (1929/1956:16–19).
8. The British Parliament to this day remains the highest court in the land; its legislation cannot be declared unconstitutional by any other judicial body.
9. Plucknett (1929/1956:152–155).
10. McDowell (1982:5).
11. Plucknett (1929/1956:144).
12. Plucknett (1929/1956:177–178).
13. Plucknett (1929/1956:148–150, 159, 177).
14. Plucknett (1929/1956:179–180).
15. Plucknett (1929/1956:163).
16. The rise of Chancery could well serve as a case study of Robert Michels's (1911) many comments on how members of permanent staffs secure power and influence.
17. Plucknett (1929/1956:180–181).
18. Plucknett (1929/1956:194). Thus, at the very outset the law that normatively mediated collective wealth as an entity (as a corporate body) also normatively mediated the family, another entity (another corporate body).
19. Parkes (1828:47).

20. Parkes (1828:55).
21. Polanyi (1944:35); see Gordon (1991) for an updated use of Polanyi.
22. Polanyi (1944:38).
23. Plucknett (1929/1956:688–689).
24. Plucknett (1929/1956:688).
25. Plucknett (1929/1956:33–34).
26. Fiduciary law has always been at the center of inheritance, imposing public obligations on what is otherwise a private matter.
27. Polanyi (1944:34–35, my emphasis).
28. Plucknett (1929/1956:27–31).
29. Brudney (1985:1407–1408, note 15). See Habermas (1962) on the rise of civil society, and then of the "bourgeois public sphere." See Stone (1982:1451, 1481–1482) on fairness constraints, beyond efficiency constraints.
30. Hoffer (1990:32–34).
31. See McClellan (1971) and Newmyer (1985) for how this brought contradictions into many of Justice Story's decisions and legal opinions. Recall the distinction that I drew in Chapter 2 between procedural normative *mediations* of how corporate power is exercised and substantive normative *limitations* on what corporations may do. The mediations may remain resilient over time, but the limitations, as we saw in Chapter 4, tend to give way with each generation.
32. Parkes (1828:xxv).
33. Plucknett (1929/1956:685); Parkes (1828:388–389).
34. Parkes (1828:xiv–xv). See Hoffer (1992) on colonial lawyers' broad sense of English law but lack of particular expertise in its details and practice.
35. Plucknett (1929/1956:184).
36. Plucknett (1929/1956:181).
37. Plucknett (1929/1956:178).
38. Plucknett (1929/1956:181–182). This left the king without an advisory council, and Henry VIII filled this administrative gap by creating a new institution that became known popularly as the Privy Council.
39. Plucknett (1929/1956:176, 187–188); this sentence and the one preceding it closely paraphrase Plucknett.
40. Plucknett (1929/1956:194–197).
41. Polanyi (1944:36). On the other hand, after the Glorious Revolution of 1689, royal charters granted more power to governors of colonies than the king possessed in England (Hoffer 1990:56–64).
42. Ernest Weinrib (1975:1) dates the institutionalization of modern fiduciary law in England to this decision. Legal scholar Deborah DeMott notes that "the trustee in Keech was . . . accountable for profit realized on the lease renewal" (private correspondence, June 14, 1994).
43. Hoffer (1990:10).
44. This explains why so many of the early U.S. corporations were transportation companies. State legislatures wanted to make sure that they truly operated as common carriers, rather than as monopolies that gouged the public (see Chapter 4, note 40).
45. DeMott (1988:880–881); see my discussion of the multidivisional form in Chapters 6–7.
46. See Breyer and Stewart (1985:23) on equity's injunctive power against unlawful official conduct. In civil law countries on the Continent, specialized tribunals were developed *within* their administrative bureaucracies to monitor the same abuses of power.
47. Clignet (1992:22).

48. DeMott raises an important point: "In nonstandardized settings in which courts hold a person to fiduciary standards on the basis of another's placing trust and confidence in him, what counts for the plaintiff is his expectations, not the more generalized trust reposed by the public. That is, does the institution of private litigation, which requires a plaintiff-specific showing in such settings, undercut the general force of your point? Likewise, and more broadly, remedies for breach of any fiduciary duty run in favor of the individual plaintiff. Only if the errant fiduciary has also committed a crime, or created some other basis for public intervention, would the social order generally, through the state, seek redress. Does the remedial aspect of this body of legal doctrine undercut your point?" (private correspondence, June 14, 1994). We saw in this chapter that Chancery acted on broader concerns, even as it heard plaintiff-specific cases. We also saw in Chapter 3, with regard to the Time-Warner case, that Delaware's Chancery does the same thing at times today.

49. I develop this point further in the section on social relationships and fiduciary law in the latter part of this chapter. This begins to address DeMott's concerns (see note 48).

50. Hoffer (1990:11).

51. Hoffer (1990:14, 82, 146).

52. Hoffer (1990:180).

53. Plucknett (1929/1956:209).

54. Haar and Fessler (1986:13–15, 56–76).

55. Plucknett (1929/1956:211–214). Hoffer notes (1990:28) that Chancery ended earlier, in 1873.

56. Hoffer (1990); see note 41.

57. Hoffer (1990:42–44).

58. Hoffer (1990:67ff).

59. Hovenkamp (1991:31).

60. Haar and Fessler (1986:149). In a major decision in 1877, Munn v. Illinois, Chief Justice Morrison Waite ruled that private property "affected with a public interest" is subject to state regulation (Newmyer 1985:133).

61. Haar and Fessler (1986:152).

62. McDowell (1982:3–4, my emphasis).

63. McDowell (1982:6–7).

64. McDowell (1982:70–72). See also Newmyer (1985) and McClellan (1971). Story remains the youngest appointee to the Supreme Court, named by Jefferson November 15, 1811, two months after his thirty-second birthday (Newmyer 1985:64).

65. Hoffer (1990:12).

66. McDowell (1982:85); also Hoffer (1990:222, note 27).

67. Hoffer (1990:222, note 27, plus 13–14, 53).

68. Hoffer (1990:93–106).

69. McDowell (1982:8). McDowell does not say specifically that this was the first decision in which this transfer occurred.

70. See Lowi (1969, 1995) more generally. For the opposite view—that Brown rests on principles of "good constitutional equity"—see Hoffer (1990).

71. See Gordon (1991) on the Delaware courts' "sociohistorical" approach. Among the colonies, Maryland had the most active Chancery, hearing thirty-two cases, for instance, in 1699 (Hoffer 1990:52–53). Delaware began its Chancery immediately after the revolution (Hoffer 1990:86–87).

72. DeMott (1988:880–881). I show elsewhere (Sciulli 1997d) that the courts hold trustees to fiduciary obligations even when beneficiaries stop paying their fees. Again, the reason for this is that the courts are concerned about the institutional

externalities of trustees' behavior, not about the immediate externalities of breaches of contract.

73. For example, Weinrib (1975).
74. See Eisenberg (1988) more generally.
75. Frankel (1983:802–803).
76. Weinrib (1975:7).
77. Frankel (1983:795–796).
78. Functionalist sociologist Barber (1963) and legal contractarians Easterbrook and Fischel (1991:259) agree on this point.
79. Frankel (1983:807–808).
80. Frankel (1983:813).
81. Frankel (1983:810); also Eisenberg (1989:1464–1466). Easterbrook and Fischel take the opposite position (1993:445): "[What] characterizes many fiduciary relations [is that] at the outset the range of contingencies is too large and information too scarce for effective contracting. During the course of performance the subjects become more concrete, options more specific."
82. Clurman (1992:240).
83. Fabrikant, *New York Times,* December 10, 1993; Janofsky, *New York Times,* November 26, 1993.
84. Fabrikant (1993).

6

The End of Doctrinal Coherence

U.S. state courts developed a third doctrinal approach to the corporation in the late nineteenth and early twentieth centuries in the midst of accelerating economic change and a general questioning of received assumptions both in economics and in law. Spanning Progressive reforms, the 1929 stock market crash, the Great Depression, and the early years of the New Deal, this period saw the supplanting of "classical" theories of political economy by Alfred Marshall's principles of "neoclassical" economics. It was also the period during which the "legal pragmatism" of Oliver Wendell Holmes and Roscoe Pound, followed by the "legal realism" of Benjamin Cardozo and Karl Llewellyn, supplanted "legal formalism."

We will see in Chapter 6 that these developments in economic theory and legal theory were related responses to U.S. industrialization, urbanization, and the rise and consolidation of the management corporation. These developments in theory encouraged the courts in practice to continue moving away from the Founders' republican vigilance and from English chancellors' general concern about the possible institutional externalities of corporate power. They encouraged the courts to drift toward liberal complacency and, at most, a "presentist" concern about the immediate externalities of corporate power. The basic tenet or working assumption of liberal complacency is that maximizing shareholders' private wealth not only increases social wealth but also automatically supports the institutional design of a democratic social order. We will therefore explore this tenet at length and see that institutional economics, the major competitor to Marshall's neoclassical economics, did not offer the corporate judiciary the concepts or doctrinal options that it needed to counter its drift from republican vigilance to liberal complacency. After presenting this brief history of ideas, we shall conclude the chapter by exploring the courts' third doctrinal approach to the corporation, namely the courts' deference to management under the business judgment rule.

Presentism in Law and in Economics

The term "legal formalism" is associated with the work and teaching of Christopher Langdell at Harvard during the 1870s and 1880s.[1] It refers broadly to the view that "individual cases, properly organized and classified, fall naturally into patterns revealing underlying principles."[2] Langdell's case method reinforced the Founders' view that law codifies a relatively resilient substantive normative framework. Tied to the Founders' particular vision of social order (revolving around yeoman farmers), legal formalism became anachronistic in the face of accelerating economic change, much like English chancellors' and U.S. republicans' earlier opposition to a rising commercial society.[3] One irony of Langdell's "conservatism," however, was that he himself had already abandoned the Founders' doctrinal grounding for the substantive norms of behavior that they valued. "[Langdell's approach] shifted the foundation [of legal theory] from principles deduced from higher-law or natural-law sources to principles derived from the study of particular cases and legal facts."[4] When Langdell sought law's *principles* in ongoing judicial behavior rather than in natural law norms, he was already adopting a variation of legal positivism. Ironically, he opened a door for pragmatists and realists to walk through when they later challenged the legitimacy of any and all resilient or "traditional" court-enforced norms.

The turn from Langdell's formalism, and the loosening hold on judicial memory of the Founders' republican vigilance and the English chancellors' social vision, was particularly evident in corporate law. We saw in Chapter 4 that U.S. judges and legal scholars increasingly questioned the merits of existing public law norms and fiduciary duties as they elaborated the courts' second or Lockean approach to the corporation. Quite purposefully, they adopted the metaphor of the corporate "natural person" because this seemed better to reflect economic "reality"—the U.S. economy's increasing complexity and dynamics. In turn, Marshall and other neoclassical economists instructed legal formalists, and later legal pragmatists and legal realists, as to the nature of economic "reality."

From Legal Formalism to Pragmatism and Realism

Writing in the 1880s and 1890s, Oliver Wendell Holmes held against Langdell and other formalists that there are no timeless legal principles to be found in judicial behavior. He insisted instead that legal principles and judicial behavior alike are best described and evaluated in terms of their current consequences in the world, not in terms of whether they are internally interrelated or form a coherent pattern. With other pragmatists, Holmes believed that "judges do and should make whatever decisions seem to them best for the community's future, not counting any form of consistency with the past as valuable for its own sake."[5] Thus, he rejected formal-

ists' reverse strategy, namely first divining legal principles from longstanding judicial behavior, and then exploring their continuing implications for
judicial practice. Holmes's view was that "the life of the law has not been
logic; it has been experience."[6] For him, Langdell's formalism "separated
law from life" and prevented judges from dealing effectively with the
"real" problems of U.S. society.[7]

Holmes and other pragmatists were convinced that "the rules of law
are the systematized and coercive embodiment of the salient opinions of the
most powerful groups in society and therefore change as those opinions and
groups change."[8] He and other pragmatists did not believe that the law can
somehow be legitimated independently.[9] Holmes's boldness in rejecting
traditionalism or classicism and his forceful advocacy of consequentialism
or presentism immediately influenced major legal scholars and very soon
informed the thinking of prominent judges.[10] "The great bulk of twentieth-
century writing on the theory of the judicial function can be viewed as an
extended commentary on his legal philosophy."[11] Holmes's presentism was
influential not simply because it offered legal scholars and judges a sound
theoretical position but also because it gave theoretical expression to developments already well under way in practice. Holmes and other pragmatists
were essentially expressing in theory what was already taking place in
Congress and state legislatures—the rise of interest group politics and the
decline of the two major political parties' "responsibility" for making and
administering law.[12]

Holmes's presentism helped to legitimate this development and, furthermore, opened the way for legal scholars to explore how to merge law
with the new "science" of economics.[13] Holmes was convinced personally
that lawyers needed greater training in economics. In the passage below he
refers to "schools of political economy"; most likely, he has in mind the
instrumentalism or means-end rationality of neoclassical economics rather
than the broader social vision of political economists. In the opening sentence he also implicitly elevates presentism above the Founders' concerns
about the direction of institutional change:

> I look forward to a time when the part played by history in the explanation
> of dogma shall be very small, and instead of ingenious research we shall
> spend our energy on a study of the ends sought to be attained and the
> reasons for desiring them. As a step toward that ideal it seems to me
> that every lawyer ought to seek an understanding of economics. The
> present divorce between the schools of political economy and law seems
> to me an evidence of how much progress in philosophical study still
> remains to be made. In the present state of political economy, indeed, we
> come again upon history on a larger scale, but there we are called on to
> consider and weigh the ends of legislation, the means of attaining them,
> and the cost. We learn that for everything we have to give up something
> else, and we are taught to set the advantage we gain against the other
> advantage we lose, and to know what we are doing when we elect. [See
> note 11]

One of the major problems that legal pragmatists soon faced, however, was whether and how to differentiate their central concept, pragmatism, from economists' basic concepts of self-interested behavior and instrumentalism, or "means-end rationality."[14] This problem persists today, as the wording of the following passage illustrates: "Viewed less an end than an instrument of social growth, the law was understood by Holmes as essentially practical, as always instrumental."[15]

One may treat legal pragmatism and neoclassical economics as related theoretical developments because at the very outset they were akin epistemologically. Legal pragmatists' concepts oriented judges to seek the most efficient or instrumental means to maximize quantitative ends or priced outcomes. Legal pragmatists assumed that "everything has a price."[16] To be sure, pragmatist philosophers—Charles Peirce and William James, George Herbert Mead and John Dewey—had broader concerns. They explored how individuals develop shared meanings of qualities in their lives, and how they then symbolize their collective efforts to maintain these qualities, as ends that elude pricing and instead are social constructions of meaning. Yet, like legal pragmatists' concepts, these philosophical concepts nonetheless bracketed republicans' central concern from view. Republicans asked: How does either instrumentally rational behavior *or symbolized-ritualistic behavior* contribute to the *institutional design* of a democratic social order, one marked by resilient normative restraints on arbitrary exercises of collective power? Rather than addressing this issue of institutional consequences at a conceptual level, legal and philosophical pragmatists simply adopted their own variant of liberal complacency: They *"presumed* a model of society characterized by stability, order, and shared values."[17]

Regardless of pragmatist philosophers' broader concerns, by the 1920s legal pragmatists and neoclassical economists had acceded to liberal complacency and presentism at a conceptual level. Legal realists, in turn, were an important subgroup within this larger pragmatist-instrumentalist movement in the law, and precisely because they were unwilling to become instrumentalists or complacent liberals. Far more than their pragmatist colleagues, realists took pride in considering how nonrational factors—from legislative coalitions to judges' personalities—affect judicial behavior and legal doctrine. In this regard they were closer to pragmatist philosophers. Driven by the pathos of the generation that fought in World War I, and informed, too, by the theoretical contributions of Max Weber and other German social theorists, legal realists added aesthetic and normative factors to legal pragmatists' basic instrumentalism. They added to pragmatism "a radical value skepticism" about the nature of democratic government and the possibility of rationally justifying any ethical propositions, "an emphasis on nonrational and even irrational factors in the judicial process," and a "realist epistemology."[18]

For example, Benjamin Cardozo was convinced that when it is unclear to judges which law to apply in a particular case—in a "close case"—the "real" source of judicial practice is "the personal and psychological predispositions of individual judges."[19] Thurmond Arnold went further, saying that "law, like most institutions in society, [is] primarily established upon a cluster of myths and folklore." Some legal realists questioned the promise of U.S. democracy itself. Fred Rodell, for instance, insisted that the U.S. legal system is unquestionably corrupt.[20] Regardless of their various impressions of U.S. legal and political practices, however, the most radical realists treated legal rules "as symbolic rhetoric performing a merely psychologically satisfying function."[21] Even with their iconoclastic view of law, most realists nonetheless exhibited fidelity to the grand mainstream of U.S. politics. Rather than moving from iconoclasm to either an elitist defense or radical debunking of mainstream politics, most realists were swept up by the spirit of the New Deal.[22] They endeavored to "do good works," as they understood it.[23]

Thus, even as realists were not complacent liberals, they nonetheless followed their pragmatist colleagues in elevating presentism and a narrow focus on the immediate externalities of local problem solving above any equivalent concern about institutional externalities. When realists brought the law's new presentism to the economic issues of the day, including the issues of corporate agency and corporate purpose, their first concern was to describe and explain how natural persons, including corporate natural persons, actually behave. After accomplishing this, they then considered how courts, corporations, or other intermediary associations might best react to "economic reality." Legal realists were not interested in independently upholding any institutional "ideals" as matters of legal principle—whether the supposed inviolability of private property or the supposed sovereignty of corporate owners within corporate governance structures.

What was the economic "reality" that realists saw by the 1920s? First, they saw that sitting management teams were gaining de facto control over corporate governance and behavior, including control over boards of directors that shareholders formally elected. Second, they saw that corporate governance structures were becoming differentiated by function, by task. This was the period, after all, when some of the most dynamic U.S. corporations, for example DuPont and General Motors, were quite pragmatically inventing what Alfred Chandler Jr. would later call the multidivisional form (to be discussed later in this chapter). Thus, realists saw middle managers at corporate divisions making important substantive decisions independently of detailed oversight by top managers at headquarters. Realists concluded from their observations that state courts needed to adjust the natural entity metaphor so that judges could approach the issues of corporate agency and corporate purpose in more "realistic" ways. They wanted to reform corporate law so that it better reflected the presence of the nascent management corporation as a new "social creation" within the U.S. economy, a new "natural person."[24]

From Political Economy to Neoclassical Economics

In the 1920s, the term "neoclassical economics" was just beginning to gain popularity.[25] Two generations earlier, Karl Marx had coined the term "classical economics" when referring to the works of Ricardo, James Mill, and their predecessors.[26] Thorstein Veblen, in turn, coined the term "neoclassical economics" at the turn of the century when referring to Alfred Marshall's (1842–1924) efforts to distance the new "science" of economics from "classical" political economy.[27] It must be kept in mind that the founders of the U.S. governmental system were classical political economists. With Locke, Mandeville, and Smith, they saw the study of economic activity as a subfield of moral philosophy, not as an independent field of study. Moral philosophy, in turn, revolved around institutional and *substantive* normative issues, in particular the interrelationship between social order and personal cultivation (or, at least, self-discipline):[28] How do individuals construct meaning or symbolize "value" in their lives, and how does the larger social order either facilitate or obstruct their efforts?

Put differently, the concepts that political economists developed to study economic activity simultaneously addressed the qualitative meaning of that activity for individuals and its qualitative significance for the institutional design of the larger social order.[29] This is illustrated well by the Founders' concern that imbalances of private wealth would likely encourage self-interested behavior (rather than self-control or cultivation), and thereby result in private disorder (rather than citizen vigilance) and public abuse (rather than limited government). Political economic approaches to economic activity were clearly more normative than "scientific."[30] This did not mean, however, that Locke, Mandeville, and Smith "moralized" about supply and demand, production and consumption, profits and employment. Nor did it mean that the Founders "moralized" about the institutions of private property and self-regulating markets. Rather, it meant that they explicitly interrelated their descriptions of economic activity and instrumentally rational behavior with a broader vision (if not theory) of institutional change, of institutional externalities.

The Continental founders of the new academic discipline of sociology (Tonnies, Pareto, Durkheim, Weber) continued this practice into the twentieth century. But the British founders of the new academic discipline of economics separated the study of the economy from any and all explicitly articulated evolutionary theories or theories of institutional change.[31]

> Economic theory based on utilitarian premises, which is to say all "economic" theory in the proper sense of the word, is purely abstract and formal, without content. It deals, in general, with certain formal principles of "economy" without reference to what is to be economized, or how; more specifically, price-economics deals with a social system in which every individual treats all others and society merely as instrumentalities and

conditions of his own *Privatwirtschaft,* a mechanical system of Crusoe economies.[32]

Thus, the basic concepts of the two new academic disciplines, sociology and economics, were diverging dramatically in the 1920s and 1930s. The founders of both disciplines, however, were responding, in their own ways, to the demise of classical political economy. The shared context of both disciplines was a general skepticism about the scientific merits—the potential explanatory power—of existing evolutionary theories.

For their part, sociology's Continental founders continued to rely on evolutionary theories, but they replaced Marxists' linear utopianism and anthropologists' linear progressivism with pathos.[33] After all, consider Durkheim's "anomie," Pareto's "instinct of combinations," and Weber's "rationalization": Each theorist was both describing how individuals actually behave within modern societies and characterizing the direction of institutional change within modern societies. What each had to say about economic activity was, respectively, interrelated at a conceptual level with the view each held of the evolution undergone by the larger social order—from *Gemeinschaft* to *Gesellschaft,* from mechanical solidarity to organic solidarity, from custom to contract—in short, from traditional norms to modern instrumentalism. Thus, each social theorist continued to work with concepts that can be characterized as political economic. None turned to the narrower means-end rationality and presentism of neoclassical economics.[34]

It bears emphasizing that with the significant exception of Auguste Comte, all major Continental social theorists were pessimistic, not sanguine, about the "natural" direction of modern institutional change.[35] Tonnies, Pareto, Durkheim, and Weber all believed, as did North American republicans, Smith, and other classical political economists, that the "natural" direction of modern institutional change is toward entropy or breakdown, not toward stability or equilibrium.[36] They portrayed modernity as an inadvertent collective drift toward private disorder and public abuse. On the one hand, they saw that classes and status groups experience breakdowns of meaning under modern conditions. Industrialization and urbanization, in turn, only accelerate this breakdown by dislodging people from once settled social arrangements. On the other hand, Continental social theorists also appreciated that elites nonetheless endeavor to maintain social order. Their great fear was that at some point elites would be willing to use any means necessary to do so, including public and private arbitrariness. All of these social theorists accepted, of course, that a robust economy might very well contribute to orderly relations of social exchange. Such an economy might thereby veil modernity's malevolent drift for a time. But they did not believe that a robust economy somehow contributes automatically to institutional equilibrium, as if the latter, too, is yielded by a "hidden hand." They did not believe, in short, that individuals' strictly self-interested and instrumentally rational efforts to solve local problems would somehow automatically establish, and then somehow maintain over time, shared meanings across classes and status groups.[37] Likewise, they did not believe that the larger social order would somehow automatically support limited government, to say nothing of citizen vigilance.[38]

By contrast to the pathos of Continental social theorists, Alfred Marshall and other neoclassical economists bracketed the matter of institutional externalities from their concerns at a conceptual level. They were on a mission. They were convinced that if the new discipline of economics was to become "scientific," was to predict and explain economic behavior, then they would have to delimit its scope of application in two fundamental ways. First, they would have to develop abstract or analytical concepts that methodically detached the irreducibly "economic" factors of modern social life from any and all "noneconomic" factors. "Economics . . . is the only one of the social sciences which has aspired to the distinction of an exact science. . . . The very conception of an exact science involves abstraction; its ideal is analytic treatment, and analysis and abstraction are virtually synonyms."[39] Second, and relatedly, they would have to substitute a more strictly presentist stance for political economists' grander social vision. That is, they would have to separate the scientific study of economic behavior from any and all explicitly articulated evolutionary theories or theories of institutional change.[40] "American economic discussion developed under the influence of [Marshall's] marginal utility theory, which is essentially a short time view of the valuation problem."[41]

Only by making both fundamental changes, neoclassicists believed, could students of the economy study scientifically the instrumental and utilitarian factors common to all team activities dedicated to maximizing production. They wanted students of economic behavior literally to "formulat[e] the data of the problem of economic organization, the unchangeable materials with which, and conditions under which, any machinery of organization has to work."[42] To this end, neoclassicists asked: What quantities of commodities are to be produced, how are they to be produced, and for whom are they to be produced?[43] How can any economic producer, whether a corporation or a small business, increase its marginal revenues and decrease its marginal costs?[44] What is the ultimate source of an entrepreneur's personal profit?[45] Under what conditions does economic growth increase, and what is the optimum rate of economic growth? Why does unemployment persist, and what for all practical purposes is the rate of full employment? How might a national economy increase the marginal productivity of its workforce and increase the marginal utility of the goods and services that it produces?[46]

Despite these sorts of questions, economists' presentism means that they bracket empirically researchable issues from their concerns. They quite consciously leave these issues to sociologists and other social scientists (including legal scholars).[47] As Paul Samuelson later put the matter: "Economics cannot try to cover every fact of the universe. It must take certain things for granted. . . . *The institutional framework of society,* the tastes of individuals, *the ends for which they strive*—all these must be taken as being given."[48] Economists thus conceptually bracket from their concerns important political economic issues by treating them as residual matters, as the noneconomic. Such questions include: How, if at all, do social institutions normatively mediate economic behavior or instrumental activity? Do corporations in particular perform a production function exclusively, or do certain changes in their governance and behavior as intermediary associations carry institutional externalities for the larger social order?[49] Even as neoclassicists bracket these "institutional" issues from their explicit concerns, their two ways of delimiting economic inquiry nonetheless commit economists to a research project that is implicitly as normative as any undertaken by any political economist. They commit economists to discovering how instrumentally to sustain a popularly acceptable rate of economic growth—the wealth of nations or social wealth—*for perpetuity.*[50] This research project is normative in two respects. First, it revolves around a teleology, an end in itself. As such, it falls outside the scope of application of neoclassicists' concepts (which are instrumentalist and presentist). Second, it assumes without argument that all institutional externalities attending instrumental efforts to maximize social wealth are inherently benign. Neoclassicists assume both points at a conceptual level, as part of their very framework of analytical concepts. They do so by neglecting at this level the possible institutional externalities of corporate governance and behavior for the larger social order. (The quotation from Samuelson in this paragraph is a case in point.)

Excursus: The Limits of Institutional Economics

Institutional economics, the discipline's own reaction against neoclassicism, fails in its own way to offer the U.S. corporate judiciary the concepts it needs to uphold the institutional design of the U.S. social order. This is the case despite the fact that Thorstein Veblen, John Commons, Clarence Ayres, and other founders of institutional economics challenged the "abstractness" of neoclassical economics in favor of a more policy-oriented approach. Indeed, they also challenged neoclassicists' implicit political economic position of liberal complacency. The problem, however, is that they did not challenge the discipline's instrumentalism and presentism. This is why their proposed alternatives to liberal complacency often sound today not only normative but speculative, strictly subjective. Institutional economists still fail to address the issue of institutional externalities methodically, as opposed to bringing it into their analyses indirectly, and strictly residually.

When John Commons points out that "the smallest unit of the institutional economics is . . . a transaction," he already brackets the matter of institutional externalities from his concerns.[51] With this conceptual decision alone, he follows neoclassicists in neglecting the institutionalized norms that frame transactions, focusing instead on the immediate externalities of economic behavior.[52]

Clarence Ayres provides a more promising opening by arguing that the "substance of institutionalism is its attempted identification and differentiation of what Veblen called 'the larger forces moving obscurely in the background' of the surface phenomena of the market place."[53] Yet, just as Veblen disclaims any interest in "moral judgment," Ayres also keeps his vision rather narrow, despite his recognition that institutionalism attempts to answer the question "what does the economy mean?" and despite his references to a "philosophy of workmanship."[54] Ayres narrows his vision to how technological change affects institutions as instrumental means to maximize production. Thus, he ends up treating "workmanship" as a synonym for technology, not as a reference to any qualities of life that particular occupations might bring into the larger social order.[55]

Edwin Witte, in turn, is forthright about institutional economists' presentism: "Institutional economists [are concerned with] the solution of particular economic problems of immediate significance."[56] One such problem might be stagflation; another might be how to continue the flow of real income "to the community."[57] For Witte, the study of "economic policy problems" moves institutional economists away from neoclassicists' "equilibrium of individualism" and "science of the price mechanism" and toward the study of the "institutional background of the time, place, and situation."[58] Yet, Witte also sees that institutional economists study this background "descriptively" and "pragmatically," not "analytically" or in conceptually rigorous ways.[59] The result is that they are not really attuned to shifts in the direction of institutional change, including increases in the scope and frequency of arbitrary exercises of collective power.

Similarly, William Dugger notes that institutional economists substitute a "descriptive realism" for neoclassicists' "predictive realism."[60] The only *changes* or *qualities* that they monitor, however, are those that occur at a social psychological level, namely individuals' transitions from "rational" motivations to "nonrational" motivations, and from utility maximization to what Dugger calls "producer of culture."[61] The qualities of social life that they study methodically, in turn, are those associated with individual effort, with internalized motivation.[62] They do not study changes or qualities associated with transitions between different institutional designs.[63] "Much institutionalist work stops at the level of pattern models based on case studies. . . . With few exceptions, modern institutionalism has not created any general theory (Myrdal's theory of circular causation is *the* exception according to Kapp) and has not even developed existing models and types."[64]

Economists' New Political Economy: Liberal Complacency

There is considerable irony hidden within the presentist stance that neoclassical economists and institutional economists share. As these economists presumably drew back from political economists' broader social vision, they nonetheless adopted implicitly one of the grandest social visions or political economic positions of all. They ironically generalized Adam Smith's quite narrow references to the "hidden hand" that brings supply and demand into equilibrium within self-regulating markets. They generalized these references to economic activity's institutional consequences for any and all modern social orders. Smith had argued, and persuasively, that the "natural" tendency of supply and demand within self-regulating markets is to reach, or to revolve around, equilibrium. This was "natural," in his view, in that *this* equilibrium is indeed strictly instrumental and utilitarian. It can conceivably occur independently of governmental oversight, of institutionalized social norms of any kind, and of any and all other extra-economic social controls.

Smith's argument was persuasive precisely because he limited himself to the economic behavior of dispersed producers who respond to the immediate, subjective preferences of dispersed consumers. He never assumed that the larger social order framing this economic behavior would also somehow tend "naturally" toward, or revolve around, an inherently benign institutional equilibrium. After all, Smith clearly appreciated the distinctiveness of the issue of institutional externalities. He appreciated that the larger social order normatively frames economic behavior and instrumental activity.[65] This is why he explicitly brought "moral" factors—extra-economic factors—into his study of the wealth of nations.[66] Smith, in short, continued to see the study of economic activity as a subfield of moral philosophy.

Ironically, when Marshall and other neoclassicists narrowed their social vision by bracketing the issue of institutional externalities at a conceptual level, they broadened Smith's notion of equilibrium into a full-blown, albeit implicit or unstated, political economic position.[67] Alongside their project of discovering how instrumentally to sustain economic growth as an end in itself, they assumed without argument—in a fashion similar to that of legal pragmatists as discussed earlier in this chapter—that the larger social order that results will *invariably* be relatively benign. Moreover, precisely because they never presented any argument to support this conceptual move, they never felt compelled to cite any theoretical rationale, nor any body of empirical research, in support of their grand political economic position. They simply assumed without argument that the "natural" tendency of market *societies* is for *their institutional design* to provide otherwise competing producers and consumers with some shared meaning automatically, as if guided by a "hidden hand." Or, alternatively, they assumed that a balance of power would somehow prevail automatically between market societies' economic and noneconomic institutions—which is still an institutional equilibrium of sorts.[68] Either way, they assumed that the results of their "scientific" project would not only advance a quantitative economic outcome (greater social wealth) but also advance a qualitative institutional outcome (a social order capable of supporting limited government and citizen vigilance). Since their liberal complacency was an implicit rather than explicit political economic position, neoclassicists also never felt compelled to address directly the concerns that Tonnies, Pareto, Durkheim, Weber, and other social theorists were raising at the time regarding modernity's systemic drift toward breakdowns of meaning and institutional "entropy."

Bringing Presentism to Corporate Law Doctrine

For all of their criticisms of abstract theory, and for all of their devotion to judicial experimentation, legal pragmatists and legal realists were instructed by neoclassical economics. Pragmatists shared neoclassicists' instrumentalism, presentism, and liberal complacency. Realists simply added an appreciation of nonrational factors, as did institutional economists and pragmatist philosophers. Yet, even as realists were somewhat reluctant to become complacent liberals, the logic of instrumentalism and presentism itself moved them steadily toward this political economic position regardless. After all, pragmatists and realists alike "substitut[ed] an empirical theory of preference for the less scientific but more conventional set of community values that traditionally served as the basis for American law."[69] Roscoe Pound's legal realism illustrates this well. He combined liberal complacency ("a belief in the natural evolution of principles over time") with instrumentalism ("a commitment to use the law as an instrument of social growth").[70] Thus, unlike the American Founders and English chancellors, Pound elevated instrumentalism above the commitment to use the law as a normative restraint on institutional externalities, on abuse and arbitrariness. Put succinctly, all pragmatists and realists "were far less concerned with *responsible* government than with *effective* government."[71]

In the field of corporation law in particular, pragmatists and realists followed neoclassical economists for as long as they could in focusing more or less exclusively on the management corporation's "production function."[72] They, too, ignored its governance function as an intermediary association. Indeed, neoclassicists saw the management corporation's "production function" as indistinguishable from that performed by any commercial enterprise, large or small. With only slight adjustments, therefore, they approached large publicly traded corporations with the same concepts with which they approached family businesses, partnerships, and all other commercial enterprises.[73] Neoclassicists were so confident that corporations' one-dimensional drive to maximize profits also automatically advances social wealth, and thereby contributes to a democratic social order, that they never really conceptualized corporations as organizations at all. They never conceptualized corporations as intermediary associations that socialize individuals, mediate constituents' exercises of positional power, and mediate management's exercise of collective power within a larger social order—and, as a result, carry consequences for the latter's institutional design. Instead, neoclassicists ironically reified their own concepts, substituting this move at a conceptual level for greater realism in empirical study.

When legal pragmatists and realists saw how economists approached the corporation, they concluded that the courts needed only to update their natural entity theory, not to abandon it. Given their own presentism and instrumentalism, it never occurred to them that the courts might also have to take a procedural turn in order to update the fiduciary law tradition (as discussed in Chapter 3), as opposed to returning to the Founders' republicanism or the chancellors' substantive social vision. Instead of taking a procedural turn, they asked: Why do the courts impose any extra-economic norms of behavior on management? "In their zeal to remedy what they considered defects in the actual operation of the legal system, realists discarded the philosophical foundations upon which constitutional limited government had been constructed."[74]

Neoclassicists' Five Assumptions About Corporations

Neoclassicists were convinced even as late as the 1920s that the management corporation would behave like any other commercial enterprise. They believed this because they were instructed by Marshall's general theory of rational (or self-interested) behavior within competitive markets. Competitive markets are distinguished from oligopolistic or monopolistic markets by at least three characteristics: multiple producers, ease of entry into and exit from any industry, and products that can be distinguished only by general type and price, not by brand name or customer loyalty.[75] This third characteristic of competitive markets permitted neoclassicists to focus exclusively on the *quantitative* outcomes of economic behavior. Once they conceptually bracketed from their concerns all references to product qualities, they simultaneously bracketed all references to other qualities, including the possible institutional externalities of corporate governance and behavior. They simply posited a priori that any commercial enterprise competes exclusively to maximize profits (a quantitative end) irrespective of how large it is or how it is organized.[76]

To say that competitive markets are marked by multiple producers is to say that each commercial enterprise accounts only for a fraction of its industry's total economic output.[77] Under such conditions, when any particular commercial enterprise retains earnings—in order to expand facilities and increase output, or in order to pursue qualitative goals of any kind (such as enhancing management's power or prestige within the firm, or enhancing a product's name recognition among consumers)—it immediately attracts new competitors to its industry. Thus, neoclassicists approach not only corporations but entire industries with the same concepts. By their account, any unit of economic production—large or small, organized or dispersed—tends toward an equilibrium state of profitability. As such, there is no incentive for any existing producer to alter its output; likewise, there is no incentive for new producers to enter an industry or for existing producers to exit.[78]

When pragmatists and realists followed neoclassicists in looking at all commercial enterprises from the outside as if they perform exclusively a production function, they ended up treating the production function as *the* corporate purpose. In effect, therefore, they replaced republican vigilance with liberal complacency. In time, they converted neoclassicists' presentism, normative project, and implicit political economic position into doctrinal options for the corporate judiciary and bar. They did so without regard for the fact that the modern corporation is an intermediary association that, as such, also performs a governance function.

Actually, pragmatists and realists had no good reason to peer inside the corporation at all—let alone to concern themselves with positional conflicts and governance disputes—given the assumptions at work when neoclassicists extended Marshall's general theory of rational behavior within competitive markets to the corporation-as-producer. We may distinguish at least five of these interrelated political economic assumptions, which were often explicit but at times implicit.[79]

First, neoclassicists assumed that the internal governance of corporations is more consensual than conflictual. Stated more precisely, they assumed that whatever the factors involved in governing a corporation, none of them is likely to bear significantly on its instrumentally rational production function.[80] They believed that corporations' ongoing competition to maximize profits is too unrelenting, too systemic a force, for governance factors to affect their production function. Indeed, even when neoclassical economists applied their general theory to joint stock companies and large publicly traded corporations *within imperfect or oligopolistic markets,* they still held fast to a comparable political economic assumption. They assumed that management's positional interests in governing the corporation remain broadly aligned with shareholders' positional interests in maximizing dividends. Alfred Marshall put this matter well in 1892:

> It is a strong proof of the marvellous growth in recent times of a spirit of honesty and uprightness in commercial matters, that the leading officers of great public companies yield as little as they do to the vast temptations to fraud which lie in their way. If they showed an eagerness to avail themselves of opportunities for wrongdoing at all approaching that of which we read in the commercial history of earlier civilizations, their wrong uses of the trust imposed in them would have been on so great a scale as to prevent the development of this democratic form of business.[81]

Paul Samuelson was more skeptical about both of Marshall's points in 1948. Regarding corporate democracy, he insisted that "the problem of keeping large corporations truly democratic is almost an insuperable one."[82] Regarding management's self-interested behavior or opportunism, he pointed out:

> Generally speaking, there will be no clash of goals between the management and stockholders. Both will be interested in maximizing the profits of the firm. However, in two important situations, there may be a divergence of interests, not infrequently settled in favor of management. First, insiders may legally or illegally vote themselves and their friends or relatives large salaries . . . at stockholders' expense. . . . The wonder is not that executives' salaries are so high but that they are not higher. . . . A second conflict may rise in connection with undistributed profits. The managers of every organization have an innate tendency to try to make it grow and perpetuate itself. . . . *There is reason to question whether profits are not plowed back into a company in many cases when the same capital could better be invested by the stockholders elsewhere, or be spent upon consumption.*[83]

Neoclassicists' second political economic assumption follows from how they applied their general theory of rational behavior to large publicly traded corporations within oligopolistic markets. They assumed that no matter who manages a corporation, and no matter how they might monitor employees and resolve disputes, corporate managers will endeavor to balance their company's marginal rates of productivity with the marginal cost of its factors of production.[84] Thus, once again, neoclassicists assumed that systemic pressures of self-regulating markets are sufficiently forceful in themselves to induce any management team to maximize shareholders' return on equity. They accepted this, curiously, even as they conceded that "realistically speaking, we must recognize that modern business firms [are so large and complicated that we] are unable to calculate their marginal revenue and marginal cost."[85] Therefore, neoclassicists' assumption that any management team will endeavor ceaselessly to balance marginal cost against marginal revenue is more an article of faith than a scientific hypothesis.[86] As we shall see in Chapter 7, economists could hold to this article of faith only until the early 1980s. One of its last expressions is the following, from 1981: "Profitable growth is a reasonable summary of the primary objective of the larger managerial corporation today."[87] With the wave of hostile takeovers and leveraged buyouts that lasted from late 1983 to 1988, even the faithful could see unambiguous evidence to the contrary.

Neoclassicists' third political economic assumption followed as a corollary to their faith in management's behavior. They assumed that rational shareholders are passive investors, not active owners. After all, why would shareholders devote their personal time to monitoring management's behavior? The systemic pressures that broadly advance their positional interests are as far beyond each manager's control as each shareholder's.

Fourth, neoclassicists looked at contracts with the same production function in view; they did not see the need to look more closely at contracts.[88] They assumed without argument that contracts are complete, unambiguous, and delimited economic arrangements—regardless of whether they are struck within a corporation or outside of it. As such, neoclassicists conceptualized contracts as promises of economic performance that are neither particularly costly to negotiate nor particularly costly to enforce. That is, they approached contracts in the same way that they approached corporations, namely, as if they are established and maintained outside of any and all institutionalized—court-enforced—norms of behavior.

Fifth, having treated corporate governance and contractual arrangements as insignificant factors "external" to production, neoclassicists treated social institutions or the larger social order accordingly.[89] Why study the institutional design of the larger social order, including how and why it changes over time, if one is already confident that such matters have no significant bearing on the production function?

Neoclassicists thus bracket from their concerns any qualities that distinguish the institutions of particular modern social orders from others, in practice. Thus, Alfred Marshall could call in general terms for "a diminution of trade secrecy" and "increased publicity in every form."[90] He had no way, however, to address methodically the possible consequences of an interrelationship between the institutions of a democratic social order and corporate governance and behavior. At best, Marshall could allude vaguely to possible institutional obstacles to "progress": "The growth of Government undertakings, as well as of giant private businesses of 'Trusts' with a partial monopoly, is full of dangers to the maintenance of a . . . free initiative which is the chief source of progress. We cannot however enter into this most important question."[91] What Marshall means by "progress," of course, is strictly utilitarian, the instrumentally rational production of quantitative ends, not any qualitative outcome or institutional arrangement.

Neoclassicist Outcomes, Revisited

As we have argued, when economists today follow neoclassicists in bracketing the institutional externalities of corporate power from their concerns at a conceptual level, they actually embrace the lofty political economic position of liberal complacency. First, they assume that corporations' maximizing behavior automatically, as if guided by a hidden hand (or isomorphic pressures), increases *social* wealth, the wealth of nations.[92] Second, they assume that corporations' maximizing behavior automatically serves the public law interest of maintaining a modern social order that is marked by shared meanings or, at the very least, by a balance of power between economic and noneconomic institutions.

This second "automatic outcome" is institutional and clearly qualitative, not presentist and quantitative. As such, any reference to this outcome, explicit *or implicit,* falls outside the scope of application of neoclassicists' concepts. The assumption, however, that a generally acceptable institutional outcome is somehow realized automatically literally underpins neoclassicists' instrumentalism and presentism. They take as given the proposition that any social order resulting from corporations' maximizing behavior will invariably institutionalize norms that mediate public and private exercises of collective power short of abuse and arbitrariness. At the very least, they assume that the existing social order will continue to support these normative mediations if they are already institutionalized within it. After all, if economists are not assuming this, how can they otherwise bracket the issue of the possible institutional externalities of corporate governance and behavior from their concerns? It is precisely because the U.S. corporate judiciary inherited the Founders' political economic position of republican vigilance as well as the English chancellors' social vision that even today it continues to resist such liberal complacency.

In sum, by treating governance as external to corporations' production function, by assuming that neither negotiating nor enforcing contracts is particularly costly (or harmful to third parties),[93] and by assuming that corporations are driven by immutable systemic pressures to maximize profits, neoclassicists gloss over three important issues, each of which begins to reveal the possible institutional externalities of corporate power. First, how is corporate production actually organized, and how can it actually be maximized instrumentally? Second, what are the bases of intracorporate conflicts of interest or positional conflicts, and how are these conflicts actually resolved? Third, how are corporate boundaries established, and how and why are they changed or maintained? Proponents of today's major economic approaches to the corporation (and of legal contractarianism) all endeavor, with varying degrees of success, to remove the gloss and to address one or more of these three issues. None of them, however, challenges neoclassicists' implicit political economic position of liberal complacency. (The contractarian approach bears examination because it is relevant to today's debate over corporate governance, and will be addressed in Chapter 7.)

The Courts' New Doctrinal Approach

The Business Judgment Rule

As corporations' size and internal complexity increased dramatically in the 1920s, management became ever more sovereign within their governance structures. Management so broadened its control over daily operations, and developed so much industry experience and expertise, that it became *the* corporate agent in fact. Management's business judgment soon became unrivaled on the board, unchallenged by shareholders in particular.[94] Correlatively, shareholders' influence within corporate governance structures withered. They indeed became absentee owners, passive suppliers of equity capital—one intermediate product among many others that constituents contribute to the corporate enterprise. Management could, and did, make many decisions without informing shareholders at all. First, it decided whether to finance corporate growth by borrowing from banks or by retaining shareholders' dividends. Second, management decided whether to integrate suppliers of intermediate products within the corporation or else to retain them as outside contractors (or subcontractors). Third, management decided where and how to invest the corporation's concentrated wealth, and where and how to exercise its collective power.

Instructed by neoclassical economics as well as by the law's pragmatic and realist turn, sitting judges in the 1920s and 1930s endeavored to accommodate at a conceptual and doctrinal level this unfolding change in the relationship between management and shareholders, between agent and principal. They certainly were not inclined to restrain this change on principle, namely by enforcing public law norms and fiduciary duties in the name of some institutional ideal, including that of keeping the legal status of shareholders' "private property" elevated above the legal status of management's "position." In truth, they were not really capable of doing so even if they had been inclined to try. Rather, it was far easier for them to push their Lockean approach to the corporate natural person as far as they could, pragmatically. Eventually judicial practice itself transformed this doctrinal approach to the corporation into a new, third approach: Whenever judges were called upon to identify the "real" corporate agent—to specify who ultimately interprets the "real" interests of the corporate natural person and who decides its "real" purpose within society—they typically pointed to management. They much preferred to defer to management's business judgment on these matters than to enforce public law norms or fiduciary duties in an effort to attain any qualitative end that might challenge management's business judgment.[95]

Indeed, the business judgment rule reflected the corporate judiciary's pragmatism and realism with regard to matters that included and went beyond management's sovereignty within corporate governance structures.[96] The judiciary recognized that even as a state legislature's standard charter may hold boards of directors formally responsible for corporate behavior, these boards nonetheless typically delegate control—"real" corporate agency—to sitting management teams. Furthermore, as pragmatists and realists, the judges now sitting on the bench were hardly inclined to second-guess any corporate agent's economic decisions. Given the dynamics and complexities of the U.S. economy, the courts as an institution lacked the capacity in any case for second-guessing.[97] It really did not matter at a doctrinal level whether "in reality" shareholder-owners (the second approach) or corporate managers (the third approach) made the decisions.[98]

There is an irony nonetheless in the courts' move from recognizing shareholder-owners as the corporate agent to recognizing sitting management teams (an irony that will ultimately explain why U.S. courts continue to resist liberal complacency). Whenever judges cite the business judgment rule and defer to management, they concede a point at a doctrinal level that moves them beyond neoclassical concepts. They concede that there is no particular corporate goal, *including that of maximizing shareholders' wealth or maximizing the corporation's growth,* that necessarily exhausts the corporation's "real" interests as a "natural person" in U.S. society. They instead grant to management broad discretion to interpret this "natural person's" "real" interests. In doing so, judges not only move beyond neoclassical concepts but also burn bridges to their second doctrinal approach to the corporation. After all, their earlier approach oriented them to uphold the integrity of investors' private property and investors' essentially Lockean contracts with their own agents.

Why were judges willing to concede such broad discretion to management as early as the 1920s? They were willing to extend the business judgment rule from investors to their agents because they were already adjusting corporate law doctrine to the "reality" of two developments taking place within corporations. Each of these developments, in turn, as we shall see, was already moving judicial behavior beyond the scope of application of neoclassical concepts.

Beyond Neoclassical Economics: Oligopolistic Firms and the Multidivisional Form

The first organizational development that pushed judges beyond neoclassical economics was the passing of competitive firms and the rise of oligopolistic firms. As a select few corporations dominated their respective industries, their management teams developed a positional interest in financing corporate growth by retaining shareholders' dividends. This positional interest is clearly inconsistent with neoclassicists' assumption that systemic pressures compel any corporate agent to maximize profits.[99] Precisely because management's new positional interest challenged a fundamental tenet of neoclassical economics, it brought considerable uncertainty into the discipline of economics itself. The uncertainty was highlighted and intensified by the work of Adlof Berle, a lawyer, and Gardiner Means, an economist, who together published *The Modern Corporation and Private Property* in 1932, pointing coldly to this implication of the management corporation. Given the uncertainty of economists, judges were left to themselves to conceptualize the relationship between management and shareholders as "realistically" as they could. The law's own turn toward pragmatism and realism offered them no compelling conceptual rationale for questioning management's business decisions, let alone for reversing them on any public law ground. Judges also were hardly in a position to anticipate how the relationship between management and shareholders might change in the future.

The second organizational development that pushed judicial behavior as well as corporate law beyond neoclassical economics was more difficult to recognize in the 1920s: the rise of the multidivisional form,[100] spearheaded, as noted earlier, by some of the country's largest and most dynamic corporations. Responding pragmatically to their own companies' growth by dedicating particular divisions to particular functions or tasks, the management teams of these corporations jettisoned the unidivisional form of organization that had marked competitive firms. They developed a new multidivisional form that would soon typify oligopolistic firms.

The multidivisional form consolidates and enhances management's positional power at the expense of shareholders' ownership. Its appearance therefore meant that the courts would eventually be asked to rule on new positional conflicts between management and shareholders (and other corporate constituents). Moreover, *at the moment that the courts intervened into these new corporate governance disputes, they would simultaneously move, in practice, outside the scope of application of neoclassical economics*—which did not envision breakdowns in intracorporate decisionmaking, either as positional conflicts or as governance disputes. As these cases came before realist and pragmatist judges, they had little choice but to develop new concepts to orient themselves. Given the collapse of republican vigilance and the rise of presentism, instrumentalism, and liberal complacency both in law and in economics, it made perfect sense for judges to build on the business judgment rule. It made less sense for them to seek their bearings in existing public law norms and fiduciary duties. They were not prepared, however, to remove the latter entirely from corporate law doctrine's core of mandatory rules.

The Rise of the Multidivisional Form: A Closer Look

Until World War II, the typical U.S. corporation centralized administration at headquarters. Within this unidivisional form, managers at headquarters were generalists. They were prepared to transfer their skills to any troubled division or operation. For that matter, they could, if necessary, transfer their skills to other firms in their industry and, at times, to firms in other industries. By the 1920s, these skills were in great demand:

> Directorships [top management's positions] were now coveted professional positions, often offering high monetary rewards. The director, rather than the owner, was the real person in power, and he was clearly in a position to control the corporation to his advantage. The development of the business judgment rule separated even further the ownership of the American business corporation from its control.[101]

As corporations gained oligopolistic control over their respective industries, they also multiplied their product lines. This multiplication soon overloaded the generalists at headquarters with governance and administrative details. No one, it seemed, had time to devote to long-term planning, and particularly to developing financial strategies to fuel corporate growth.

Top managers developed the multidivisional form pragmatically as a problem-solving device. It met their needs as they diversified their corporations' product lines; enlarged their corporations' physical facilities; and broadened their corporations' markets for supplies, sales, and capital.[102] Starting slowly in the 1920s,[103] and constrained for a time by the Depression and World War II,[104] this organizational transformation accelerated rapidly in the 1950s. From 1949 to 1969, for instance, the number of major U.S. corporations that could qualify as a "single business" fell from 28 percent to only 7 percent. For that matter, only 36 percent of *Fortune* 500 firms could qualify any longer as having a single "dominant product."[105]

Alfred Chandler Jr. describes the new governance structure in terms of tiers or levels (see Figures 6.1 and 6.2):[106] Operational units are at the lowest administrative level. Each such unit has its own administrative office, its own managers and staff, its own bookkeeping system, and its own resources (whether operating capital, physical facilities, or human capital). Thus, each unit might include within its local governance: manufacturing plants; finance, sales, purchasing, and marketing offices; and research and development facilities. The on-site managers of these units are the corporation's lower-level managers.

The corporation's middle-level managers govern the divisions, and from this transoperational level they monitor lower managers' decisions and the performance of operational units. At the divisions, middle

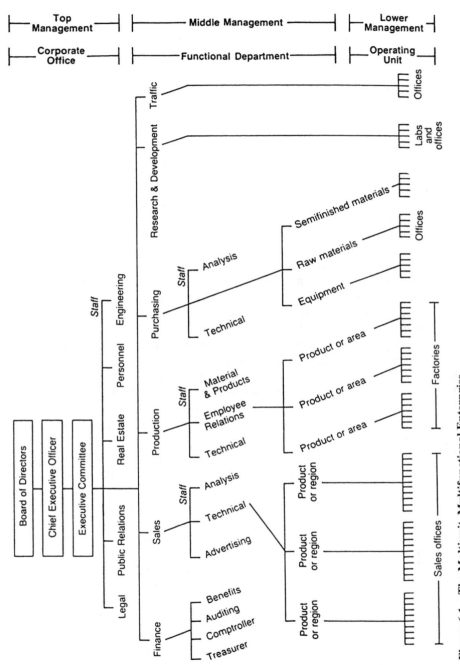

Figure 6.1   The Multiunit, Multifunctional Enterprise
(Reprinted by permission of the publisher from *Scale and Scope: The Dynamics of Industrial Capitalism* by Alfred D. Chandler, Jr., Cambridge, Mass.: Harvard University Press. Copyright © 1990 by Alfred D. Chandler, Jr.)

managers administer the corporation's major product lines, administer the divisional office itself, and both recruit and motivate lower managers. Each division within the multidivisional form is defined by function, by the sets of tasks that it is responsible for performing. It is not defined by physical location or where the units happen to be that perform these tasks.[107] Thus, in DuPont there are divisions dedicated, respectively, to chemicals, plastics, finishes, fibers, films, and explosives; there are no divisions called East Coast, Midwest, or Overseas. Each functional division competes against its own previous quarterly performance, and against that of its counterparts in its industry. Divisional quarterly reports contain financial data about a division's inputs and outputs, and rarely do top managers at headquarters augment this quantitative information with more qualitative information gathered from on-site visits.[108]

Finally, at headquarters, the corporation's top managers and directors monitor divisional quarterly reports and middle managers' behavior. Yet, middle managers' behavior often eludes them: "The performance measures that the general office gets about the inferior level in a decentralized organization carry few details that would enable them to penetrate the veil shielding the division manager from close inspection of his or her subordinates."[109] At headquarters, all major decisions by management are formally ratified by the board, which typically meets monthly. Corporate boards are formally responsible not only for ratifying such decisions but also for monitoring *the process* by which sitting management teams arrived at them as well as *the process* by which they intend to implement them.[110] Their legal mandate, as shareholders' elected agent, is ultimately to represent and promote shareholders' positional interests.[111] That is, board powers are formally delegated by shareholders, not by top management.[112] Top management, however, supplies the board with most of the information upon which it makes decisions.[113] This information is often incomplete, unclear, and less than candid; the inscrutability of corporate proxy statements and quarterly reports is notorious.[114]

Corporate boards are composed of both "inside" and "outside" directors. The insiders are drawn from the corporation's sitting management team itself, whereas the outsiders are typically drawn from the top managers of financial institutions and other corporations. Outsiders may well include a prominent individual drawn from the arts or higher education (recent examples include Beverly Sills of the Metropolitan Opera and sociologist Harriet Zuckerman of Columbia University).[115] Shareholder majorities formally approve all appointments to the board and, until very recently, shareholders so infrequently initiated their own slates of candidates that the predictability of board elections would have made a Stalinist apparatchik envious.[116]

Headquarters does not dictate divisional policy. Rather, it establishes long-term strategies of corporate growth, including investment and finance

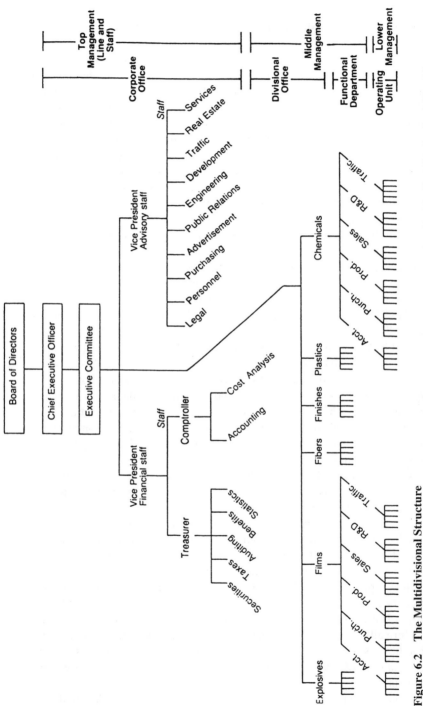

Figure 6.2   The Multidivisional Structure
(Reprinted by permission of the publisher from *Scale and Scope: The Dynamics of Industrial Capitalism* by Alfred D. Chandler, Jr., Cambridge, Mass:
Harvard University Press, Copyright © 1990 by Alfred D. Chandler, Jr.)

strategies; allocates resources to each division based on these strategies and the strengths of each division's own quarterly reports; coordinates activities across divisions; and both recruits and motivates middle managers.[117] Top management clearly has a positional interest in improving its monitoring of middle managers' behavior. The same is true, of course, about middle management. It has a positional interest in improving its monitoring of lower managers' behavior at the operational units. Thus, management has something of a shared positional interest, which has inclined it to: (1) align managers' incentives across the firm; (2) establish mechanisms of internal review at each lower level; (3) ensure reliable auditing (at least for management's own internal reviews); and (4) *establish governance structures that can effectively coordinate management's activities and resolve its internal disputes.*[118]

At least on its face, management's shared positional interest in improved monitoring across a corporation is consistent with shareholders' positional interest in reducing a corporation's agency costs and increasing its profits. Indeed, this explains why, until late 1983, management's collective efforts in the four areas just noted were sufficient to assure shareholders that their own positional interests were being at least broadly advanced. Shareholders could reasonably assume, along with neoclassical economists, that management would have little interest in wasting corporate assets and every interest in maximizing dividends. We shall see in Chapter 7 how the wave of hostile takeovers and leveraged buyouts that rose in late 1983 revealed for all to see that neither assumption held true in practice.

Notes

1. Legal historian Herbert Hovenkamp (1991) chronicles the rise of "classicism" or formalism in U.S. law during the period of Jacksonian democracy, and then its consolidation and dominance up to the New Deal.
2. Aichele (1990:12–13).
3. Aichele (1990:6); Posner (1990:14–17).
4. Aichele (1990:13). This is precisely why the great U.S. legal proceduralist, Lon Fuller, opposed legal formalism and supported legal realism early in his career: He, too, wished to detach the law from its anachronistic, substantive normative foundations. Fuller differed from other legal realists, however, in endeavoring to attach the law to a set of procedural norms that could still support—or "ground"—citizen vigilance over arbitrary exercises of collective power (see Chapter 2). By contrast, legal realists generally opposed the effort to "ground" any set of norms, whether substantive *or procedural.* They instead insisted that, in "reality," all norms are as negotiable and renegotiable as interests. Put differently, they did not believe that norms could resiliently frame or mediate individuals' ongoing instrumental behavior and conflicts of interest.
5. Smith (1990:413). Smith is quoting approvingly a critical definition of legal pragmatism offered by Ronald Dworkin.
6. Quoted by Aichele (1990:5).

7. Posner (1990:15–17).

8. Posner (1990:16); also Aichele (1990:23).

9. This view of powerful groups' opinions is precisely what Fuller challenged. He insisted that U.S. common law is grounded on nonnegotiable *procedural* norms, not more directly on substantive beliefs or material interests.

10. I borrow the term "presentism" from Alexander (1989), who uses it in discussing symbolic interaction, ethnomethodology, and dramaturgy. These approaches in sociology, along with the Chicago school's case studies, are very similar to economics, both epistemologically and methodologically, even as they develop a more "nonrational" theory of action. They, too, study individual and group behavior independently of any explicitly articulated evolutionary theory or theory of institutional externalities. See Hans Joas's collected essays (1993) for explorations of pragmatism's relationship to symbolic interactionism in particular. See Fine (1993) for an excellent review of the latter's place in the discipline of sociology today.

11. Aichele (1990:14); see White (1993) for an intellectual biography of Holmes. Summers (1982:25) sees legal pragmatism's major ideas in Oliver Wendell Holmes's "The Path of the Law," published in the *Harvard Law Review* in 1897, and Felix Cohen's "The Problems of a Functional Jurisprudence," published in 1937.

12. Aichele (1990:34); Lowi (1969).

13. Aichele (1990:20). Legal formalists held a few basic economic principles themselves. They believed, first, that self-regulating markets work pretty well if left alone; second, that "the best legal rules enlarge total social wealth"; and third, that governmental intervention into the economy is not an evil in and of itself, but the state should not intervene in favor of the rich or privileged. It should intervene, if at all, to expand opportunities for everyone (Hovenkamp 1991:4–5).

14. Aichele (1990:42).

15. Aichele (1990:25). Consider Joas's efforts to distinguish pragmatism from instrumentalism and utilitarianism: "[Pragmatism] does not conceive of action as a pursuit of ends that the contemplative subject establishes a priori and then resolves to accomplish; the world is not held to be mere material at the disposal of human intentionality. Quite to the contrary, pragmatism maintains that we find our ends in the world, and that prior to any setting of ends we are already, through our praxis, embedded in various situations. . . . The course followed by an action then . . . must be produced over and over again by construction and is open to continual revision. . . . Playful self-development and creative solution of problems . . . repudiate the primacy of an instrumentalist concept of labor for action just as radically as does [Habermas's] adducing of interaction and communication as kinds of action not accounted for by a model based upon labor" (1986:131–132). Also: "The pragmatism that arose in the United States constitutes an entirely original and autonomous way of interpreting the creativity of action. For pragmatism, the guiding metaphor is neither poetic expression nor material production nor revolutionary transformation of society, but instead the creative solution of problems by an experimenting intelligence" (1990:247–248).

16. Summers (1982:278–279); Samuelson (1948:37).

17. Aichele (1990:42, my emphasis). See page 144 for neoclassical economists' equivalent assumption. See Janowitz (1975) for an influential postwar example of liberal complacency in sociology, and recall Powell's characterization of institutionalists' view of stability and consensus within organizations (Chapter 3, page 55). Consider how C.E. Ayres worded his challenge to neoclassicists' presentism and complacent liberalism in 1934–1935, a particularly embarrassing time to be assuming without argument that local problem solving and complacency about

institutional outcomes somehow results automatically in a benign social order: "The 'Neo-classicist' does quite right to challenge the *assumption* of imminent calamity, but the mere show of intellectual calm does not altogether dispose of the *possibility*" (1934–1935:23).

18. Summers (1982:36–37); Aichele (1990:56, 72); see Fine (1993:70–71) on today's "social realists" in sociology.

19. Aichele (1990:45). Posner (1990:17–19) sees Cardozo as consolidating Holmes's ideas, and he points out that both legal pragmatism and legal realism are uniquely American. English law remains more formal and Continental law remains tied to natural law principles (1990:19, note 30).

20. Aichele (1990:61–62).

21. Aichele (1990:71). Niklas Luhmann (1972) continues this approach to law in sociology.

22. Aichele (1990:43, 52–56).

23. This was strictly fortuitous, and distinctively American (see Selznick on Dewey, 1992:172–173). German social theorist Hans Joas appreciates that American pragmatists' unyielding support for democracy is a distinctively *American* product, one yielded, ironically, by the "tension" between utilitarianism *and republicanism* (1992:85). He sees, that is, that pragmatism's concepts and presentism in themselves are not somehow tied exclusively to liberal or social democracy. "The first time I read it, I therefore felt that the National Socialist objections to Dewey . . . must have been opportunistic gestures to appease the censors. . . . However, a look at [Eduard Baumgarten's] preparatory publications and the framework in which the book was written soon showed this assumption to be false: when Baumgarten praises the spirit of pragmatism, he really does so from a National Socialist standpoint" (Joas 1993:109). Seeing this, Joas can only conclude that "as a philosophy of action, pragmatism became caught up in the enthusiasm for decisiveness, action, and power which characterized National Socialist intellectuals. Its democratic ideal was redefined in terms of the ideology of a national racial community and derived from common ancient Germanic origins" (1993:111). Joas also agrees with Carl Friedrich Gethmann that Heidegger's *Being and Time* contains the "earliest conception of consistent pragmatism in the German-speaking world" (1993:106, quoting Gethmann). See Bourdieu (1988) for the argument that National Socialist principles may be found at the center of *Being and Time*.

24. See Blumberg (1993:27–30).

25. Frank Knight, for instance, does not yet use the term in 1921. Sociologist Severyn Bruyn (1991:18–19) notes that Paul Samuelson institutionalized the term in 1955 in his college introductory text. The term does not appear in the first edition of 1948.

26. Keynes (1936:3, note 1).

27. Bruyn (1991:18–19). Keynes, however, claimed the "neoclassical" title for himself, and he placed Alfred Marshall, along with John Stuart Mill and others, in the "classical school" (1936:3, note 1; see also, for example, 177–179). It seems that each great economist considers his predecessors' ideas to be anachronistic, thereby "classical."

28. This interrelationship, captured well by the German term *bildung,* preoccupied Tönnies, Weber, and other founders of German sociology (Ringer 1969).

29. McCoy (1980:5–7, 19–20).

30. The most reflective neoclassical economists, however, have never abandoned political economists' concerns. Consider the following passage from Keynes (1936:374): "For my part, I believe that there is social and psychological justification for significant inequalities of incomes and wealth, but not for such large dispar-

ities as exist today. There are valuable human activities which require the motive of money-making and the environment of private wealth-ownership for their full fruition. Moreover, dangerous human proclivities can be canalised into comparatively harmless channels by the existence of opportunities for money-making and private wealth, which, if they cannot be satisfied in this way, may find their outlet in cruelty, the reckless pursuit of personal power and authority, and other forms of self-aggrandisement. It is better that a man should tyrannize over his bank balance than over his fellow-citizens; and whilst the former is sometimes denounced as being but a means to the latter, sometimes at least it is an alternative. But it is not necessary for the stimulation of these activities and the satisfaction of these proclivities that the game should be played for such high stakes as at present. Much lower stakes will serve the purpose equally well, as soon as the players are accustomed to them."

31. With exceptions, of course, on both sides. Within economics, there was the institutional economics of John Commons, Wesley Mitchell, Morris Copeland, Clarence Ayres, and others (see Samuels's three-volume collection, 1988). Within sociology, there was the Chicago school's emphasis on local ethnographies, detached from the broader concerns of European social theorists. See Joas (1987) on this issue.

32. Knight (1921/1948:xii).

33. This pathos is consistent with the only law of evolution that holds true both in physical and life sciences, the Second Law of Thermodynamics, the law of entropy. Thermodynamics originated in a memoir of Sadi Carnot in 1824 on the efficiency of steam engines and the fact that heat moves inexorably from hotter to colder bodies (Georgescu-Roegen 1971:129). This insight introduced "the greatest transformation ever suffered by physics" because the laws of classical mechanics cannot account for unidirectional movement; they instead assume that all movement is reversible (Georgescu-Roegen 1971:8, 129). German physicist Rudolf Clausius introduced the term "entropy" in 1865 and "gave the first two laws of thermodynamics their classic formulation" (Georgescu-Roegen 1971:129–130). As economist Nicholas Georgescu-Roegen puts the matter (1971:9): "The Entropy Law is neither a theoreum deducible from the principles of Classical mechanics nor a reflection of some of man's imperfections or illusions. On the contrary, it is as independent a law as, for example, the law of universal attraction, and just as inexorable." The term "entropy" is derived from the Greek term for "evolution."

34. This was one of Parsons's central arguments in *The Structure of Social Action* (1937). See Zukin and DiMaggio (1990) on sociologists' continuing opposition to neoclassical economics, and see Etzioni (1988) for an important argument regarding the different social psychologies that drive the two disciplines.

35. See Ringer (1969) for the Germans' pathos.

36. For example, see Parsons (1937:739, 752).

37. Compare this to institutionalists' views today; see Chapter 3, page 55).

38. After World War II, U.S. social theorist Talcott Parsons continued to rely on an evolutionary theory (as did Jurgen Habermas in Germany), but, for whatever reason, he stripped away social theorists' earlier pathos (Sciulli and Gerstein 1985). Parsons insisted that "functional differentiation" was more likely to result in a benign "directionality" than in a malevolent "drift," at least within the United States.

39. Knight (1921/1948:3).

40. As Georgescu-Roegen (1971) would put the matter, economists remained tied at a conceptual level to the notion of locomotion in classical mechanics, even as physics itself was accommodating—in one way or another—an evolutionary theory, namely the Second Law of Thermodynamics.

41. Knight (1920/1948:303). See note 69 below for Keynes's version of presentism. As in other matters, Veblen was well aware that economics was moving toward presentism. He wrote a paper titled "Why Is Economics Not an Evolutionary Science?" (Gordon 1976:133). Knight's accommodation of presentism is curious. On the one hand, his work is refreshing in that he acknowledges forthrightly that it is an error to treat "historical changes as tending toward an equilibrium," and he is personally pessimistic about the prospects for liberal democracy or "free discussion" (1920/1948:xix, xxxiv–xxxvi). Yet, having expressed these essentially political economic concerns, Knight then brackets the issue of institutional change from his study of risk and uncertainty. Indeed, Knight argued in his 1948 preface (at pages xlii–xliii) that the scientific study of economics needed to become even more "presentist" than Marshall had thought: "There is no period of production or time interval separating production and consumption. . . . In a stationary or progressive economy, investment is in fact permanent, and in reality most single items are committed with a presumption of permanence. . . . Production of capital cannot be treated as indirect production of its future yield; two productive operations must be recognized, even though this seems to involve double counting. The result of production, either in consumed service or growth of capital, is then always strictly simultaneous with production itself, from instant to instant."

42. Knight (1920/1948:viii).

43. These are Samuelson's "triplet of basic problems of economic organization" (1948:12).

44. Marshall (1892/1919).

45. Knight (1920/1948).

46. The last three questions are Keynes's (1936).

47. This bracketing is a product of economists' methodological individualism. We will explore this issue in Chapter 7; see note 58 there on this term.

48. Samuelson (1948:14, my emphasis).

49. See Chapter 4, note 28. The concept "production function" was introduced to economics by Philip Wicksteed in 1894, thereby pushing economists' approach to production closer to concepts of classical mechanics and further away from those of classical political economy. "The product being a function of the factors of production we have $P = f(a,b,c, . . .)$" (Georgescu-Roegen 1971:234). This narrow approach to production rests on a fallacy, however, in that "a flow [of factors of production] does not necessarily represent either a decrease or an increase in a stock [of commodities] of the same substance." Put differently, the fallacy is that it reduces change to locomotion rather than including also qualitative change in actual production which also affects workers, their households, and then the larger social order (Georgescu-Roegen 1971:223). Influenced by this narrow approach to production, Samuelson (1948:15) reduces political economy to appraising and improving "the efficiency with which a community mobilizes its means to achieve the prescribed ends." Elsewhere (1948:131, note 1) he dismisses out of hand the possibility of conceptualizing corporations as intermediary associations that exercise collective power within a larger social order. In dismissing this, however, he reduces the whole matter to business lobbying, neglecting the governance of corporations: "It would take us too far afield away from economics and into politics to discuss business as a system of power: how special-interest groups have occasionally lobbied, bribed, and agitated in order to influence public policy. Of course, the same has been known to be true of farmers and labor unions."

50. Keynes forcefully advocated this strategy in 1936. The concluding chapters of *The General Theory of Employment Interest and Money* include not only a defense of Smith's concern about national wealth *but also a defense of certain tenets of mercantilism.* They also include trenchant criticisms of free trade, even as

he calls "a policy of trade restrictions . . . a treacherous instrument" (1936:339). Consider the following passage in light of the U.S. trade imbalance today, and the recent passage of NAFTA: "Nevertheless, if we contemplate a society with a somewhat stable wage-unit, with national characteristics which determine the propensity to consume and the preference for liquidity, and with a monetary system which rigidly links the quantity of money to the stock of the precious metals, it will be essential for the maintenance of prosperity that the authorities should pay close attention to the state of the balance of trade. For a favourable balance, provided it is not too large, will prove extremely stimulating; whilst an unfavourable balance may soon produce a state of persistent depression" (1936:338).

    51. Commons (1931:22–24).

    52. Dragun does the same (1983:332–333).

    53. Ayres (1951:12).

    54. Ayres (1951:14, 16).

    55. Ayres (1951:12–15); Tool (1981:114–117) sees Veblen and Keynes sharing an "instrumental value theory," and Rutherford (1981) adds Ayres. For a broader use of Veblen's term "workmanship," see Anderson (1996).

    56. Witte (1954:30).

    57. For example, see Toole (1981:117–118, 121).

    58. Witte (1954:30); Witte takes the last two phrases from Frank Knight.

    59. Witte (1954:31–32).

    60. Dugger (1979:87).

    61. Consider how this relates to Perez-Diaz's social psychological definition of institutionalized democracy (see Chapter 2, pages 33–34). Similarly, Etzioni (1988) treats the "moral dimension" of economic activity as more social psychological than institutional.

    62. This was Parsons's point of departure in challenging Marshall (1937:148–150, 161–164).

    63. For example, see Toole (1981:122–123) and Parsons (1937:155–158).

    64. Wilber and Harrison (1978:112–113). Robert Gordon (1976:129) decries "the failure of economic theory to adapt its analytical tools to the changing institutional environment." Charles Wilber and Robert Harrison (1978:61) summarize the "methodological basis of institutional economics" as "pattern model, storytelling, and holism."

    65. Consider how Frank Knight puts the matter: "The more vital problems are not problems of economy, but of maintaining social unity in the face of economic interests. And the foundations of unity lie not in intelligence, but in habit, emotion, and ideals of value" (1920/1948:xxx).

    66. Smith is best remembered for his appreciation of how military preparedness inculcates norms of self-discipline. Knight considers normative or institutional factors precisely because he is pessimistic rather than sanguine about modernity's "natural" direction of change (e.g., 1920/1948:xiii–xv). But, again, these normative factors do not play a role in his study of risk and uncertainty; rather, here he reduces all "aesthetic" and "nonrational" elements to instrumental means and quantitative ends.

    67. See Parsons (1937:159–161) on "natural order" in Marshall.

    68. See Hechter (1983:185–186) on these assumptions in rational choice theory.

    69. Aichele (1990:xvi–xvii). Ironically, by 1936 Keynes would remind his fellow economists of the importance of *convention* for "economic progress," and this passage also nicely captures economists' presentism: "In practice we have tacitly agreed, as a rule, to fall back on what is, in truth, a convention. The essence of this

convention . . . lies in assuming that the existing state of affairs will continue indefinitely, except in so far as we have specific reasons to expect a change. This does not mean that we really believe that the existing state of affairs will continue indefinitely. We know from extensive experience that this is most unlikely. . . . Nevertheless the above conventional method of calculation will be compatible with a considerable measure of continuity and stability in our affairs, *so long as we can rely on the maintenance of the convention.* . . . But it is not surprising that a convention, in an absolute view of things so arbitrary, should have its weak points. It is its precariousness which creates no small part of our contemporary problem of securing sufficient investment" (1936:152–153).

70. Aichele (1990:31).

71. Aichele (1990:72).

72. See note 49.

73. See Marshall (1892:139–178, 287–302); Knight (1920/1948:291–312); Samuelson (1948:108–132, 491–532). For comments, see Jensen and Meckling (1976:306–307) and Williamson (1988b:569). Easterbrook and Fischel continue this practice by saying (1991:10): "Corporations are a subset of firms. The corporation is a financing device and is not otherwise distinctive."

74. Aichele (1990:56).

75. By contrast, under oligopolistic conditions: (1) each firm's output is a significant part of its industry's total; (2) a great deal of material and human capital is needed to enter any industry; and (3) products may be distinguished by qualities or brand names touted in advertising. This is why managers of oligopolies find it rational to retain earnings: They wish to expand their firms' facilities (and advertising budgets) and thereby to compete for market share over time as opposed to maximizing immediate earnings.

76. Easterbrook and Fischel at times continue this practice today; again, see, for example 1991:136.

77. Heilbroner and Thurow (1978:210).

78. Heilbroner and Thurow (1978:193).

79. See Easterbrook and Fischel's discussion (1991:166–171).

80. Easterbrook and Fischel assert that corporate governance is transparent, irrespective of whether it is consensual or not (1991:7): "Governance structures are open and notorious, unlike the conduct they seek to control. Costs of knowing about a firm's governance are low."

81. Marshall (1892/1919:169).

82. Samuelson (1948:121).

83. Samuelson (1948:130–131, my emphasis).

84. Marshall (1892/1919:176–178, 287–293); Williamson (1985:209).

85. Samuelson (1948:510).

86. Samuelson (1948:502).

87. Herman (1981:86); compare to Samuelson (1948:519).

88. The term does not appear in Marshall's index (1892/1919), nor in Samuelson's (1948).

89. Williamson (1985:240); Brudney (1985:1438–1439).

90. Marshall (1892/1919:169–170).

91. Marshall (1892/1919:170).

92. More specifically, they are assuming that maximizing shareholder wealth or corporate growth *results automatically in Pareto optimal outcomes* (see Easterbrook and Fischel 1991:126, 145).

93. "All the terms in corporate governance are contractual in the sense that they are fully priced in transactions among the interested parties. . . . [I]t is unim-

portant whether knowledge about the nature or effect of the terms is widespread, at least for public corporations. The mechanism by which stocks are valued ensures that the price reflects the terms of governance and operation, just as it reflects the identity of the managers and the products the firm produces" (Easterbrook and Fischel 1991:17–18).

94. Hovenkamp (1991:60–63).

95. Friedman (1973/1985:520); Johnson (1990:899–900); Hovenkamp (1991:62–63). The courts similarly defer to administrative agencies. Here they acknowledge that they lack any special competence to assess the longer-term costs or benefits of any given agency's decisions (Breyer and Stewart 1985:371). The courts might take a "hard look" at *how* a particular agency arrived at a particular decision, but they rarely challenge the decision itself in content or substance. Easterbrook and Fischel, however, illustrate well the even greater discretion that the courts accord to corporate management: "The same judges who aggressively review the design of aircraft (in product-liability cases) and the decisions of disinterested administrative agencies react in horror at the prospect of deciding whether a manager was negligent when introducing a new product after test-marketing in only two cities" (1991:vii). I have converted this passage from a question into a statement.

96. Loewenstein (1989:70).

97. Easterbrook and Fischel reject this explanation for the business judgment rule: "The business judgment rule must rest on something more. It reflects limits on the use of liability rules to assure contractual performance" (1991:94). I address their view of the business judgment rule elsewhere, in the context of exploring their redefinition of the fiduciary law tradition (see Sciulli 1997d).

98. The same is true of creditors when firms run into financial difficulties. In extreme situations, for example the case of Memorex in 1973–1974, major creditors such as Bank of America may replace the CEO and top management team (Herman 1981:124). But typically even bankers follow a tradition of not challenging management's prerogative (Herman 1981:128). The situation is quite different in Japan (Kester 1991).

99. Berle and Means (1932); Mark (1987:1474–1475). This is the problem that Japan is beginning to face today (Kester 1991:269–279). Even Easterbrook and Fischel hedge on this issue by not emphasizing immediate profits and instead referring at times to investors' longer-term calculations of gain—even as this is inconsistent with their own framework of concepts. "For most firms the expectation is that the residual risk bearers have contracted for a promise to maximize long-run profits of the firm, which in turn maximizes the value of their stock" (1991:36, also 183); this wording is not consistent with their wording at 206–207.

100. The significance of the multidivisional form was not really appreciated until 1962, with the publication of Alfred Chandler's *Strategy and Structure* (Williamson 1985:278–280). See Sobel (1984:52–75) for a short history of this period of corporate consolidation.

101. Hovenkamp (1991:63).

102. Chandler (1990:618–619); Bratton (1989a:1492); Williamson (1985:278–285).

103. Until 1929, over two-thirds of the industrial output of the entire world was produced by three countries: Germany, the United Kingdom, and the United States (Chandler 1990:3–13).

104. James Burk notes (1988) that the impact of the Depression was not necessarily one-sided, and so does Sobel (1984:122–152). On the one hand, the stock market lost 90 percent of its value from 1929 to 1931 (Burk 1988:23); branch offices of the New York Stock Exchange fell from 1,658 in 1930 to 1,215 in 1934,

and to 1,057 in 1940 (Burk 1988:60). On the other hand, the number of individual shareholders actually rose from 9–11 million in 1930 to 10–12 million in 1932, doubling the number in 1927 (Burk 1988:32; see also Sobel 1984:84–98).

105. Chandler (1990:617–618).

106. Chandler (1990:14–16).

107. Chandler (1990:31, 36).

108. Chandler (1990:44).

109. Stinchcombe (1990:114).

110. Butler (1989:118). I show elsewhere (Sciulli 1997a) that the most important corporate governance disputes of the 1980s and 1990s revolved around these process issues.

111. Williamson (1985:298, 305, 316–317).

112. Japanese corporations also vest control in a board elected by shareholder-owners (banks and trading partners). A major shareholder from an owning *family* is usually appointed to the figurehead position of president and chairman of the board. The group of "executive directors" that actually runs the corporation is comprised of well-educated managers. By the 1930s, the entire board was comprised of such inside managers, except for the figurehead president-chairman; there were no outside directors. Shareholders' interests were protected because management then received 10 percent of company profits. Today it receives 15–20 percent (Kester 1991:38–39). This organizational arrangement is "available" for management eventually to transfer *its positions* by inheritance, by more or less absolute control over succession.

113. Japanese management teams offer much more information, and to many more corporate constituents, than do U.S. management teams (Kester 1991:68–69).

114. The Financial Accounting Standards Board, which oversees accounting rules in the United States and is itself overseen by the Securities and Exchange Commission, has been endeavoring since 1984 to improve the accuracy of managers' reported salaries and earnings (Cowan 1992). See note 116.

115. During early 1994, the *New York Times* investigated whether W. Ann Richards, Chancellor of City University of New York, spent too much time on five corporate boards (Newman and Weiss, February 22, 1994, pages 1, 8). Whether this charge holds up or not, her compensation for each board is instructive: For Abbott Laboratories (since 1980), Richards receives $3,750 a month, plus $625 a month as a committee chair; for Owens-Corning Fiberglas Corp. (since October 1993), $20,000 a year, plus $800 a meeting; for American Electric Power (since 1981), $20,000 a year, plus $1,000 a meeting and $1,000 a day for any inspection trip or conference; for Humana Inc. (since 1991), $22,000 a year, plus $1,000 a meeting, $4,217 for each special meeting, and $550 for each committee meeting; and for Maytag Corp. (since 1988), $22,000 a year, plus $1,000 a meeting, $1,000 for each committee meeting, and $750 for each telephone meeting.

116. The Securities and Exchange Commission recently developed new proxy rules designed to increase shareholders' ability to challenge management's slate of candidates. For three reasons, however, this is not likely to affect corporate governance or corporate performance very much.

First, outside directors are typically dedicated full-time to managing their own corporations or financial institutions. At best, they work only part-time in shareholders' interests.

Second, outsiders' *position* within the corporation's governance structure, as monthly participants on its board, offers them few incentives to assert their independence from the insiders who manage the company. A significant exception took place on April 6, 1992: John G. Smale, a former chairman of Procter & Gamble

Company, led General Motors' outside directors in a successful effort to control the board's executive committee, which is mandated to monitor the company's management (Lohr 1992). This successful effort, however, came many years after GM resisted trimming its managerial ranks despite increasing foreign competition.

Third, all directors share one overriding positional interest as directors (Anders 1992:114): to avoid making any costly mistakes for which they can potentially be held *personally* accountable (as was the case in Smith v. Van Gorkom). Thus, directors ultimately share top managers' aversion to risk, and this *shared positional interest* in avoiding risk is not likely to be affected by increasing the number of outsiders on corporate boards. Indeed, boards with outsider majorities neither financially outperform insider-dominated boards nor exhibit greater social responsibility (Dent 1989:897–899). Moreover, most of the boards of the largest public corporations in the United States have had outsider majorities for the past fifteen years.

117. Chandler (1990:594); see also Williamson (1985:284) and Stinchcombe (1990:122–125) for lists of top management's activities.

118. Williamson (1985:283).

7

Doctrinal Fissures: Corporate Law and Judicial Practice Today

When top management granted discretion to middle managers at divisions, this greatly complicated corporate governance. It also greatly complicated the courts' efforts to identify the corporate agent, to identify who "really" gets things done in the corporation's name and thereby bears legal responsibility for its behavior. The extent to which the rise of the multidivisional form complicated this issue may be appreciated by considering that *all* of the tasks assigned to managers at both middle and top levels were new. As such, these tasks had to be delineated and coordinated. Their coordination, in turn, had to be routinized. It had to be institutionalized by a governance structure, a workable system of monitoring and incentives.

Developing such a system was, and remains, more difficult to accomplish than might at first appear. On the one hand, as top management entrusted middle managers with governing and administering divisions, shareholders understandably became interested in reducing what economists call management's "moral hazard" at all levels of the multidivisional form. On the other hand, top management understandably became interested in narrowing middle managers' scope of moral hazard at divisions but in broadening its own discretion at headquarters. Moral hazard is an immediate externality of the multidivisional form and, therefore, of contemporary corporate governance. This chapter will trace how this immediate externality metamorphoses into positional conflicts and governance disputes, and then metamorphoses again into institutional externalities. We shall see as well why the U.S. corporate judiciary has lost its moorings in the business judgment rule and the fiduciary law tradition, and why, as a result, it is adrift as an institution.

Immediate Externalities of the Multidivisional Form

From Moral Hazard to Positional Conflict

Consider the dilemma that outside suppliers face when top management offers them either a long-term contract or some other opportunity to enter the corporation as a new constituent.[1] Suppliers know that if they accept either offer, management will tailor suppliers' intermediate products—whatever they are—to the corporation's particular needs. Using economists' terminology, suppliers know that their intermediate products will become fixed assets for the corporation and sunk costs for them: They will not be able to redeploy them easily or costlessly later. Thus, suppliers know that if they accept either offer, their *position* will change. In effect, their position will move from (1) its current fluid sites of contracting in competitive markets, from which suppliers can exit relatively easily and costlessly, to (2) a more structured situation in which the obstacles to, and costs of, exiting are literally prohibitive. In a structured situation, the supplier's position is itself vulnerable to management's self-interested behavior—opportunism—at all three levels of the multidivisional form. Thus, suppliers who enter a structured situation unprotected are essentially trusting managers at all levels to exhibit "good will," to act "disinterestedly" on their behalf. This is a gamble, of course, and economists refer to it as a "moral hazard."[2]

The term is used broadly. Economists employ it to refer to any team activity in which agents cannot fully price, easily monitor, or effectively control subordinates' performances. As one example, consider Frank Knight's use of the term:

> The classification or grouping [of the risks involved in relying on others' discretion or judgment] can only to a limited extent be carried out by any agency outside the person himself who makes the decisions, because of the peculiarly obstinate connection of a *moral hazard* with this sort of risk. The decisive factors in the case are so largely on the inside of the person making the decisions that the "instances" are not amenable to objective description and external control.[3]

In a situation characterized as a moral hazard, individuals have no alternative other than to trust others to carry out their assigned duties on time and with sufficient levels of motivation and creativity. Economists perceive this as "hazardous," as a risky gamble, precisely because they are so skeptical that most people will act "morally" when left on their own, as opposed to acting strategically or self-interestedly.

When people do in fact take advantage of a moral hazard—take advantage of gaps in a pricing system, a monitoring regime, or a control mechanism—economists use the terms "shirking," "self-dealing," or "opportunism." Shirking refers to goldbricking, or the failure to fulfill assignments on time. Self-dealing refers to stealing, or the behavior of those who line their own pockets at the team's expense. Opportunism encompasses these two sets of behavior and refers in addition to the failure to maximize team performance that occurs when leaders take advantage of subordinates or otherwise fail to provide effective leadership.[4] As examples, managers and other agents may badger subordinates in ways that do not improve their performance but are instead gratuitous or self-aggrandizing; here they "self-deal," albeit in a social psychological way rather than a more pecuniary way. Or, they may fail to monitor subordinates effectively even when this is possible; here managers shirk in the amount of motivation and creativity that they dedicate to their duties.

Economists today appreciate that moral hazard, structured situations in which individuals have no alternative other than to trust others to contribute their best performance, is intrinsic to any team activity. Moral hazard becomes particularly intractable when a team's very success hinges on the *quality* of each individual's contribution, on how much motivation and creativity each team member dedicates to his or her assigned task. The term refers generally, therefore, to any structured situation in which individuals must rely on others prospectively (or *ex ante*) to expend their best effort because they are unable to monitor a more modest effort retrospectively (or *ex post*) by pricing their contribution. *Thus, moral hazard is intrinsic to most professional work.*

In the case of the suppliers who are offered a long-term contract or some other opportunity to enter a corporation, these corporate constituents have not only a rational self-interest but also a positional interest in counterbalancing their exposure to management's opportunism. For instance, suppliers may reject the offer unless they are guaranteed special compensation packages in the event that (1) their position is later eliminated or (2) managers overuse their fixed assets and thereby depreciate them sooner than expected. More important for present purposes, suppliers may reject the offer unless management grants them some control over how managers at all levels use their intermediate products. After all, this is the only way in which they can prevent management from unnecessarily tailoring their intermediate products to the corporation's specific needs, from unnecessarily "fixing" or "sinking" their assets.

From management's point of view, however, *this second concession brings suppliers into the corporation's governance structure.* Clearly, a rational management team will agree to this only if convinced that securing the same intermediate products elsewhere, under different contract provisions, will take far more time and be far more costly. This illustrates well not only the general problems of moral hazard and opportunism but also the general way in which the multidivisional form complicates corporate governance. Each concession that management grants to each constituent simultaneously complicates a corporation's governance structure. Management may nonetheless grant many such concessions in its ongoing effort to recruit expert personnel and secure an uninterrupted flow of specialized intermediate products.

Consider, for instance, that one significant part of middle managers' duties in governing and administering divisions is ceaselessly to monitor regional markets in search of new raw materials and intermediate products. What this means, in practice, is that middle managers are the group of constituents most conversant with a corporation's particular technologies, particular manufacturing facilities, and particular product lines.[5] Theirs is the constituency with the most knowledge and expertise specific to the firm, the division, and even the product.[6] Thus, in practice, the success of a corporate enterprise as a whole hinges in some significant part on the motivation and creativity that middle managers bring to their assigned duties at divisions. Middle managers therefore operate within a scope of moral hazard that top management must contend with in one way or another.

Middle managers too are exposed to uncertainties—in fact, the same uncertainties that suppliers face when they bring their intermediate products into a corporation. Middle managers' experience and expertise—their human capital—becomes tailored to one corporation's particular needs as time passes. Their operational skills become fixed assets for the corporation and sunk costs for them. With each passing year, their "intermediate product" of human capital becomes more difficult and costly for them to transfer to any other corporation. Thus, like the suppliers, middle managers also have both a self-interest and a positional interest in gaining some "control" over their future. Ultimately, they have an interest in gaining some representation within their corporations' governance structures and, of course, in gaining compensation guarantees in the event that they are fired or their positions are eliminated.

In this context moral hazard and the fear of opportunism begin to metamorphose into positional conflicts. Middle managers are understandably anxious about their vulnerability to top managers' discretion. Top managers, in turn, are understandably anxious about the scope of moral hazard within which middle managers operate at divisions. Top management's dilemma is to find some way, on the one hand, to assure middle managers of its "good will" or disinterestedness and, on the other hand, to narrow middle managers' scope of moral hazard. The dilemma is that "good will" can only be demonstrated over time. Moreover, if top management instead grants middle managers representation within the governance structure, *the moral hazard is shifted to headquarters,* which becomes vulnerable to judicial interventions into the corporation's governance structure, in response to charges of breach of contract, to conflicts of interest between top management and middle management that escalate into positional conflicts.

Furthermore, top management's dilemma does not end here. If it denies middle managers representation, it then reduces their rational incentives for performing well, for fully dedicating their skills to the company. Top management in this case leaves each middle manager with only two "rational" choices. He or she can exit the corporation at the moment that a suitable opportunity becomes available. Or, when none is available, he or she can shirk, self-deal, or otherwise take advantage of gaps in top management's monitoring and control. For example, each middle manager may provide only that level of motivation and creativity that top management is capable of pricing or otherwise noticing at headquarters. Indeed, economists insist that it is not rational for middle managers within this structured situation to perform at a level that is closer to their true capacities.[7]

Top management has a clear positional interest in denying middle managers, suppliers, and all other corporate constituents new protections or guarantees. Any new protection or guarantee simultaneously constricts top management's positional power. It not only narrows its discretion but also, as we have seen, exposes its business judgment and the corporation's governance structure to monitoring and intervention by state courts. Any new protection or guarantee, after all, is a promise or "contract" that, as such, can be converted into a formal appeal to state courts to scrutinize top management's behavior. Such protections can only remind shareholders and other investors of the scope of moral hazard to which they already have exposed themselves by hiring an agent rather than managing the corporation themselves. "The first question facing entrepreneurs [or corporate agents] is what promises to make, and the second is how to induce investors to believe them. Empty promises are worthless promises."[8]

From Moral Hazard to Governance Dispute

Investors' general worry that corporate agents might take advantage of moral hazards across the multidivisional form, whether by making promises or by breaking promises, begins to reveal why top management's exposure to *investors'* "opportunism" increased in the 1980s in the form of hostile corporate takeovers and leveraged buyouts. The irony is that top management's very successes increased its exposure to these changes in corporate control.

As we saw in Chapter 6, the multidivisional form freed top management from most divisional and operational responsibilities, enabling it to dedicate its time and resources at headquarters to developing finance strategies.[9] At first glance it would seem that top managers' strategic skills are therefore more transferable or fungible on the labor market than are middle managers' operational skills. We also saw in Chapter 6, however, that the day of the generalist at headquarters is over. Each top manager's strategic skills, like the operational skills of each middle manager, also become tailored to a particular corporation as time passes. His or her human capital becomes a fixed asset for the corporation, a sunk cost for the top manager. Thus, most top managers' prospects for career mobility outside their corporation steadily decline over the course of their careers.

Under the multidivisional form, then, top management developed a self-interest and a positional interest in arranging routine career advancement for itself within the corporation, if it could. Unlike middle management, moreover, top management often succeeded in creating for itself what sociologists and economists call a "firm internal labor market."[10] The irony, again, is that its very successes—dedicating itself at headquarters to finance strategies, and establishing for itself a firm internal labor market—inadvertently exposed the top management *position* to "opportunism" by shareholders and other investors. This only became apparent, however, in late 1983 when a wave of hostile takeovers and leveraged buyouts began to sweep across the U.S. corporate world. Until then, Oliver Williamson and other economists saw takeovers and buyouts as a means by which the management teams of innovative conglomerates extended the multidivisional form to their backward, recalcitrant counterparts in smaller firms.[11] Three important countertrends initiated in late 1983, however, forever shattered this imagery of linear "progress." First, small corporations as well as underwritten raiders and buyout specialists began putting together credible hostile bids for even the largest conglomerates. Second, hostile takeovers and leveraged buyouts often resulted in deconglomeration—in a selling off of the target corporation's divisions in order to finance the change in corporate control itself. Third, with deconglomeration, corporations often "restructured" in ways that benefited shareholder majorities immediately but that typically eliminated many managerial positions, at headquarters and divisions alike.

What hostile takeovers and leveraged buyouts revealed for all to see was the gap, at a frozen moment in time, between the liquidation value of a target corporation's existing assets and the resale value of its stock. To be sure, knowledgeable shareholders accept that stock is typically traded at some significant discount of corporations' liquidation value.[12] Nonetheless, the new market for corporate control revealed that this gap was considerably wider than shareholders had been led to believe by management. It was so wide, in fact, that all of the uncertainty and risk attending leveraged buyouts and raids financed by junk bonds seemed well worth taking.[13] Indeed, the risks faced later by raiders and buyout specialists, as they arranged the simultaneous resale of their targets' parts, *still* seemed to make sense given the returns that were possible.

Examples across the decade and into the 1990s illustrate why so many investors were willing, and remain willing, to live with greater uncertainties and risks. DuPont's friendly takeover of Conoco for $7.68 billion in 1981 marked the start of the decade's accelerating pace of changes in corporate control. The value of Conoco stock rose from under $50 a share to

$98 for a total increase in premium of $3.2 billion; DuPont's premium fell $800 million. Ivan Boesky earned $40 million on this single deal in arbitrage.[14] In 1984, CBS shares were selling at $72 when Ted Turner presented a bid for the company. Securities analysts then set its break-up value at around $200 a share.[15] As late as 1988, RJR Nabisco shares were selling below $50, but shareholders received $109 after its leveraged buyout by Kohlberg, Kravis, Roberts & Co. in November of that year.[16] Even today shareholders can benefit considerably from the market for corporate control. Viacom stock rose from $37 on April 22, 1993, when Martin Davis and Sumner Redstone began exploring the possibility of a merger, to $67.50 on September 13, 1993, the day after they publicly announced their plans. On Labor Day 1993, before the Paramount-Viacom saga began, Paramount stock was worth $6.7 billion; three months later, by January 1994, its value had increased another $2.8 billion. Likewise, Paramount shares were selling for $69 when the Viacom-Paramount merger was announced; by the time the bidding war between Viacom and QVC network ended, on February 15, 1994, its shares had risen again, now between $78 and $82.[17]

In other words, by late 1983, once entrenched (and often arrogant) management teams were suddenly fighting for their very positions and careers. In essence, *shareholders' private property began challenging management's positional power for "sovereignty" within corporate governance structures.* Moreover, not only were management's positions jeopardized by the very real threat of takeovers or buyouts, but their business judgment was also exposed to scrutiny by institutional investors. Of course, top managers reacted accordingly in the 1980s, as they do today. They restructured their firms in an effort both to please (and lull) institutional investors and to preempt surprises. "A corporate restructuring is any transaction that could have an effect on equity ownership, including a merger, a management buyout or a recapitalization."[18] Managers restructured their respective corporations in an effort to remove raiders' or buyout specialists' incentives to approach stockholders bilaterally with alternative plans and finance strategies. Put differently, management everywhere endeavored to bring the value of corporate stock more clearly into line with the liquidation value of corporate assets.[19]

> If the market price does not fully reflect the firm's value, the managers, faced with a bid, can reveal the news on which the bidder is acting. Investors may evaluate it for themselves. . . . By and large, managers are the mistaken parties—for they have their egos on the line, while professional investors are betting their wallets.[20]

Management-initiated restructurings were extremely rare occurrences before 1984.[21] In that year they began to proliferate and they remain common today. In just an eighteen-month period, between January 1984 and mid-July 1985, 398 of the 850 largest corporations in North America restructured. Only 52 of these restructurings were initiated in response to actual tender offers or credible takeover threats.[22] Actually, even when hostile takeovers peaked, in 1986, they affected only 40 of 3,300 corporate equity ownership transactions; only 110 others were affected by voluntary or unopposed tender offers.[23] Nonetheless, throughout the 1980s, 2,300 U.S. companies restructured or were otherwise touched in one way or another by raids and buyouts; $180 billion was borrowed to finance these transactions.[24] Even when the market for corporate control eventually declined, after 1988, restructurings of one kind or another remained prominent features of the corporate landscape. They continued to be favored by institutional investors as well as bondholders.

Piore and Sabel capture well how disruptive even at the outset were the three trends we noted earlier that countered the linear "progress" or extension of the multidivisional form:

> The current reorganization within mass producers is confusing the relationship between corporate headquarters and the productive units that it coordinates. There is a chance that efforts to break with mass-production patterns of control will produce chaos, rather than a system of coordination for flexible specialization. This danger that corporate reforms could end in chaos is increased by the potentially contradictory nature of the reforms.[25]

This is the point at which moral hazard and opportunism begin to metamorphose not only into positional conflicts but into full-blown governance disputes.[26] The takeovers and buyouts fueling the new market for corporate control revealed for all to see that top management had inadvertently exposed its position to shareholders' "opportunism." When top management dedicated itself at headquarters to developing finance strategies, it became vulnerable to alternative finance strategies that raiders and buyout specialists would eventually propose to shareholder majorities bilaterally. Sociologist Arthur Stinchcombe writes that his own "theory of market uncertainty and market information segregation does not predict anything about the general office, except that if it exists it will tend to restrict itself to investment, profit assessment, and performance measurement functions, *much as the stock market or investment bankers do.*"[27] In the context of the events under discussion here, then, a management team's substantive grasp of its own corporation's product lines, divisions, regional markets, and operational units was no longer necessarily any greater than that of any investment banker—or any raider.[28] At the same time, raiders' willingness to maximize shareholders' dividends immediately (and, of course, to maximize their own private wealth) often proved, not surprisingly, to be more attractive to shareholder majorities than a sitting management team's longer-term strategies of corporate growth.[29]

In this way, top management's very successes in gaining sovereignty within the multidivisional form prepared the way both organizationally and institutionally for deconglomeration, for "opportunism" by shareholders, raiders, and other investors.[30] This is what Williamson had in mind in 1988 when he noted that hostile takeovers became possible only because a suitable corporate governance structure was in place. By late 1983, raiders and buyout specialists could indeed negotiate alternative finance strategies bilaterally with shareholder majorities without seeming to disrupt anything other than top management's positions at headquarters and middle management's at divisions. "Hostile tender offers are responses to the failures of the target's managers."[31] Hostile tender offers demonstrated quite compellingly for everyone to see, particularly shareholder majorities, that top management had indeed taken advantage of investors within its own scope of moral hazard. "A tender offer gives the shareholders a chance to go over the head of managers when agency costs become too high."[32] Top management had often advanced its own positional interests opportunistically, as opposed to acting more disinterestedly on behalf of shareholders or, arguably, the corporate entity.

The Normative Dilemma of the 1920s that Judges Face Again Today

Two Bases of Doctrinal Continuity: Business Judgment and Fiduciary Law

Judges could keep their rulings relatively consistent even as the rise and consolidation of the multidivisional form greatly complicated corporate governance because they were able pragmatically to adjust some of corporate law's basic concepts to accommodate this new "reality." From the 1920s through the 1970s, they found two particularly important bases of conceptual continuity: the business judgment rule and the fiduciary law tradition. By clinging to the business judgment rule even as they transferred their deference from shareholder-owners to sitting management teams, the courts could keep their decisions linked, however tenuously at times, to their second, Lockean approach to corporate agency. We saw in Chapter 5 that as early as the mid-nineteenth century the courts were beginning to defer to shareholder-owners' interpretations of the corporate entity's "real" interests. The courts simultaneously were losing their institutional memory of the Founders' republican concerns. By the end of the century, judges began transferring the courts' then established practice of deference to management's interpretations. With one significant exception, judges thereby transferred to management the discretion—the scope of moral hazard—to determine the corporation's place and purpose within society.

The exception was that judges continued to prohibit management, as they had earlier prohibited shareholder-owners, from encroaching against those public law norms and fiduciary duties still at the core of corporate law doctrine. Indeed, the courts' long tradition of enforcing fiduciary duties within structured situations of dependence and trust was the courts' second base of conceptual continuity. Following the practice of England's Chancery, U.S. state courts held anyone who occupies a position of power within such situations legally responsible for acting "fairly" or "equitably." Transferring this tradition's norms of behavior to corporate governance in particular, U.S. judges held the corporate agent legally responsible for bearing two fiduciary duties.[33] First, they held the corporate agent responsible for bearing a duty of care, a court-enforced normative duty not to self-deal or otherwise waste corporate assets. Second, and more important, they held the corporate agent responsible for bearing a duty of loyalty, a court-enforced normative duty to exhibit fidelity to the corporate entity. Corporate agents bear this second duty by advancing the corporate entity's "real" interests "disinterestedly," as opposed to acting either more instrumentally on behalf of shareholders or more strategically in their own positional interests. However, with the courts' increasing loss of institutional memory of the Founders' republican concerns about corporate power, and the increasing hold of neoclassicists' and pragmatists' liberal complacency, judges became uncertain why they should continue to enforce either duty. Why not simply enforce management's contractual obligations to shareholders and to other corporate constituents, stakeholders?

From Immediate Externalities to Institutional Externalities

Elsewhere I show that the duty of care turns out not to be a fiduciary duty at all.[34] For present purposes we may simply recognize that the duty of care is adequately covered by civil and criminal sanctions against destroying or stealing others' property. Thus, one of the bases of conceptual continuity for U.S. state courts—the fiduciary law tradition—ultimately stands or falls on whether and how the duty of loyalty is enforced. After the turbulence of the 1980s, this base is now crumbling.[35] This is so because the state courts have failed at a doctrinal level to distinguish (1) their pragmatic tendency to extend the duty of loyalty to long-term enterprises (as if corporations are endangered species or historical landmarks) from (2) the more principled practice of English chancellors. Following this latter tradition, they could extend the duty of loyalty to structured situations in civil society—wherein corporate agents' internal governance and external behavior result in institutional externalities that bear on the larger social order.

Like other sociologists, William Roy is unfamiliar with the fiduciary law tradition. He therefore cannot account for the efforts of U.S. state courts—as opposed to European judicial systems—to maintain directors' relative autonomy from both shareholders and sitting management teams. He also cannot account for why the states—again, unlike European countries—"actively chipped away at the rights of ownership and fortified the powers given to officers and directors."[36]

We noted this peculiarly American tendency in Chapter 3. We observed that the U.S. corporate judiciary monitors generally how corporations are governed and at times intervenes into "governance disputes" between corporate boards and sitting management teams on one hand and shareholders and stakeholders on the other. Roy understands this type of intervention. The corporate judiciary also, however, monitors how managers structure the relationship between their own positions of power and the positions occupied by shareholders and stakeholders with an eye to preventing managers from insulating their positions from others' oversight and from the discipline of market forces. Despite Roy's otherwise informed analysis of the pressures that powerful groups place on U.S. state courts as they oversee corporate power, this is a sphere of judicial concern that he does not see—the courts' own public law concern about the possible institutional externalities of private governance structures in U.S. civil society.

The courts do not simply favor management's positions over shareholders' ownership, nor do they try to insulate corporate performance from the discipline of market forces as if corporations are national landmarks. Rather, the courts try to ensure, first, that corporate managers act disinterestedly on behalf of shareholders and stakeholders alike, and second—even more basically—that corporate managers do not exercise their positional power unfairly or arbitrarily in structured situations in civil society. To this end they discipline managers when a corporation's governance structure makes it difficult for shareholders, bondholders, or long-term suppliers objectively to monitor their performance, or when managers erect high barriers to their own removal for poor performance.[37] The courts intervene in such situations because they do not want managers to "have the power to unilaterally determine or materially vary the rules that govern those divergencies of interest."[38] Their public law concern in these cases is institutionalized in the "relative autonomy" of U.S. law.

In sum, by the 1970s the U.S. corporate judiciary had failed to distinguish at a doctrinal level between extending the duty of loyalty to long-term enterprises and extending it to structured situations whose governance can alter the institutional design of the larger social order. In the absence of an explicit and unambiguous understanding of this distinction, the duty of loyalty could remain in effect only as long as judges could be reasonably certain that U.S. corporations *were* long-term enterprises, in "reality." From World War II through the 1970s, this was a reasonable assumption. But as the wave of hostile takeovers and leveraged buyouts altered the very landscape of the corporate world, judges now had difficulty enforcing management's supposed duty of loyalty to *the* corporate entity as a long-term enterprise. They had lost sight of their more important responsibility as an environmental agent, namely to monitor how positional power is exercised at least in certain structured situations in civil society.

Immediately after World War II U.S. courts had developed a renewed, albeit short-lived, interest in enforcing public law norms and fiduciary duties, although these decisions continued to overlook the doctrinal traditions that had once undergirded such enforcement. The corporate judiciary's renewed interest in this sphere emerged particularly in its general support of U.S. corporations that in fact were long-term enterprises. This renewed interest was short-lived because it was a product of developments entirely exogenous to the ongoing evolution of judicial practice from republican vigilance to liberal complacency.

Legal pragmatism and legal realism were momentarily driven out of favor during and then immediately after World War II in the wake of the political disintegration of Europe. The meaning of events seemed unambiguous then: Fascism and Nazism reminded U.S. judges about the courts' role as an institution in somehow supporting limited government and citizen vigilance—in articulating publicly, and then enforcing with consistency, "the moral claims of settled law."[39] During this period it was once again clear that institutional externalities may indeed attend modern social change, particularly if the courts as an institution operate on the narrower assumption of pragmatists and realists—that all moral claims are reducible to local problem solving and to groups' ongoing competition for influence and power.[40]

Through their grounding in the traditional fiduciary duty of loyalty to the corporate entity, therefore, the corporate judiciary's rulings remained joined, albeit tenuously, to a larger social vision,[41] to an implicit, vaguely sensed concern about the possible institutional externalities of corporate power. This concern derives, of course, from a perspective more political economic than neoclassical, more republican than either liberal or pragmatic. The traditional fiduciary duty of loyalty maintained the link between the corporate judiciary's rulings and the Founders' concerns about maintaining an institutional design, extending from state to civil society, capable of keeping government limited and of supporting citizen vigilance. This same link extends to English chancellors' earlier concerns about holding barons to "fair" or "equitable" behavior even in their private affairs. The corporate judiciary enforced this existing duty of corporate law, this existing norm of corporate governance and behavior, independently of private law contracts and whatever immediate externalities befell particular corporate constituents. Moreover, it enforced it *independently of the public law norms that state legislatures placed in their standard charters by statute.* Even today, this court-enforced norm of corporate power marks the outer limit of *any* corporate agent's discretion in maximizing profits or market share. *It marks the outer limit of management's contractual obligations to share-holders and all other corporate constituents.*[42]

At a doctrinal level it did not much matter that U.S. judges were now imposing the longstanding fiduciary duty of loyalty on management whereas earlier they had imposed it on shareholder-owners (the second approach), and even earlier on state legislatures themselves (the first approach). What mattered is that U.S. judges continued to insist that *the* corporate agent, whoever it is, is obligated by law to advance the "real" interests of the corporate entity "disinterestedly." Nonetheless, in otherwise deferring to management's business judgment in bearing this court-enforced normative obligation, judges thereby deferred as well to management's interpretions of what the corporate entity's "real" interests are.

By the 1920s, management was becoming virtually sovereign within private enterprises that it did not own. The courts' retention of their second base of conceptual continuity, the fiduciary law tradition, was not a simple matter of transferring the business judgment rule to management in an effort to enforce management's contractual obligations to shareholders. Ultimately the courts were encouraging management to behave in a quite different, seemingly nonrational way,[43] that is, to subordinate all of its contractual obligations, including those to shareholders, to its purported normative obligations to the corporate entity as a long-term enterprise.

The courts encouraged this extracontractual, normative behavior, ironically, even as they themselves had already turned their backs on the Founders' political economic position of republican vigilance. The courts as an institution had already moved toward the political economic position of liberal complacency, following neoclassical economics as well as legal pragmatism and realism. Consider, then, what this meant in practice: The courts as an institution were no longer willing to identify the "real" interests of the corporate natural person independently of management's business judgment. On the contrary, they were willing to leave this matter to management, at least as long as it did not act in egregious ways, as long as it *seemed* to act "disinterestedly" and therefore consistently with the corporate agent's fiduciary duty of loyalty to the corporate entity as a long-term enterprise.

Thus, whenever a sitting management team failed to maximize profits in practice and instead decided to retain shareholders' dividends to finance corporate growth, it could credibly claim that it was advancing "disinterestedly" the corporate entity's "real" interests as a long-term enterprise. If a particular judge wished to dispute this claim, he or she would have to demonstrate that the courts are capable of identifying the "real" interests of the corporate entity independently of management. Given that economists themselves were finding it difficult after World War II to describe and explain corporate behavior at a conceptual level, and given that the courts continued to move toward liberal complacency despite their brief renewal of interest in enforcing norms of behavior, individual judges were understandably reticent to challenge management's business judgment.

From Private Property to Positional Power

Taken together, the courts' two bases of doctrinal continuity—the business judgment rule and the fiduciary law tradition—accorded greater legal status to management's position than to shareholders' ownership.[44] In a market society where private property, self-regulating markets, and Lockean contracts are not only economic institutions but valued, nearly sacred, substantive norms, this landed the courts squarely in the middle of a public law dilemma. The courts were essentially declaring at a doctrinal level that *positional power* (management's interpretations of the corporation's "real" interests) merits higher legal standing than *private property* (management's contractual obligations to shareholders). Berle and Means's *The Modern Corporation and Private Property* became controversial immediately upon publication in 1932 precisely because it drew attention to this fact. Their thesis was that the management corporation itself endangers the institution of private property.[45]

Surprisingly, U.S. state courts were not particularly troubled by any of this until much later. To be sure, Berle and Means's thesis was debated for decades by economists and legal scholars alike. Not until the mid-1970s at the earliest, however, did legal scholars begin considering seriously its implications for corporate governance and behavior. Then the relationship between the management corporation and private property literally polarized the major law journals.[46]

Prior to that time, judges saw themselves as simply continuing what their predecessors had done in each of the courts' two earlier approaches to the corporation. They saw the corporation's "real" interests as essentially no different from those that a unitary agent would ultimately interpret more or less unilaterally. And they had a point. They were simply transferring their traditional deference to a unitary corporate agent from shareholder-owners to management. Moreover, judges had another sound reason for not questioning what they were doing: A management team is typically appointed by a board of directors that, in turn, is formally elected by a shareholder majority. Thus, the corporation still seemed to be "a representative democracy, of an indirect type."[47] Most fundamentally, though, what unambiguous public law interest could judges say they were serving by challenging management's interpretations of its corporation's "real" interests? In short, U.S. judges imposed fiduciary duties and public law norms on the new corporate agent more out of a lingering respect for traditional judicial practice than out of any clear sense that doing so served an unambiguous public law interest.

As the multidivisional form was increasingly adopted after World War

II, management's sovereignty became ever more secure, ever more insulated from both external and internal challenges.[48] From the 1950s through the mid-1970s, three interrelated processes were at work to shore up this sovereignty. First, U.S. corporations' dominant position in the world economy seemed to indicate to judges management's success in achieving long-term corporate growth. Second, as U.S. corporations grew into conglomerates, management's sovereignty or positional power was even more dramatically increased. Third, assured of the merit of their third doctrinal approach, the corporate judiciary as an institution dutifully broadened its deference to management's business judgment.[49]

As the immediate postwar decades passed and U.S. corporations moved ever more forcefully into world markets, management teams had little reason even to consider strategies of maximizing short-term profit in shareholders' interests. Legal scholar John Coffee Jr. captures well why management routinely dismissed such strategies out of hand: Shareholders can always diversify their investment portfolios by buying the stocks (and bonds) of various corporations. The only way, however, that management can diversify its more fixed asset of human capital *is to diversify the corporation itself.*

> Some economists, such as Robin Marris and William Baumol, have argued that corporate managers maximize sales or growth, not profits [or dividends]. In part, such an empire-building policy is pursued, they claim, to increase the security of the corporation's managers, because the acquisition of additional divisions and product lines both reduces the risk of insolvency and provides opportunities for personal advancement. This claim can be understood as an assertion that managers seek to build a diversified portfolio *within their firm.* Exactly this specific claim has been made by financial economists, most notably by Amihud and Lev, who marshall evidence that "managers, as opposed to investors . . . engage in conglomerate mergers to decrease their largely undiversifiable 'employment risk.'" Where these different writers share a common ground is in their mutual recognition that empire building may be rational for managers but inefficient for shareholders.[50]

It would seem at first that reducing a corporation's debt or leverage benefits every corporate constituent. Economists and legal contractarians point out, however, that when management finances corporate growth by retaining dividends rather than by borrowing or leveraging, it not only fails to maximize shareholders' private wealth but also insulates its plans for long-term growth from the scrutiny of investment bankers. In short, management is not compelled automatically by market forces to act disinterestedly, particularly when markets are oligopolistic rather than competitive. Nor is it any more likely to act disinterestedly because the courts have deferred to its business judgment and declared it *the* corporate agent.

Fissures in Corporate Law Doctrine

The Rise of Legal Contractarianism

Earlier we noted in passing that the courts' public law dilemma—management's position subordinating shareholders' private property—did not overly concern legal scholars and sitting judges until the mid-1970s. At that time, however, one set of critics—legal contractarians—began pointing to corporate law doctrine's seemingly untenable mix of concepts and principles.[51] Legal contractarians noted that corporate law doctrine spans (1) private law contracts, as common law rulings; (2) public law norms, as state legislative statutes; and (3) fiduciary duties, as norms of equitable or disinterested behavior that the courts enforce independently of contracts and statutes. Moreover, by the mid-1980s, three developments made it impossible for judges any longer to ignore the fissures latent in corporate law doctrine. First, the courts were enforcing management's fiduciary duties with less and less consistency. Second, the new market for corporate control revealed for all to see that management had indeed financed corporate growth at shareholders' expense. Third, legal contractarians had steadily grown more successful in convincing legal scholars, and many judges, that the courts' third doctrinal approach could no longer orient the courts toward consistent rulings. Eventually they convinced them that corporate law doctrine is inimical to U.S. corporations' future domestic profitability and international competitiveness.[52] Led by Judge Frank Easterbrook and legal scholars Daniel Fischel, Henry Butler, Bernard Black, Roberta Romano, and others, legal contractarians' growing influence within the corporate judiciary and bar was enhanced dramatically in late 1983 when the new market for corporate control burst onto the scene.

A few years before the turbulence of the 1980s, legal contractarians began encouraging the courts to accord greater legal status to management's contractual obligations to shareholders than to its purported fiduciary duties to the corporate entity. In effect, they have advocated yet a fourth doctrinal approach to the corporation, one in which the longstanding entity metaphor is replaced by an altogether new metaphor, namely the concept of the "nexus of contracts" that Michael Jensen and William Meckling were then consolidating in economics.[53] This new approach is influenced considerably, however, by the legacies of neoclassical economics and legal pragmatism. It builds more directly on neoclassical concepts and assumptions than does any other current economic approach to the corporation.[54] It is also more consistent with the law's turn to pragmatism and realism in theory as well as the courts' increasing presentism, instrumentalism, and liberal complacency in practice. Moreover, it responds directly to Berle and Means's concern that the management corporation endangers the institution of private property. Indeed, contractarians' shareholder-centered approach to the corporation is largely consistent at a conceptual level with the courts' second doctrinal approach to the corporation. Unlike the latter, however, contractarians' concepts are sufficiently sophisticated to accommodate the changes that have affected U.S. corporations since the mid-1970s, including ongoing domestic deregulation and intensifying international competition.[55]

Contractarians' central thesis is that a corporation is quite literally an aggregate of transactions, a "nexus of contracts." "Most organizations are simply legal fictions which serve as a nexus for a set of contracting relationships among individuals."[56] Contractarians purposefully reduce the corporation to a site in a market society at which a flurry of more or less patterned contractual arrangements happens to coalesce for some passing period of time. They refuse to acknowledge at a conceptual level that the corporation *or any other organization* is also an intermediary association. That is, they reject the idea that the corporation exercises collective power in the larger social order and thereby invites judicial monitoring and intervention on any public law ground. "Taken to its limits, the contract approach implies that anything goes—that managers should be allowed to exploit any available devices to respond to [tender] offers, while being bound to respect any contractual limits on their powers. Courts' only role would be to enforce the contracts."[57]

With their nexus metaphor, contractarians bring neoclassicists' liberal complacency, presentism, instrumentalism, and methodological individualism forcefully into the study of corporate governance and behavior.[58] They do so even as they are quite aware that some corporations are conglomerates, and that their governance structures are greatly complicated by the contracts management has struck with suppliers and other constituents.[59] Indeed, for Jensen and Meckling, as for Alchian and Allen earlier, methodological individualism is appropriate irrespective of whether one is studying the behavior of corporations, hospitals, commercial banks, philanthropic foundations, insurance companies, cooperatives, or private clubs. For Jensen and Meckling:

> The private corporation or firm is simply one form of legal fiction which serves as a nexus for contracting relationships and which is also characterized by the existence of divisible residual claims on the assets and cash flows of the organization which can generally be sold without permission of the other contracting individuals.[60]

Economists Alchian and Allen stated the same basic methodological principle more generally over a decade earlier:

> [Businesses] do not constitute a different system of production control. Unless one can see through this organizational facade, he may confound specific means of communication and contracting with the general underlying principles of control of production.[61]

Jensen and Meckling go so far as to say that the corporation is no more a natural person, no more a personality with motivations, intentions, or "real" interests, than the wheat market or the stock market.[62] As a corollary, they also insist, often implicitly but at times explicitly, that the corporation is no more capable of exercising collective power arbitrarily than the wheat market or the stock market. Indeed, they rarely find it useful even to take note of a corporation's form of organization.[63] The only exceptions that they acknowledge are when a corporation's form of organization reflects the boundaries that state legislatures have set artificially, by statute, on the kinds of contracts that corporate constituents may strike in their own interests without fear of judicial sanction.[64] In self-regulating markets, therefore, where such boundaries do not exist, they insist that a corporation's form of organization carries neither any legally significant meanings for the individuals involved nor any legally significant externalities for the larger social order. Put most bluntly, contractarians see corporate governance and behavior as a strictly private matter, not as something that merits judicial intervention on any public law ground.[65]

Thus, contractarians' most basic unit of analysis is neither the corporate entity nor the corporate division and the forms in which either unit may be organized; it is individuals' contracts and self-interested behavior. In contractarians' view, consistent with their methodological individualism, as long as state courts and state legislatures do not impose "artificial" (that is, extracontractual) burdens on individuals, the systemic pressures of self-regulating markets—including the market for corporate control—are sufficient in themselves to induce everyone to maximize his or her own private wealth independently.[66] Government imposes such burdens whenever it attempts to advance any public law interest, whenever it defines corporate purpose as anything other than maximizing the private wealth of shareholders, as the principal and "bearer of residual risk."[67] Shareholders' equity, after all, is the ultimate source of revenue covering the corporation's outstanding debts. Contractarians are convinced that whenever government imposes "artificial" burdens on individuals' self-interested contracting, it "distorts" the priced outcomes of self-regulating markets. This imposition in turn opens the door for government to pursue *qualitative* ends of one kind or another *on public law grounds.* Once this door opens to the state, the state can then seek ever greater involvement in the economy.[68]

Contractarians also believe, as a corollary, that when government suspends its "artificial" activities—leaving corporations and all other sites of contracting to the free play of individuals' self-interested behavior—systemic pressures of self-regulating markets automatically align corporate agents' *behavior* with shareholders' *positional* interests.[69] Contractarians thus need not even argue their case for a shareholder-centered approach to the corporation; shareholders' presentism and subordination of all considerations of quality to the size of their dividends will infuse the very ethos of corporate governance and behavior. Moreover, contractarians are convinced that the easiest way to sidestep government's "artificial" activities, and instrumentally to advance shareholders' positional interests, is to change the corporation's investment structure, not its governance structure:[70] If managers invest their own private wealth in the company, as an equity stake, this should be sufficient to align their behavior with shareholders' positional interests. Like Berle and Means, contractarians do not believe that any possible changes in a corporation's governance structure would produce this alignment.

At times contractarians add a twist to their basic argument that in a curious way links maximizing shareholders' private wealth to democratic values, a "public law interest" as they understand it.[71] In updating neoclassicists' fourth and fifth assumptions about the corporation, they restate neoclassicists' implicit political economic position of liberal complacency:[72] When shareholders' private wealth is being maximized, this simultaneously (1) benefits the corporate aggregate (such as it is);[73] (2) increases social wealth;[74] and (3) contributes *invariably* to a benign social order.[75] Thus, they see shareholders' positional interests as quite literally isomorphic with the public law interest in supporting the institutional design of a democratic social order.[76]

Contractarians view the corporation as an entity without boundaries, that is, a transitory site of individual contracting. Much like Marshall had done in the 1890s, they treat the "corporation" at a conceptual level as if it lacks all qualities of "firmishness" or "personhood" in the larger social order. Barely an identifiable association, it is certainly not an intermediary association at all, but rather a power-neutral—or, at most, power-balanced—aggregation of individuals. "Because power has no place in neoclassical theory . . . the actual history of market forms remains outside the purview of economics."[77] Contractarians believe that the rise of any corporate aggregate out of individuals' ongoing self-interested behavior has little to do with anyone's wish to exercise collective power over others. Rather, it has everything to do with one basic economic fact: At any given moment, the benefits of team production at this site of contracting will outweigh the costs, including all moral hazards and all shirking, self-dealing, and opportunism.[78]

Contractarians also believe that any corporate aggregate will grow only to that point at which this cost-benefit relationship begins to reverse.[79] By the late 1970s, however, it was clear to them that U.S. corporations had reached this point of reversal and nonetheless continued to grow. The culprit, they believed, was government or, more particularly, the corporate judiciary. It continued to impose "artificial" burdens on individuals' self-interested behavior by enforcing management's purported fiduciary duties of care and loyalty to the corporate entity as a long-term enterprise. For contractarians, this is what prevented market forces from "naturally" sanctioning corporate growth at the moment that the cost-benefit relationship began to reverse.

In short, contractarians insist that nothing positive results from the enforcement of the public law norms and fiduciary duties of corporate law doctrine. Once a market for control over the corporation itself is in place, they see no good reason why the courts should bother to restrain management *even from exercising its positional power capriciously or arbitrarily in shareholders' interests.*[80] They refuse to accept that a corporate aggregate, whether long-term or not, contains *entrenched* positional interests. Put differently, they do not see any positions of dependence and trust within corporations. As a result, they do not see any possible institutional externalities for the larger social order in how management or shareholder majorities exercise positional power. With their nexus metaphor, contractarians see everything as too fluid for any of this to matter. Shareholders delegate control over daily operations to a management team (through an elected board). Management remains shareholders' agent, bound to advance their positional interests by contract. Management does not occupy a superordinate position within an independent structure of authority; the corporation does not possess qualities of "firmishness" or "personhood." It is not an independent entity, an organization, an intermediary association. It is strictly a voluntary commercial enterprise: "The analogy to contract focuses attention on the voluntary and adaptive nature of any corporation. . . . Contract means voluntary and unanimous agreement among affected parties."[81]

Contractarians' prescription for modernizing corporate law, and improving U.S. corporations' domestic profitability and international competitiveness, then, is both direct and seemingly practicable. They are convinced that state legislatures must remove all remaining public law norms from corporate law doctrine, and also that the corporate judiciary must either redefine or else jettison its own fiduciary law tradition.[82] They believe, moreover, that when state legislatures and state courts become more "realistic" in these ways, they finally will facilitate rather than needlessly obstruct two other beneficial developments. First, they will encourage shareholders to pressure management teams relentlessly to maximize dividends. Again, in terms of contractarians' implicit political economic position, this simultaneously increases social wealth and contributes automatically to a relatively benign social order. Second, courts and legislatures will also bring greater coherence to corporate law doctrine. This, in turn, can only orient individual judges toward more consistent rulings, thereby increasing the courts' integrity and legitimacy as an institution.[83]

From Private Law Controversy to Public Law Controversy

We have seen that contractarians began to expose the fissures in corporate law doctrine before hostile takeovers and leveraged buyouts challenged management's sovereignty in practice. In essence, contractarians challenged management's sovereignty in principle. They did so by posing three questions to the corporate judiciary based on their view that the courts' traditional enforcement of the fiduciary duty of loyalty to the corporate entity "artificially distorts" the priced outcomes of self-regulating markets. They asked:

1. Does management ever *misinterpret* the corporation's "real" interests, either purposefully or inadvertently, when fulfilling this duty in the absence of a market for corporate control?
2. Is management ever driven by its own self-interests when the courts "artificially" insulate its business judgment from the market's discipline?
3. Is management even capable of acting disinterestedly when such "artificial" judicial protections are in place?

With these three questions, contractarians not only pushed judges to face an already controversial matter of private law. They also pushed them to face an extraordinarily controversial public law issue.

The courts had been endeavoring to address a private law issue since the 1920s, namely: Does management in fact develop strategies that advance the corporate entity's "real" interests? Once the courts conceded in the late 1970s and early 1980s that management often acts more self-interestedly, they lost the business judgment rule as one of their two bases of conceptual continuity. They then turned to their other base of conceptual continuity, corporate law's core of public law norms and fiduciary duties. When they imposed these norms and duties on management, however, they elevated some unidentified *qualitative* standard of corporate governance above all *quantitative* standards or priced outcomes of corporate performance. Instead of asking whether management maximizes profits and dividends, they now ask if it acts "disinterestedly" in advancing the corporate entity's "real" interests.

With this second question, judges face a public law issue. After all, how can judges themselves recognize with consistency, both over time and across the courts, when sitting management teams are actually advancing corporations' "real" interests *by any qualitative standard?* Any qualitative standard of corporate performance is a norm of behavior. And the only good reason judges can have for imposing any norm of behavior on corporate agents is that they believe this serves some unambiguous public law interest.[84] Put differently, judges must believe that some normatively unmediated changes in corporate governance and behavior can carry institutional externalities for the larger social order.

This lingering public law issue may be visualized by considering how family courts also often move from private law concerns over immediate externalities to public law concerns over institutional externalities. This happens whenever a family court judge is called upon to determine when an adult is no longer capable of formulating, articulating, and acting upon his or her own interests. Once a judge believes that an adult has lost this capacity, the judge may place this person in a mental hospital against his or her own will. Admitting adults involuntarily to mental hospitals raises an endless number of public law issues. At least within institutionalized democracies, these decisions are not restricted to immediate externalities, to relatives' claims of harm. These decisions carry institutional externalities because how they are resolved can broaden the scope and increase the frequency of private arbitrariness across sectors of civil society.[85]

In the case of the corporate judiciary, we may ask whether judges are in fact capable of recognizing and understanding in common when a management team is actually advancing its corporation's "real" interests "disinterestedly" by any qualitative standard of behavior. By late 1983, hostile takeovers and leveraged buyouts left judges with no alternative other than to face this public law issue head on. Would they continue enforcing the public law norms and fiduciary duties on the books, or would they broaden shareholders' (and stakeholders') contractual freedom in the new market for corporate control?

Why Legal Contractarians Are So Influential

Whatever merits the nexus of contracts approach may have in updating neoclassical economics and the courts' second doctrinal approach to the corporation, contractarians' influence within the corporate judiciary and bar has also been augmented by two practical developments. First, the domestic policy environment has since the late 1970s favored deregulation and private contracts. Even with a Democratic administration in the 1990s, policymakers remain disposed to deregulate banking. Second, and more significantly, with the new market for corporate control that emerged in the 1980s, even the largest U.S. corporations were treated, in practice, as passing sites of decentralized contracting.[86] Corporate restructurings remind everyone of this today, and also that the market for corporate control remains in place.

These two developments so emboldened legal contractarians that by the late 1980s they began challenging corporate law's very legitimacy. Moreover, they added an important element to Jensen and Meckling's basic position, pointing out that state courts as an institution are capable of enforcing only private law contracts with consistency, not norms of behavior. Once again, contractarians have a point and, once again, it may be visualized by considering the workings of family courts. When family court judges attempt to enforce norms of behavior in the family governance disputes that come before them, they also find it difficult to keep their rulings consistent. These norms instruct them to intervene into family affairs when, for example, parents fail to fulfill their status obligations to children and as a result harm the larger social order.[87] In fact, however, aside from the most egregious misconduct (which is often covered by criminal law in any case), it is difficult for judges to demonstrate when parents actually shirk their (extracontractual) obligations.[88] What these norms of behavior actually require of parents is open to interpretation.

When corporate judges attempt to enforce public law norms and fiduciary duties in the governance disputes that come before them, they too face the problem of securing intersubjective recognition and understanding for their decisions. Fiduciary law in particular instructs them to intervene into intracorporate affairs when a board, sitting management team, or shareholder majority fails to fulfill its extracontractual obligations to the corporate entity and thus brings harm to the larger social order. How do judges know when a particular management team is no longer advancing its corporation's "real" interests "disinterestedly"? After all, whenever a judge defers to management's business judgment, he or she defers to its interpretations of the corporation's *qualitative* "real" interests or "intrinsic value."[89] When can a judge question these interpretations? By what *independent* standard can a judge identify a corporation's qualitative "real" interests or "intrinsic value"? Can judges even recognize and understand any such standard *in common,* let alone apply it with any consistency?

In addition to these questions, judges also bear the burden of proving that any standard that they bring to corporate governance disputes advances some unambiguous public law interest—that is, that unacceptable institutional externalities can result if they fail to apply their qualitative standard of corporate governance to the disputes that come before them. In other words, they bear the burden of identifying the purpose (or purposes) they expect corporations to serve other than to maximize dividends, or else to maximize their own growth.

Contractarians' response to the question of corporate purpose is both simple and direct: The only economically practicable *and legally enforceable* standard of corporate performance is whether management maximizes shareholders' private wealth. When contractarians insist that the courts as an institution are only capable of enforcing *quantitative* standards of corporate performance with consistency, they have a point. In 1988, for example, the Omnibus Trade Act "allowed the United States government to block foreign investors from obtaining a controlling interest in an American company," but it was not clear to anyone what "national security" interest this act actually served.[90] Consider how Labor Secretary Reich put the general issue involved before he took office:

> Nor, in this global economy, is it clear, in any event, how the top executives of American-owned corporations could be made to take on . . . national responsibilities. Regulations governing how corporations should operate in the United States are applicable to all firms doing business

here, regardless of the nationality of their shareholders. The American system has no special means of alerting the top executives of American-owned . . . corporations to the existence of public goals, or of mandating that they pursue these goals. In fact, were American-owned corporations subject to special burdens and obligations, they would be put at a distinct disadvantage relative to foreign-owned companies doing business in the United States, who would be free to maximize their profits . . .[91]

Contractarians could not agree more. Indeed, they go further. Because they assume that a market for corporate control simultaneously maximizes private wealth and social wealth, they also assume that judicial enforcement of any norms of behavior only adds unnecessary costs to the mix. Thus, they insist that the corporate judiciary accomplishes only one thing when it imposes norms of behavior on management: It shields inefficient management teams from the impersonal discipline of the new market for corporate control.[92] When contractarians insist that the corporate judiciary currently encourages management to shirk, self-deal, and otherwise engage in opportunistic conduct at shareholders' expense, once again they have a point. Judges and legal scholars alike are well aware that corporate law's basic concepts and principles fail to come to terms with the complex dynamics of the U.S. economy.[93] Judges appreciate that corporate law is not sufficiently sophisticated to allow them somehow to anticipate how U.S. corporations might best compete in today's global economy. And again, Reich agrees: "Corporate nationality is becoming irrelevant. . . . Nations can no longer substantially enhance the wealth of their citizens by subsidizing, protecting, or otherwise increasing the profitability of 'their' corporations; the connection between corporate profitability and the standard of living of a nation's people is growing ever more attenuated."[94]

Notes

1. See Williamson (1988a, 1988b).
2. Economists also call situations of moral hazard "the residual loss of an agency relationship," and lawyers call them "structured situations that contain positions of dependence and trust." Legal contractarians, of course, prefer economists' narrower view (e.g., Easterbrook and Fischel 1991:260). Economists want the principal (shareholders) to reduce the residual loss by ending the agency relationship (with management) outright. They want owners to be active managers, not passive investors; or, alternatively, they want managers to own substantial shares of stock. By contrast, fiduciary law instructs the courts to impose norms of "fair" or "equitable" conduct on anyone who holds positions of power within structured situations. Legal traditionalist William Bratton (1993) sees the notion of "good will" as central to fiduciary law, but we saw in Chapter 5 that fiduciary law stands or falls on whether the courts can identify in common those structured situations that contain positions of dependence.
3. Knight (1921/1948:251).

4. My use of the term "opportunism" is broader than DeMott's and closer to Oliver Williamson's and George Cohen's. DeMott writes: "'Opportunism' is not a technical term of art for purposes of legal analysis; its evident meaning as used in judicial opinions and in academic writing is highly variable. All such meanings convey moral disapproval, however. My definition is the deliberate and successful pursuit of an unbargained-for advantage. Whether the law permits the advantage to be retained is a separate question, the answer to which varies enormously with the circumstances" (1994:71). For Williamson and his co-authors, opportunism is "an effort to realize individual gains through a lack of candor or honesty in transactions" (1975:258, quoted by DeMott 1994:72, note 20). Finally, for George Cohen, opportunism encompasses "any contractual conduct by one party contrary to the other party's reasonable expectations based on the parties' agreement, contractual norms, or conventional morality" (1992:957, quoted by DeMott 1994:72, note 20).

5. See Stinchcombe (1990:chap. 3) for a rich account of middle managers' "information-systems."

6. For example, see Anders (1992:177). Middle managers differ from top managers in having control over operations. They thereby differ from top managers in their responsibilities, language, goals, and experience. Lower managers and other employees also face moral hazards, but those that middle managers face are unique in two respects. On the one hand, their positional interest in protecting themselves from top management's opportunism can complicate corporate governance structures far more than, say, the presence of labor unions. On the other hand, middle managers are typically subjected to more intense performance monitoring than lower managers or other employees. Given these pressures, they are also more "available" to engage in corporate crimes (Coffee 1981:399).

7. Williamson (1985:243).

8. Easterbrook and Fischel (1991:3).

9. Fligstein (1985, 1990); Stinchcombe (1990:124–126).

10. An internal labor market is "any cluster of jobs, regardless of occupational titles or employing organizations, that have three basic structural features: (a) a job ladder, with (b) entry only at the bottom and (c) movement up this ladder, which is associated with a progressive development of knowledge and skill" (Knoke, Kalleberg, Marsden, and Spaeth 1993:5, note 1, quoting Althauser and Kalleberg in 1981). Some observers argue that top management is currently endeavoring to go even further, that is, to pass along its positions by inheritance, either intrafamilial or extrafamilial, much as shareholders pass along their stocks by inheritance. See Clignet (1992) for a discussion of inheritance and Easterbrook and Fischel (1991:132–134) on managers selling their offices.

11. Bratton (1989a:1518–1519). Even as late as 1990, sociologist Neil Fligstein (1990) still saw the multidivisional form largely as the means by which finance managers came to dominate headquarters and to perpetuate their positions.

12. Coffee (1981:1500).

13. See Easterbrook and Fischel (1991:193–205) for a survey of the literature.

14. Stewart (1991:3–4); Easterbrook and Fischel (1991:196).

15. Coffee (1986:4–5, note 6).

16. Anders (1992:131).

17. Norris, *New York Times,* January 30, 1994. Viacom stock fell nearly back to its April price in November 1993, in the midst of its bidding war with QVC Network. And the latter's stock also fell. On Labor Day 1993, Viacom's stock was worth $7.6 billion, and by January 1994 its value had fallen $3 billion; QVC Network's stock was worth $2.6 billion, and its value fell $800 million.

18. Rinaldi (1990:760, note 1). Since 1981 restructuring has included tenden-

cies toward deconglomeration, even as it continues to include horizontal and vertical integrations, product line extensions, and market extensions (Yago 1991:110).

19. Coffee (1986:4–5).
20. Easterbrook and Fischel (1991:178).
21. Coffee (1990:1505–1506).
22. Coffee (1986:5–6, citing *Wall Street Journal,* August 12, 1985).
23. Jensen (1988:22).
24. Anders (1992:280–281).
25. Piore and Sabel (1984:283).
26. See Easterbrook and Fischel (1991:162–211).
27. Stinchcombe (1990:149, my emphasis).
28. Anders (1992:xix, 39, 160–164).
29. See Anders (1992:156–157, 161) on how Kohlberg, Kravis, Roberts & Company, the leveraged buyout specialists, coopted the top management of the firms it acquired and induced them to invest their own life savings in the firms' stock.
30. Williamson (1988a, 1988b).
31. Easterbrook and Fischel (1991:171).
32. Ibid.
33. See Chapter 4, pages 92–93.
34. See Sciulli (1997d).
35. Easterbrook and Fischel *reduce* the duty of loyalty to the duty of taking care in using investors' wealth (1991:103).
36. Roy (1997:155–158).
37. I cited Eisenberg (1989:1472) on these two points in Chapter 3, and added three other examples from Eisenberg of judicial interventions into corporate governance disputes.
38. I also quoted this passage from Eisenberg (1989:1474) in Chapter 3.
39. Aichele (1990:75).
40. Harvard legal theorist Lon Fuller was particularly influential after World War II precisely because he had warned U.S. judges about this during the early 1940s. He pointed to the nihilism implicit in American "bastard pragmatism," the drift of normatively unmediated pluralist politics (the phrase, however, is Hurst's). He encouraged U.S. courts to continue enforcing normative mediations on all exercises of collective power, public or private, although Fuller had fundamental *procedural* norms in mind, *not the substantive norms at the core of the Founders' natural law understanding of social order.* In the debate between legal formalists and legal realists, Fuller sided squarely with the latter. He saw that Langdell had already abandoned the Founders' *substantive* natural law norms. He also appreciated that neither he nor any other legal theorist could somehow return directly to the Founders' republican vigilance. See Sciulli (1992) on the importance of Fuller's distinction between procedural "natural law" norms and substantive natural law norms.
41. *Why* this was the case is a matter that I address elsewhere (Sciulli 1997d).
42. This is precisely why Easterbrook and Fischel and other legal contractarians go to such lengths to redefine this tradition—in order to reconcile it with simply upholding contracts and maximizing investors' wealth. See Sciulli (1997d).
43. Easterbrook and Fischel (1991:93).
44. Again, this is what Roy (1997) sees, following Berle and Means.
45. Dent (1989:883–884).
46. In 1983 the *Journal of Law and Economics* published a 250-page symposium assessing the significance of Berle and Means's book.

47. Knight (1920/1948:291).
48. Galbraith (1967) remains the strongest statement of management's sovereignty during this period.
49. Bratton (1989a:1494).
50. Coffee (1986:20, my emphasis).
51. The most important early articles are Fischel (1978, 1982); Easterbrook and Fischel (1981, 1982, 1983); Klein (1982); and Carlton and Fischel (1983). See Butler (1989) for a review and assessment of this literature, and Easterbrook and Fischel (1991) for the most methodical statement of the contractarian position. Klein was one of the first legal scholars to advocate that the courts encourage corporate governance structures to balance constituents' competing interests as a substitute for enforcing management's traditional fiduciary duties. Rational choice sociologist James Coleman develops this position (1990:561–572).
52. For example, see Chancellor Allen (1993).
53. Jensen and Meckling (1976) built on Alchian and Allen (1964/1972).
54. Millon (1990:229, note 113); Bratton (1989a:1476–1477); Coffee (1986:25–28).
55. For instance, legal contractarians support maximizing shareholders' private wealth *and yet they do not hypostatize corporate ownership*. "Because private property is such a profound part of the American ethos, [the neoclassical] model's normative implications long dominated our approach to corporate law. [The neoclassical] model broke down when confronted by the new contractarian model. The old model depended upon the corporation being a thing capable of being owned. In other words, it required one to reify the corporation: to treat the firm as an entity separate from its various constituents. As we have seen, however, nexus of contracts theory squarely rejects this basic proposition. By throwing the concept of ownership out the window, along with its associated economic and ethical baggage, the contractarian model also eliminates [Milton] Friedman's principal argument for favoring shareholders over nonshareholders" (Bainbridge 1993:1428).
56. Jensen and Meckling (1976:310).
57. Easterbrook and Fischel (1991:166).
58. Economist Joseph Schumpeter is believed to have coined the term "methodological individualism," but Hobbes was the first modern theorist to adopt it (Elster 1990:48–49; Bhargava 1992:1). Economic and social theorists who adopt this approach "explain collective (macroscopic) phenomena on the basis of individual (microscopic) behavior and strategies" (Birnbaum and Leca 1990:3). Thus, as Jon Elster puts it (1990:47): "Methodological individualism is a form of reductionism. . . . [I]t claims that all social phenomena—whether process, structure, institutions, or habitus—can be explained by the actions and properties of the participating individuals" (see also Elster 1985:5). For Steven Lukes (1973:122) it is "a prescription for explanation, asserting that no purported explanations of social (or individual) phenomena are to count as explanations . . . or as rock-bottom explanations, unless they are couched wholly in terms of facts about individuals" (quoted by Bhargava 1992:19). Contrary to neoclassicists' liberal complacency, Elster follows Schumpeter in pointing out that there is no necessary link between methodological individualism and liberalism or political individualism (1990:49). Rational choice sociologist James Coleman supposes at the very outset that there is such a link, but he never explains why (see e.g., 1990:4–5, 11–19). Regardless, methodological individualism is a researcher's attribution; it is a researcher's choice of a unit of analysis, not an ontological quality of the phenomenon being studied (Birnbaum and Leca 1990:3). Thus, researchers who employ this approach cannot describe or explain a society's systemic properties, including its institutional exter-

nalities. Coleman, for instance, says candidly that "there is no tangible macro level" of analysis (1990:12) and that he does not assume system integration at all (1990:15). Nonetheless, no assumes system equilibrium (1990:38–40), and a general consensus over rights (1990:54). Nor can those who adopt this approach describe or explain processes of self-identification or collectivity-identification (Birnbaum and Leca 1990:11–13; Coleman 1990:31–32, 53, 75–77). In other words, they have difficulty explaining how individuals symbolize together and socially construct the meaning of qualities in the world, and then how they symbolize and socially construct their own collective efforts to attain these qualities. Rational choice sociologist Michael Hechter concedes this (1983:185–186).

59. For examples, see Fama and Jensen (1983); Kraakman (1984); Bratton (1989b:409).

60. Jensen and Meckling (1976:311); also Easterbrook and Fischel (1991:12).

61. Alchian and Allen (1964/1972:281).

62. They are correct, of course, when the matter is put in this way. Corporations and organizations do not have motivations, intentions, or "real" interests. When individuals internalize norms in primary or secondary socialization, these norms become their motivations of behavior. Corporations and organizations do, however, institutionalize *normative orientations* in their various divisions. This happens at the moment that divisional managers and administrators adopt any *form* of organization—whether the bureaucratic, the democratic, the patron-client, or the collegial. When forms of organization institutionalize norms at particular divisions or sites of team activity, these norms become their constituents' orientations of behavior. Individuals can indeed be *oriented* by the same norms in common, as corporate constituents with positional interests. This can hold true even if they have internalized different and possibly competing norms as individuals, and even if they pursue different and possibly competing interests.

63. Consider the following statement by Easterbrook and Fischel (1991:12): "Corporations sometimes are organized as hierarchies, with the higher parts of the pyramid issuing commands; sometimes they are organized as dictatorships; sometimes they are organized as divisional profit centers with loose or missing hierarchy. The choice of organization and compensation devices will depend on the size of the firm, the identity of the managers, and the industry (or spectrum of industries) in which the corporation participates."

64. Jensen and Meckling (1976:311, note 14).

65. For examples, see Easterbrook and Fischel (1991:21–23, 35, 39). Once we identify the institutional externalities of changes in corporate governance and behavior at a conceptual level, we expose the greatest weaknesses in economists' (and rational choice theorists') implicit political economic position of liberal complacency. These externalities exceed the scope of application of methodological individualism. Thus, the latter is contractarians' Achilles' heel in accounting for the actual behavior of the corporate judiciary.

66. Jensen and Meckling (1976:307); Easterbrook and Fischel (1991:96, 113, 182).

67. Easterbrook and Fischel (1991:93); for the phrase, see Marshall (1892/1919:168).

68. Recall Milton Friedman's view as described in Chapter 3 of this volume (at page 70).

69. For examples, see Jensen (1988:28) and Easterbrook and Fischel (1991:142).

70. For example, Demsetz and Lehn (1985:1159).

71. Of course, any reference to a public law interest, whether explicit or

implicit, exceeds the scope of application of contractarians' methodological individualism.

72. See Chapter 6, page 144.

73. And yet, ironically, in their influential paper of 1976, Jensen and Meckling do not apply their analysis of agency costs "to the very large modern corporation whose managers own little or no equity" (1976:356). They apply it to close corporations, whose owners are also its managers.

74. When Jensen states, "takeovers do not waste credit or resources but instead generate substantial gains," his evidence is that takeovers typically increase the total value of both companies by 8 percent (1988:23; see also Easterbrook and Fischel 1991:196). Critics counter that shareholders in both companies involved in the takeover cash in managers' and other employees' firm-specific human capital and pension plans. They do not fulfill the terms of their implicit contracts to ensure longer-term employment and to deliver benefits. Jensen and other contractarians respond that the market for corporate control benefits not only shareholders but the economy as a whole by loosening control over resources. This permits investors to move capital quickly "to its highest-valued use" (see Easterbrook and Fischel 1991:198–205). Jensen's other arguments regarding social wealth are indirect. For instance, he concedes that there is actually little evidence that managers are more shortsighted than markets, and yet he "believes that this phenomenon does occur." He then adds that there is no evidence that markets are shortsighted, and instead much evidence that they are not (1988:25–26).

75. For examples, see Jensen and Meckling (1976:355); Jensen (1988:21, 28); and Easterbrook and Fischel (1991:6–7, 30–31, 37–39, 170–171).

76. Dent (1989:895, citing Manning).

77. Friedland and Robertson (1990:7).

78. Alchian and Demsetz (1972); see also Alchian and Allen (1964/1972:282); and Easterbrook and Fischel (1991:8–9).

79. Jensen and Meckling (1976:310); Butler (1989:104).

80. Bratton (1989b:454–456); Easterbrook and Fischel (1991:4, 99–100, 253–275, 316–319).

81. Easterbrook and Fischel (1991:15); these two sentences span half a page and a chapter subheading.

82. Contractarians try to help by defining what they call the "fiduciary principle" in terms that are consistent with maximizing shareholders' private wealth (see Sciulli 1997d). Richard Posner, a contemporary legal pragmatist, goes further (1990:353–392). He characterizes the common law as steadily enhancing and promoting economic efficiency. He fails to appreciate that the common law (to say nothing of fiduciary law) has always *mediated* individuals' self-interested behavior under certain conditions. It has done so in an effort to sustain a more benign civil society than market exchanges alone can reasonably be expected to yield automatically, by a hidden hand. Even those early U.S. legal theorists who were most drawn to neoclassical economics "conceded that the common law required certain firms such as common carriers to charge only reasonable rates" (Hovenkamp 1991:31). Melvin Eisenberg (1988) captures the common law's capacity to institutionalize normative mediations or restraints by seeing its connection both to broad "social propositions" and to the courts' own "institutional principles."

83. Bratton (1989a:1473, 1513); see also Clark (1989:1707–1708).

84. My point in Chapter 2 in distinguishing procedural normative mediations from substantive normative limitations is to isolate those institutionalized norms that do indeed advance an unambiguous public law interest, at least within any democratic social order.

85. Scheff (1964); Rosenhan (1973); Scull (1989); Bach (1989). Isaac and Armat (1990) are unique in bracketing this issue.

86. Again, contractarians also inherited the influence of legal pragmatism and the central place that private property and the private law of contracts have had in corporate law doctrine since the courts' second approach to corporate agency (Bratton 1989a:1473; see also Bainbridge's comment in note 55).

87. Because fiduciary law revolves around public law concerns rather than private law contracts, it is difficult to understand why rational choice sociologist James Coleman brings the issue of the care of children into his discussion of corporations in his major theoretical work (1990:579–609).

88. This is because the fiduciary law norms applicable to family governance disputes are substantive. Therefore, unlike the case of corporate governance disputes, it is not possible to bring the "procedural turn" that we discussed in Chapter 2 to family governance disputes.

89. See Easterbrook and Fischel (1991:136, 206–209).

90. Reich (1991:157–158).

91. Reich (1991:141–142).

92. For example, Easterbook and Fischel (1991:93, 206, 227).

93. For example, Chancellor Allen (1992a, 1992b).

94. Reich (1991:153).

PART 3

Conclusion

8

Reconsidering Institutionalism

Before exploring some implications for the new institutionalism of our discussion of corporate governance and the corporate judiciary, let us broadly summarize six major points of that discussion:

1. Corporations are intermediary associations, not simply commercial enterprises; they perform a governance function, not simply a production function.

2. Private governance structures in civil society do not automatically support the institutional design of a democratic social order. There is no theory or body of research in economics that establishes that competitive markets ensure such a result automatically. Moreover, there is no theory or body of research in political science or sociology that establishes that pluralist (or corporatist) group competition within either private or public governance structures ensures such a result automatically.

3. The founders of the U.S. constitutional system and, earlier, English chancellors saw the need to extend fiduciary law, the law of trusts, to certain structured situations in civil society in order to maintain a democratic (or, earlier, a benign) social order.

4. This historical legacy lingers still in the U.S. corporate judiciary's oversight of corporate governance disputes. This legacy is under assault today by legal contractarians and by events, that is, by the market for corporate control and increasing competition in global markets.

5. The corporate judiciary qualifies uniquely as an "environmental agent." It not only monitors corporate governance for its immediate externalities—the harms it can cause to discrete constituents—but for its institutional externalities as well—the harms it can cause to the institutional design of a democratic social order.

6. Whether we study the corporate judiciary or not, we must account at a conceptual level for the fact that advanced societies vary empirically,

across their sectors, in terms of the extent to which they institutionalize democracy in civil society.

By way of further summary, we review four orienting hypotheses proposed in our discussion for the empirical study of institutional change:

1. The governance of intermediary associations in democratic social orders differs empirically from the governance of intermediary associations in formal democracies and imposed social orders (from Chapter 2, page 44).

2. The procedural normative mediations discussed in Chapter 2 (a) will be found in a large and increasing number of sectors within institutionalized democracies; (b) will be found in a small and decreasing number of sectors within formal democracies; and (c) will be in even more rapid decline in more imposed social orders, those undergoing a transition toward an "iron cage" (from Chapter 2, page 44).

3. Collegial formations (a) will be found in great and increasing numbers within the corporate and association divisions and sectors of institutionalized democracies; (b) will be found in far fewer and decreasing numbers within the divisions and sectors of formal democracies; and (c) will be in even more rapid decline within the divisions and sectors of more imposed social orders (from Chapter 3, page 65).

4. When anyone who holds a position of power within an intermediary association socializes constituents to tolerate and accommodate arbitrariness, this carries institutional externalities for any existing democracy, whether formal or institutionalized (from Chapter 3, page 70).

Institutional Drift or Procedural Turn?

The corporate judiciary is adrift as an institution, as an important environmental agent in U.S. civil society. It has been dislodged from its twin moorings in the business judgment rule and its own fiduciary law tradition. As a result, managers and shareholder majorities have greater leeway, in principle, to experiment with corporate governance structures than at any time since the 1920s. Everyone involved, however, is operating with the faith that this decentralized, ad hoc experiment will increase social wealth and support the institutional design of a democratic social order. Because there is neither theoretical nor empirical support for this faith, it qualifies in the most classic sense as an ideology. It is more a collective prejudice than a reasoned point of departure in identifying the relationship between changes in the governance of intermediary associations and institutional change in the larger social order.

In a separate book manuscript, titled "Corporate Power in Civil Society," I explore at length legal scholars' debate over corporate law and judicial practice in an effort to identify a new mooring for the corporate judiciary. In order to secure a hearing among legal scholars and sitting judges, any such alternative must be consistent with the courts' fiduciary law tradition and yet also be "realistic." That is, any doctrinal mooring today must serve two goals. First, it must facilitate, not needlessly obstruct, corporations' efforts to compete effectively in domestic and international markets. Second, it must nonetheless normatively mediate corporations' ongoing competition in ways that reduce arbitrariness by corporations and other intermediary associations, and yet not do so in ways that otherwise "buffer" management from the discipline of the market for corporate control.

The doctrinal mooring I have proposed requires the corporate judiciary to take a "procedural turn" in updating its fiduciary law tradition, as presented more generally in Chapters 2 and 3. The corporate judiciary would bring a concern for the presence of collegial formations in corporate governance structures as it intervenes into governance disputes. I show in my book manuscript that this procedural turn serves the two goals just noted and is consistent with a significant set of judicial decisions. For present purposes, we can conclude our discussion here by exploring how ongoing institutional change in the economy and corporate judiciary (as presented in Chapters 4–7) supports our earlier discussion (Chapters 1–3) of the promise and limits of the institutional approach to organizations.

The new institutionalism is advanced in specific ways when sociologists acknowledge at a conceptual level that (1) some organizations are intermediary associations and that (2) certain qualities of intermediary associations and their institutionalized environments are unique to democratic social orders. First, a focus on these qualities reduces, and in some cases eliminates, the four difficulties with which institutionalists have been grappling in theory and in research for nearly two decades (see Chapter 1, pages 22–26). Second, such a focus allows social scientists to connect institutionalists' empirical findings in the study of organizations to the "larger concerns of sociology," including the issue of institutional change. Once social scientists appreciate that the presence of collegial formations within corporations and other intermediary associations is contingent, and that the judiciary's enforcement of any mandatory rules for corporate and association governance is also contingent, they may then empirically investigate instances when changes in corporate governance and judicial behavior challenge the institutional design of democratic social orders.

Institutionalist Difficulties Revisited

We can begin to illustrate our proposed contributions to the institutional approach by showing how the conceptual distinctions we drew in Chapters 1–3 and the example of institutional change presented in Chapters 4–7 address the four difficulties that institutionalists themselves experience when they apply their approach to organizations. As we review these difficulties, we employ the terminology used in this volume rather than institutionalists' own.

Institutionalists' first difficulty, the one that they inherited from open systems theory, is in distinguishing between the effect of economic and technical factors upon intermediary associations and the effect upon them of cultural factors in institutionalized environments. DiMaggio continues to insist today, for instance, that it is "fruitless" to generalize about culture and economy, and that he cannot isolate effects on economic behavior that are unambiguously "cultural" from those that are due more narrowly to economic competition itself.[1] We may pursue both of these lines of inquiry, however, by focusing on whether and when corporations and other intermediary associations (1) exhibit fidelity to corporate law doctrine's existing public law norms and fiduciary duties; and (2) exhibit fidelity to the threshold of procedural norms as presented in Chapter 2.

This focus for empirical research allows social scientists to generalize across modern societies. In turn, it directs their attention to the behavior of the corporate judiciary over time: When does the corporate judiciary approach the corporation as a set of structured situations whose governance may carry institutional externalities for the larger social order? When does it approach the corporation as a long-term enterprise that merits judicial protection, as if it were a historical monument or endangered species? And when does it approach the corporation as a nexus of contracts that, at most, carries immediate externalities for sitting management teams? These questions can focus the attention of social scientists such that their work is not limited to (1) whether corporations economize over time or, for that matter, (2) whether corporations' prospects for survival improve over time (see Chapter 3, page 56).[2]

Moreover, the fidelity of corporations and other intermediary associations to existing public law norms and fiduciary duties accounts in some part for how corporate agents and corporate constituents establish and maintain a sense of shared purpose or meaning even when their behavior is not instrumentally rational. In turn, their fidelity to the threshold of procedural norms accounts for how corporate agents and corporate constituents can maintain a sense of shared purpose apart from its imposition by mechanisms of social control, whether those employed within corporations or those employed by "environmental agents" (see Chapter 3, pages 50–53 for the integration/control distinction). This second type of normative behavior by corporate agents and corporate constituents also accounts for how innovative corporations can enhance their legitimacy in the eyes of influential outsiders, at least within institutionalized democracies. By definition, innovative corporations challenge those *substantive* routines—whether instrumental or normative—typically followed by other corporations in their sector. They may *legitimate* their new routines and "cultures" by conveying to influential outsiders—particularly the corporate judiciary—that they are by no means challenging the *procedural* norms unique to the institutional design of democratic social orders.[3] Whether corporate agents seek legitimacy in this sense for their governance structures and divisions and, more important, whether the corporate judiciary oversees corporate governance with an eye to agents' fidelity to procedural norms, are both empirical variables. Neither the behavior of managers of multinational corporations in this regard nor that of state judges is overdetermined by isomorphic pressures. Nonetheless, this behavior is clearly normative or "ritualistic," not instrumentally rational or directly economizing.

Institutionalists' second difficulty is in recognizing or identifying the contexts in which corporate agents' concerns about legitimacy take precedence over their more immediate efforts to economize.[4] These concerns take precedence within those corporate divisions—not only research divisions but also corporate boards and other governance structures—wherein constituents are expected by outside influentials (particularly the corporate judiciary) as well as by organization agents in their public statements to deliberate over the meaning of qualitative outcomes (such as changes in the governance structure). The value of these outcomes to the larger social order eludes pricing in stock and bond markets.

In democratic social orders this expectation can be institutionalized, but only contingently. When institutionalized, it can range widely from the meaning (and value) of maintaining deliberation itself to the meaning (and value) of maintaining the institutional design of a democratic social order. Only ongoing deliberation within corporations and other intermediary associations can maintain the integrity of scientific research (whether within universities or within corporate research divisions), the integrity of professional practice (again, irrespective of site of professional practice), and the integrity of corporate and association governance. These are all qualities whose meaning (for participants) and value (for the larger social order) cannot be reduced to changing prices in stock and bond markets. After all, the institutional design of a democratic social order not only limits government. Equally important, it maintains organizational support in civil society—in private governance structures and the corporate judiciary—for citizen vigilance. We proposed in Chapter 3 that this particular standard of legitimacy is not relative to time and place. Rather, it is generalizable across institutionalized democracies. This standard can be a guide to empirical investigation insofar as it addresses (1) whether collegial formations are present within corporations and other intermediary associations and (2) whether private governance structures exhibit fidelity to the threshold of procedural norms.

Institutionalists' third difficulty is in explaining why state or industry associations ever reward corporations whose behavior is not instrumentally rational or maximizing. Institutionalists also have difficulty identifying the "myths" that advance corporate or institutional goals and identifying the goals themselves. Thus they fail to see that corporate agents' fidelity to the threshold of procedural norms advances the corporate goal of establishing and maintaining meaning and legitimacy in possibly integrative ways rather than in demonstrably controlling ways. It also advances the institutional goal of mediating public *and private* power short of arbitrariness, thereby contributing to limited government and citizen vigilance. By contrast, corporate agents' fidelity to the public law norms passed by state legislatures are most likely "myths" in Meyer and Rowan's sense. They frequently advance the organizational goal of insulating management from the discipline of the market for corporate control, and it is not clear that they serve any significant institutional goal.

Institutionalists' final challenge is to characterize at least in broad terms the direction of change of intermediary associations, social sectors, and the larger social order.[5] We propose, on the one hand, that organizational homogeneity only brings institutional externalities into a democratic social order when it involves encroachments against the threshold of procedural norms. When this occurs, the direction of social change shifts, such that a democratic social order takes on characteristics of a formal democracy that, in turn, is itself in transition to a more imposed social order. We also propose, on the other hand, that organizational heterogeneity cannot be said automatically to support the institutional design of a democratic social order. When it involves increasing encroachments against the threshold of procedural norms, it too challenges the institutional design of democratic social orders. It too can push formal democracies toward a transition to more imposed social orders.

Furthermore, just as social scientists may identify increases or decreases in any corporate division's efficiency and profitability over time, they may also identify increases or decreases in any corporate division's *behavioral* fidelity to the threshold of procedural norms. They may isolate both sets of practices in both historical and crossnational perspective. Thus, they may identify when corporations and other intermediary associations bring institutional externalities into the larger social order and when they do not. They may also identify when the corporate judiciary endeavors to mediate institutional externalities and when it does not.

In this way we are connecting an institutional approach to intermediary associations to sociology's "broader concerns." Social scientists may well find increasing arbitrariness within certain social sectors of the United States and decreasing arbitrariness within certain social sectors of Mexico, Brazil, or Iran.[6] They may also find either increases or decreases in arbitrariness within a particular social sector of the United States over the course of a given chronological period. They might ask, for example, if there is more or less arbitrariness in the corporate research divisions of the pharmaceutical industry today than ten, twenty, or thirty years ago.[7] They might investigate changing levels of arbitrariness in the corporate boards of the communications industry or, for that matter, in the boards of either private or public universities. Our point is that we can now see that these are empirically researchable issues. These are not matters that social scientists can settle, or assume a priori, by simply labeling a social order democratic, pluralist, corporatist, or statist.[8] These are also not matters that institutionalists can settle or assume by simply referring generically to isomorphic pressures, or to "institutionalization" and "rationalization."[9] They can only settle these matters by exploring how corporations and other intermediary associations actually exercise collective power within different social sectors. An institutional approach to organizations, understood in this way, will necessarily broaden into the historical and crossnational study of institutional change in modern social orders.

Notes

1. DiMaggio (1994:47).

2. DiMaggio opens his impressive review of the literature on "culture and economy" by saying that economy refers to production, exchange, and consumption (1994:28). This leaves out the matter of governance, precisely the area of greatest concern to the corporate judiciary, the most important "environmental agent" in U.S. civil society.

3. DiMaggio defines "culture" as revolving around "constitutive" and "regulatory" norms (1994:27, plus 30, 36, 42). This distinction, however, neglects whether either type of norm is directly substantive and therefore not only regulatory but limiting; or procedural and, at most, mediating. Procedural norms are possibly integrative in modern, pluralistic societies; substantive norms are typically controlling. Whether and when they are integrative is an open question, one subject inherently to competing interpretations.

4. Again, DiMaggio acknowledges that he cannot identify these contexts (1994:47).

5. Powell and Smith-Doerr note that institutionalists and other sociologists of organizations have yet to identify the consequences for U.S. civil society of recent corporate downsizing and the "flattening" and decentralization of corporate hierarchies (1994:380–384).

6. I doubt that this is the case, but my point is that at every place and time this is an empirical issue, and we may as well begin treating it as one.

7. See Braithwaite (1984).

8. For such labeling, see Jepperson and Meyer (1991:220–225).

9. See Sciulli (1997c).

Bibliography

Aichele, Gary J. 1990. *Legal Realism and Twentieth-Century American Jurisprudence.* New York: Garland Publishing, Inc.

Alchian, Armen A. and William R. Allen. 1964/1972. *University Economics: Elements of Inquiry,* 3d ed. Belmont, CA: Wadsworth.

Alchian, Armen A. and Harold M. Demsetz. 1972. "Production, Information Costs and Economic Organizations." *American Economic Review* 62:777–795.

Alexander, Jeffrey C. 1989. *Twenty Lectures.* New York: Columbia University Press.

Allen, (Chancellor) William T. 1992a. "Our Schizophrenic Conception of the Business Corporation." *Cardozo Law Review* 14:261–281.

———. 1992b. "Corporate Directors in the Dawning Age of Post-Managerialism." Paper presented at Stanford University, Center for Economic Policy Research, May 1 (15 pages).

———. 1993. "Contracts and Communities in Corporation Law." *Washington and Lee Law Review* 50:1395–1408.

Anders, George. 1992. *Merchants of Debt: KKR and the Mortgaging of American Business.* New York: Basic.

Anderson, Charles W. 1979. "Political Design and the Representation of Interests." In Philippe C. Schmitter and Gerhard Lembruch, eds., *Trends Toward Corporatist Intermediation,* pp. 271–297. Beverly Hills, CA: Sage.

———. 1996. "How to Make a Good Society." In Karol Edward Soltan and Stephen L. Elkin, eds., *The Constitution of Good Societies,* pp. 103–117. University Park: Pennsylvania State University Press.

Appleby, Joyce. 1984. *Capitalism and a New Social Order: The Republican Vision of the 1790s.* New York: New York University Press.

Archer, Melanie and Judith Blau. 1993. "Class Formation in Nineteenth-Century America: The Case of the Middle Class." *Annual Review of Sociology* 19:17–41.

Ayres, Clarence E. 1934–1935. "Moral Confusion in Economics." *Ethics* 45:170–199. Reprinted 1988 in Warren J. Samuels, ed., *Institutional Economics,* vol. 2, pp. 20–49. Hants, UK: Edward Elgar.

———. 1951. "The Co-ordinates of Institutionalism." *American Economic Review* 41:47–55. Reprinted 1988 in Samuels, *Institutional Economics,* vol. 1, pp. 9–17.

Bach, Jonathan P. 1989. "Requiring Due Care in the Process of Patient

Deinstitutionalization: Toward a Common Law Approach to Mental Health Care Reform." *Yale Law Journal* 98:1153–1172.

Bainbridge, Stephen M. 1993. "In Defense of the Shareholder Wealth Maximization Norm: A Reply to Professor Green." *Washington and Lee Law Review* 50:1423–1447.

Banfield, Edward C. 1958. *The Moral Basis of a Backward Society.* New York: Free Press.

Banning, Lance. 1978. *The Jeffersonian Persuasion: Evolution of a Party Ideology.* Ithaca, NY: Cornell University Press.

Barber, Bernard. (1963) 1993. "Is American Business Becoming Professionalized?: Analysis of a Social Ideology." In Barber, *Constructing the Social System,* pp. 145–163. New Brunswick, NJ: Transaction.

Barenberg, Mark. 1994. "Democracy and Domination in the Law of Workplace Cooperation: From Bureaucratic to Flexible Production." *Columbia Law Review* 94:753–983.

Baum, Joel A.C. and Walter W. Powell. 1995. "Cultivating an Institutional Ecology of Organizations: Comment on Hannan, Carroll, Dundon, and Torres." *American Sociological Review* 60:529–538.

Bell, Daniel. 1976. *The Cultural Contradictions of Capitalism.* New York: Basic.

Bellah, Robert N., Richard Madsen, William M. Sullivan, Ann Swidler and Steven M. Tipton. (1985) 1986. *Habits of the Heart: Individualism and Commitment in American Life.* New York: Harper and Row.

Berle, Adolf, Jr. and Gardiner C. Means. (1932) 1967. *The Modern Corporation and Private Property.* Reprint ed. New York: Harcourt Brace and World.

Bhargava, Rajeev. 1992. *Individualism in Social Science: Forms and Limits of a Methodology.* Oxford, UK: Clarendon.

Birnbaum, Pierre and Jean Leca. 1990. Introduction to Birnbaum and Leca, eds., *Individualism: Theories and Methods,* pp. 1–14. Oxford, UK: Clarendon.

Black, Bernard S. 1990. "Is Corporate Law Trivial?: A Political and Economic Analysis." *Northwestern University Law Review* 84:542–597.

Blumberg, Phillip I. 1993. *The Multinational Challenge to Corporation Law: The Search for a New Corporate Personality.* New York: Oxford University Press.

Bourdieu, Pierre. (1979) 1984. *Distinction: A Social Critique of the Judgment of Taste.* Cambridge MA: Harvard University Press.

———. (1988) 1991. *The Political Ontology of Martin Heidegger.* Stanford: Stanford University Press.

———. (1989) 1996. *The State Nobility: Elite Schools in the Field of Power.* Stanford: Stanford University Press.

Bourgin, Frank. (1945) 1989. *The Great Challenge: The Myth of Laissez-Faire in the Early Republic.* New York: George Brazilier.

Braithwaite, John. 1984. *Corporate Crime in Pharmaceutical Industry.* London: Routledge & Kegan Paul.

———. 1985. "White Collar Crime." *Annual Review of Sociology* 11:1–25.

Bratton, William W., Jr. 1989a. "The New Economic Theory of the Firm: Critical Perspectives from History." *Stanford Law Review* 41:1471–1527.

———. 1989b. "The 'Nexus of Contracts' Corporation: A Critical Appraisal." *Cornell Law Review* 74:407–465.

———. 1993. "Self Interest and Good Will in Corporate Fiduciary Law." Paper presented at Fifth Annual Meeting of the Society for the Advancement of Socio-Economics, New York, March 1993.

Breyer, Stephen G. and Richard B. Stewart. 1985. *Administrative Law and Regulatory Policy: Problems, Text, and Cases,* 2d ed. Boston: Little, Brown.

Brudney, Victor. 1985. "Corporate Governance, Agency Costs, and the Rhetoric of Contract." *Columbia Law Review* 85:1403–1444.

Bruyn, Severyn T. 1991. *A Future for the American Economy: The Social Market.* Stanford: Stanford University Press.

Buchanan, Scott. 1958. "The Corporation and the Republic." New York: Fund for The Republic (28-page pamphlet).

Burk, James. 1988. *Values in the Marketplace: The American Stock Market Under Federal Securities Law.* Berlin and New York: Walter de Gruyter.

Burt, Ronald S. 1983. *Corporate Profits and Cooperation: Networks of Market Constraints and Directorate Ties in the American Economy.* New York: Academic Press.

Butler, Henry N. 1989. "The Contractual Theory of the Corporation." *George Mason University Law Review* 11:99–123.

Calhoun, Craig. 1995. *Critical Social Theory.* Boulder, CO: Westview.

Calhoun, Craig, Edward LiPuma and Moishe Postone, eds. 1993. *Bourdieu: Critical Perspectives.* Chicago: University of Chicago Press.

Carlton, Dennis W. and Daniel R. Fischel. 1983. "The Regulation of Insider Trading." *Stanford Law Review* 35:857–895.

Chandler, Alfred D., Jr. 1962. *Strategy and Structure: Chapters in the History of the American Industrial Enterprise.* Cambridge, MA: MIT Press.

———. 1977. *The Visible Hand: The Managerial Revolution in American Business.* Cambridge, MA: Harvard University Press.

———. 1990. *Scale and Scope: The Dynamics of Industrial Capitalism.* Cambridge, MA: Harvard University Press.

Cicourel, Aaron V. 1993. "Aspects of Structural and Processual Theories of Knowledge." In Calhoun, LiPuma and Postone, *Bourdieu: Critical Perspectives,* pp. 89–115.

Clark, Robert C. 1989. "Contracts, Elites, and Traditions in the Making of Corporate Law." *Columbia Law Review* 89:1703–1747.

Clignet, Remi. 1992. *Death, Deeds, and Descendants: Inheritance in Modern America.* New York: Aldine de Gruyter.

Clurman, Richard M. 1992. *To the End of Time: The Seduction and Conquest of a Media Empire.* New York: Simon and Schuster.

Cocks, Geoffrey. 1985. *Psychotherapy in the Third Reich: The Goring Institute.* New York: Oxford University Press.

Coffee, John C., Jr. 1981. "'No Soul to Damn: No Body to Kick': An Unscandalized Inquiry into the Problem of Corporate Punishment." *Michigan Law Review* 79:386–459.

———. 1986. "Shareholders Versus Managers: The Strain in the Corporate Web." *Michigan Law Review* 85:1–109.

———. 1990. "Unstable Coalitions: Corporate Governance as a Multi-Player Game." *Georgetown Law Journal* 78:1495–1549.

Cohen, George M. 1992. "The Negligence-Opportunism Tradeoff in Contract Law." *Hofstra Law Review* 20:941–1016.

Coleman, James S. 1990. *Foundations of Social Theory.* Cambridge, MA: Harvard University Press.

Commons, John R. (1931). "Institutional Economics." *American Economic Review* 21:648–657. Reprinted 1988 in Samuels, *Institutional Economics,* vol. 3, pp. 18–27.

Cowan, Alison Leigh. 1992. "Executive Stock Rule Considered." *New York Times,* January 22, pp. C1, C14.

Dahl, Robert. 1971. *Polyarchy.* New Haven: Yale University Press.

Delaney, Kevin J. 1992. *Strategic Bankruptcy: How Corporations and Creditors Use Chapter 11 to Their Advantage.* Berkeley: University of California Press.

Demo, David H. 1992. "The Self-Concept over Time: Research Issues and Directions." *Annual Review of Sociology* 18:303–326.

DeMott, Deborah A. 1988. "Beyond Metaphor: An Analysis of Fiduciary Obligation." *Duke Law Journal* 1988:879–924.

———. 1994. "Do You Have the Right to Remain Silent?: Duties of Disclosure in Business Transactions." *Delaware Journal of Corporate Law* 19:65–102.

Demsetz, Harold and Kenneth Lehn. 1985. "The Structure of Corporate Onwership: Causes and Consequences." *Journal of Political Economy* 93:1155–1177.

Dent, George W., Jr. 1989. "Toward Unifying Ownership and Control in the Public Corporation." *Wisconsin Law Review* 1989:881–924.

Diggins, John P. 1984. *The Lost Soul of American Politics: Virtue, Self-Interest, and the Foundations of Liberalism.* New York: Basic.

DiMaggio, Paul J. 1988. "Interest and Agency in Institutional Theory." In Lynne G. Zucker, ed., *Institutional Patterns and Organizations: Culture and Environment,* pp. 3–21. Cambridge, MA: Ballinger.

———. 1994. "Culture and Economy." In Neil Smelser and Richard Swedberg, eds., *The Handbook of Economic Sociology,* pp. 27–57. Princeton: Princeton University Press.

DiMaggio, Paul J. and Walter W. Powell. 1983. "The Iron Cage Revisited: Institutional Isomorphism and Collective Rationality in Organizational Fields." *American Sociological Review* 48:147–160.

———. 1991. Introduction to Powell and DiMaggio, eds., *The New Institutionalism in Organizational Analysis,* pp. 1–38. Chicago: University of Chicago Press.

Douglas, Mary. 1986. *How Institutions Think.* Syracuse, NY: Syracuse University Press.

Dragun, Andrew K. 1983. "Externalities, Property Rights, and Power." *Journal of Economic Issues* 17:667–680. Reprinted 1988 in Samuels, *Institutional Economics,* vol. 3, pp. 324–337.

Dugger, William M. 1979. "Methodological Differences Between Institutional and Neoclassical Economics." *Journal of Economic Issues* 13:899–909. Reprinted 1988 in Samuels, *Institutional Economics,* vol. 2, pp. 84–94.

Easterbrook, Frank H. and Daniel R. Fischel. 1981. "The Proper Role of a Target's Management in Responding to a Tender Offer." *Harvard Law Review* 94:1161–1204.

———. 1982. "Corporate Control Transactions." *Yale Law Journal* 91:698–737.

———. 1983. "Voting in Corporate Law." *Journal of Law and Economics* 26:395–428.

———. 1991. *The Economic Structure of Corporate Law.* Cambridge, MA: Harvard University Press.

———. 1993. "Contract and Fiduciary Duty." *Journal of Law and Economics* 34:425–446.

Eisenberg, Melvin Aron. 1988. *The Nature of the Common Law.* Cambridge, MA: Harvard University Press.

———. 1989. "The Structure of Corporation Law." *Columbia Law Review* 89:1461–1525.

Elkin, Stephen L. 1993. "Constitutionalism's Successor." In Elkin and Soltan, eds., *A New Constitutionalism: Designing Political Institutions for a Good Society,* pp. 117–143. Chicago: University of Chicago Press.

Elkin, Stephen L. and Karol Edward Soltan, eds. 1993. *A New Constitutionalism: Designing Political Institutions for a Good Society.* Chicago: University of Chicago Press.

Elster, John. 1990. "Marxism and Methodological Individualism." In Birnbaum and Leca, *Individualism: Theories and Methods,* pp. 46–61.

Epstein, Cynthia Fuchs. 1990. "The Cultural Perspective and the Study of Work." In Kai Erikson and Steven Peter Vallas, eds., *The Nature of Work: Sociological Perspectives,* pp. 88–98. New Haven: Yale University Press, American Sociological Association Presidential Series.

Etzioni, Amitai. (1961) 1975. *A Comparative Analysis of Complex Organizations: On Power, Involvement, and Their Correlates,* rev. ed. New York: Free Press.

———. 1988. *The Moral Dimension: Toward a New Economics.* New York: Free Press.

Fabrikant, Geraldine. 1993. "Delaware Court Ruling Aids QVC in Struggle to Acquire Paramount." *New York Times,* December 10, p. 1.

Fama, Eugene F. and Michael C. Jensen. 1983. "Separation of Ownership and Control." *Journal of Law and Economics* 26: 301–325.

Fine, Gary Alan. 1993. "The Sad Demise, Mysterious Disappearance, and Glorious Triumph of Symbolic Interactionism." *Annual Review of Sociology* 19:61–87.

———. 1996. *Kitchens: The Culture of Restaurant Work.* Berkeley: University of California Press.

Fischel, Daniel R. 1978. "Efficient Capital Market Theory, the Market for Corporate Control, and the Regulation of Cash Tender Offers." *Texas Law Review* 57:1–46.

———. 1982. "The Corporate Governance Movement." *Vanderbilt Law Review* 35:1259–1292.

Fligstein, Neil. 1985. "The Spread of the Multidivisional Form Among Large Firms, 1919–1979." *American Sociological Review* 50:377–391.

———. 1990. *The Transformation of Corporate Control.* Cambridge, MA: Harvard University Press.

Frank, David John, John W. Meyer and David Miyahara. 1995. "The Individualist Polity and the Prevalence of Professionalized Psychology: A Cross-National Study." *American Sociological Review* 60:360–377.

Frankel, Tamar. 1983. "Fiduciary Law." *California Law Review* 71:795–836.

Friedland, Roger and Robert R. Alford. 1991. "Bringing Society Back In: Symbols, Practices, and Institutional Contradictions." In Walter W. Powell and Paul J. DiMaggio, eds. *The New Institutionalism in Organizational Analysis*, pp. 232–263. Chicago: University of Chicago Press.

Friedland, Roger and A.F. Robertson, eds. 1990. *Beyond the Marketplace: Rethinking Economy and Society.* New York: Aldine de Gruyter.

Friedman, Debra and Michael Hechter. 1988. "The Contribution of Rational Choice Theory to Macrosociological Research." *Sociological Theory* 6:201–218.

Friedman, Lawrence M. (1973) 1985. *A History of American Law.* New York: Simon and Schuster.

Friedman, Milton. (1962) 1982. *Capitalism and Freedom.* Chicago: University of Chicago Press.

Fuller, Lon L. (1964/1969) 1975. *The Morality of Law,* rev. ed. New Haven: Yale University Press.

Galbraith, John Kenneth. (1967) 1971. *The New Industrial State.* Boston: Houghton Mifflin.

Gans, Herbert. 1986. *Middle American Individualism.* New York: Free Press.

Georgescu-Roegen, Nicholas. 1971. *The Entropy Law and the Economic Process.* Cambridge, MA: Harvard University Press.

Gibbs, Jack P. 1981. *Norms, Deviance and Social Control: Conceptual Matters.* New York: Elsevier.

Giddens, Anthony. 1979. *Central Problems in Social Theory: Action, Structure and Contradiction in Social Analysis.* Berkeley: University of California Press.

———. 1984. *The Constitution of Society: Outline of the Theory of Structuration.* Cambridge, UK: Polity Press.

Gordon, Jeffrey N. 1991. "Corporations, Markets, and Courts." *Columbia Law Review* 91:1931–1988.

Gordon, Robert A. (1976) 1988. "Rigor and Relevance in a Changing Institutional Setting." *American Economic Review* 66:1–14. Reprinted 1988 in Samuels, *Institutional Economics,* vol. 2, pp. 124–137.

Goodrich, Carter. 1960. *Government Promotion of American Canals and Railroads, 1800–1890.* New York: Columbia University Press.

Granovetter, Mark. 1990. "The Old and the New Economic Sociology: A History and an Agenda." In Friedland and Robertson, *Beyond the Marketplace,* pp. 89–112.

Granovetter, Mark and Richard Swedberg, eds. 1992. *The Sociology of Economic Life.* Boulder, CO: Westview.

Gutmann, Amy. 1995. "The Virtues of Democratic Self-Constraint." In Amitai Etzioni, ed., *New Communitarian Thinking: Persons, Virtues, Institutions, and Communities,* pp. 154–169. Charlottesville: University of Virginia Press.

Haar, Charles M. and Daniel Wm. Fessler. 1986. *The Wrong Side of the Tracks: A Revolutionary Rediscovery of the Common Law Tradition of Fairness in the Struggle Against Inequality.* New York: Simon and Schuster.

Habermas, Jurgen. (1962) 1989. *The Structural Transformation of the Public Sphere.* Cambridge, MA: MIT Press.

Halbwachs, Maurice. 1992. *On Collective Memory.* Edited and with an introduction by Lewis Coser. Chicago: University of Chicago Press.

Hannan, Michael T., Glenn R. Carroll, Elizabeth Dundon and John Charles Torres. 1995. "Organizational Evolution in a Multinational Context: Entries of Automobile Manufacturers in Belgium, Britain, France, Germany and Italy." *American Sociological Review* 60:509–528.

Hannan, Michael T. and Glenn R. Carroll. 1995. "Theory Building and Cheap Talk About Legitimation: Reply to Baum and Powell." *American Sociological Review* 60:539–544.

Hart, Keith. 1990. "The Idea of Economy: Six Modern Dissenters." In Friedland and Robertson, *Beyond the Marketplace,* pp. 113–136.

Hayek, Friedrich A. 1973–1979. *Law, Legislation and Liberty: A New Statement of the Liberal Principles of Justice and Political Economy,* 3 vols. Chicago: University of Chicago Press.

Hechter, Michael. 1983. "Karl Polanyi's Social Theory: A Critique." In Hechter, ed., *The Microfoundations of Macrosociology,* pp. 158–189. Philadelphia: Temple University Press.

———. 1987. *Principles of Group Solidarity.* Berkeley: University of California Press.

Heilbroner, Robert L. and Lester C. Thurow. 1978. *The Economic Problem,* 5th ed. Englewood Cliffs, NJ: Prentice-Hall.

Herman, Edward S. (1981) 1982. *Corporate Control, Corporate Power: A Twentieth Century Fund Study.* Cambridge, UK: Cambridge University Press.

Hirschman, Albert. 1970. *Exit, Voice and Loyalty: Responses to Decline in Firms, Organizations and States.* Cambridge, MA: Harvard University Press.

Hoffer, Peter Charles. 1990. *The Law's Conscience: Equitable Constitutionalism in America.* Chapel Hill: University of North Carolina Press.

———. 1992. *Law and People in Colonial America.* Baltimore: Johns Hopkins University Press.

Hovenkamp, Herbert. 1991. *Enterprise and American Law, 1836–1937.* Cambridge, MA: Harvard University Press.

Hurst, James Willard. 1970. *The Legitimacy of the Business Corporation in the Law of the United States 1780–1970.* Charlottesville: University of Virginia Press.

Irwin-Zarecka, Iwona. 1996. "Memory Criticism, or How We Know the Right from Wrong." In David Sciulli, ed., *Comparative Social Research,* Supplement 2, *Normative Social Action,* pp. 23–30. Greenwich, CT: JAI Press.

Isaac, Rael Jean and Virginia C. Armat. 1990. *Madness in the Streets: How Psychiatry and the Law Abandoned the Mentally Ill.* New York: Free Press.

Janofsky, Michael. 1993. "Ruling on QVC Bid Faces an Expert Review." *New York Times,* November 26, p. C1.

Janowitz, Morris. 1975. "Sociological Theory and Social Control." *American Journal of Sociology* 81:82–108.

Jensen, Michael C. 1988. "Takeovers: Their Causes and Consequences." *Journal of Economic Perspectives* 2:21–48.

Jensen, Michael C. and William H. Meckling. 1976. "Theory of the Firm: Managerial Behavior, Agency Costs and Ownership Structure." *Journal of Financial Economics* 3:305–360.

Jepperson, Ronald L. 1991. "Institutions, Institutional Effects, and Institutionalism." In Powell and DiMaggio, *The New Institutionalism in Organizational Analysis,* pp. 143–163.

Jepperson, Ronald L. and John W. Meyer. 1991. "The Public Order and the Construction of Formal Organizations." In Powell and DiMaggio, *The New Institutionalism in Organizational Analysis,* pp. 204–231.

Joas, Hans. (1986) 1993. "The Unhappy Marriage of Hermeneutics and Functionalism: Jurgen Habermas's Theory of Communicative Action." In Joas, *Pragmatism and Social Theory,* pp. 125–153. Chicago: University of Chicago Press.

———. (1987) 1993. "Pragmatism in American Sociology." In *Pragmatism and Social Theory,* pp. 14–51.

———. (1990) 1993. "Conclusion: The Creativity of Action and the Intersubjectivity of Reason—Mead's Pragmatism and Social Theory." In *Pragmatism and Social Theory,* pp. 238–261.

———. (1992) 1993. "An Underestimated Alternative: America and the Limits of 'Critical Theory.'" In *Pragmatism and Social Theory,* pp. 79–93.

———. 1993. "American Pragmatism and German Thought: A History of Misunderstandings." In *Pragmatism and Social Theory,* pp. 94–121.

———. 1993. *Pragmatism and Social Theory.* Chicago: University of Chicago Press.

Johnson, Lyman. 1990. "The Delaware Judiciary and the Meaning of Corporate Life and Corporate Law." *Texas Law Review* 68:865–936.

Journal of Law and Economics. Symposium. 1983. *Corporations and Private Property.* Symposium. *Journal of Law and Economics* 26:235–496.

Kamens, David H., John W. Meyer and Aaron Benavot. 1996. "Worldwide Patterns in Academic Secondary Education Curricula." *Comparative Education Review* 40:116–138.

Kammen, Michael. 1986. *Spheres of Liberty: Changing Perceptions of Liberty in American Culture.* Madison: University of Wisconsin Press.

Keane, John. 1988. *Democracy and Civil Society: On the Predicaments of European Socialism, the Prospects for Democracy, and the Problem of Controlling Social and Political Power.* London: Verso.

Kennedy, Robert Dawson, Jr. 1991. "The Statist Evolution of Rail Governance in the United States, 1830–1986." In John L. Campbell, J. Rogers Hollingsworth and Leon N. Lindberg, eds., *Governance of the American Economy,* pp. 138–181. Cambridge, UK: Cambridge University Press.

Kester, W. Carl. 1991. *Japanese Takeovers: The Global Contest for Corporate Control.* Boston: Harvard Business School Press.

Keynes, John Maynard. 1936. *The General Theory of Employment Interest and Money.* New York: Harcourt, Brace.

Klein, William A. 1982. "The Modern Business Organization: Bargaining Under Constraints." *Yale Law Journal* 91:1521–1564.

Knight, Frank. (1921) 1948. *Risk, Uncertainty and Profit.* Boston: Houghton Mifflin.

Knoke, David. 1981. "Power Structures." In Samuel L. Long, ed., *Handbook of Political Behavior,* vol. 3, pp. 275–332. New York: Plenum.

———. 1990. *Political Networks: The Structural Perspective.* Cambridge, UK: Cambridge University Press.

Knoke, David, Arne L. Kalleberg, Peter V. Marsden and Joe L. Spaeth. 1993. "Job Training in U.S. Organizations." Unpublished manuscript, 33 pages.

Kohn, Melvin. 1977. *Class and Conformity: A Study in Values,* 2d. ed. Chicago: University of Chicago Press.

———. 1990. "Unresolved Issues in the Relationship Between Work and Personality." In Kai Erikson and Steven Peter Vallas, eds., *The Nature of Work: Sociological Perspectives,* pp. 36–68. New Haven: Yale University Press, American Sociological Association Presidential Series.

Kraakman, Reiner H. 1984. "Corporate Liability Strategies and the Costs of Legal Controls. *Yale Law Journal* 93:857–898.

Lasch, Christopher. (1990) 1991. *The True and Only Heaven: Progress and Its Critics.* New York: Norton.

Lijphart, Arend. 1984. *Democracies: Patterns of Majoritarian and Consensus Government in Twenty-One Countries.* New Haven: Yale University Press.

Lipset, Seymour Martin. 1960. *Political Man: The Social Bases of Politics.* Garden City, NJ: Doubleday.

———. 1994. "The Social Requisites of Democracy Revisited." *American Sociological Review* 59:1–22.

Loewenstein, Mark J. 1989. "Toward an Auction Market for Corporate Control and the Demise of the Business Judgment Rule." *Southern California Law Review* 63:65–105.

Lohr, Steve. 1992. "Pulling Down the Corporate Clubhouse." *New York Times,* April 12, section 3, pp. 1, 5.

Lowi, Theodore. 1969. *The End of Liberalism: Ideology, Policy and the Crisis of Public Authority.* New York: Norton.

———. 1995. *The End of the Republican Era.* Norman: University of Oklahoma Press.

Lukes, Steven. 1973. "Methodological Individualism Reconsidered." In A. Ryan, ed., *The Philosophy of Social Explanation,* pp. 119–129. Oxford UK: Oxford University Press.

Luhmann, Niklas. (1972) 1985. *A Sociological Theory of Law.* London: Routledge & Kegan Paul.

Mark, Gregory A. 1987. "The Personification of the Business Corporation in American Law." *University of Chicago Law Review* 54:1441–1483.

Marshall, Alfred. (1892) 1919. *Elements of Economics of Industry.* London: Macmillan and Co.

McClellan, James. 1971. *Joseph Story and the American Constitution: A Study in Political and Legal Thought.* Norman: University of Oklahoma Press.

McCoy, Drew R. 1980. *The Elusive Republic: Political Economy in Jeffersonian America.* Chapel Hill: University of North Carolina Press.

McDowell, Gary L. 1982. *Equity and the Constitution: The Supreme Court, Equitable Relief, and Public Policy.* Chicago: University of Chicago Press.

————. 1988. *Curbing the Courts: The Constitution and the Limits of Judicial Power.* Baton Rouge: Louisiana State University Press.

McWilliams, Wilson Carey. (1973) 1974. *The Idea of Fraternity in America.* Berkeley: University of California Press.

Meyer, John. 1983. "Conclusion: Institutionalization and the Rationality of Formal Organizational Structure." In Meyer and W. Richard Scott, eds., *Organizational Environments: Ritual and Rationality,* pp. 261–282. Beverly Hills, CA: Sage.

Meyer, John and Brian Rowan. 1977. "Institutionalized Organizations: Formal Structure as Myth and Ceremony." *American Journal of Sociology* 82:431–450.

Meyer, John W., W. Richard Scott and Terrence E. Deal. (1981) 1983. "Institutional and Technical Sources of Organizational Structure: Explaining the Structure of Educational Organizations." In Meyer and Scott, *Organizational Environments,* pp. 45–67.

Michels, Robert. (1911) 1949. *Political Parties.* Glencoe, IL: Free Press.

Millon, David. 1990. "Theories of the Corporation." *Duke Law Journal* 1990:201–262.

Milner, Murray. 1996. Presentation in Department of Sociology, Texas A&M University.

Mitchell, Lawrence E. 1990. "The Fairness Rights of Corporate Bondholders." *New York University Law Review* 65:1165–1229.

Mizruchi, Mark. 1982. *The American Corporate Network, 1904–1974.* Beverly Hills, CA: Sage.

————. 1992. *The Structure of Corporate Political Action.* Cambridge, MA: Harvard University Press.

Morrill, Calvin. 1995. *The Executive Way: Conflict Management in Corporations.* Chicago: University of Chicago Press.

Muller, Ingo. (1987) 1991. *Hitler's Justice: The Courts of the Third Reich.* Cambridge, MA: Harvard University Press.

Newman, Maria and Samuel Weiss. 1994. "CUNY Chancellor's Time Spent with Corporate Boards Is at Issue." *New York Times,* February 22, p. 1.

Newmyer, R. Kent. 1985. *Supreme Court Justice Joseph Story: Statesman of the Old Republic.* Chapel Hill: University of North Carolina Press.

Norris, Floyd. 1994. "Can't Tell Viacom from QVC?" *New York Times,* January 30, section 4, p. 3.

Note. 1982. "Constitutional Rights of the Corporate Person." *Yale Law Journal* 91:1641–1658.

Offe, Claus. 1981. "The Attribution of Public Status to Interest Groups: Observations on the West German Case." In Suzanne Berger, ed., *Organizing Interests in Western Europe: Pluralism, Corporatism, and the Transformation of Politics,* pp. 123–158. Cambridge UK: Cambridge University Press.

————. 1983. "Political Legitimation Through Majority Rule?" *Social Research* 50:709–756.

Orts, Eric W. 1992. "Beyond Shareholders: Interpreting Corporate Constituency Statutes." *George Washington Law Review* 61:14–135.

————. 1993. "The Complexity and Legitimacy of Corporate Law." *Washington and Lee Law Review* 50:1565–1623.

Ouchi, William G. and Alan L. Wilkins. 1985. "Organizational Culture." *Annual Review of Sociology* 11:457–483.

Palmiter, Alan R. 1989. "Reshaping the Corporate Fiduciary Model: A Director's Duty of Independence." *Texas Law Review* 67:1351–1464.

Parkes, Joseph. 1828. *A History of the Court of Chancery.* London: Longman, Rees, Orme, Brown and Green.

Parsons, Talcott. (1937) 1968. *The Structure of Social Action,* 2 vols. New York: Free Press.

Perez-Diaz, Victor M. 1993. *The Return of Civil Society: The Emergence of Democratic Spain.* Cambridge, MA: Harvard University Press.

Piore, Michael and Charles Sabel. 1984. *The Second Industrial Divide: Possibilities for Prosperity.* New York: Basic.

Plucknett, Theodore F.T. (1929) 1956. *A Concise History of the Common Law.* London: Butterworth and Co.

Polanyi, Karl. (1944) 1957. *The Great Transformation: The Political and Economic Origins of Our Time.* Boston: Beacon.

Posner, Richard A. 1990. *The Problems of Jurisprudence.* Cambridge, MA: Harvard University Press.

Powell, Walter W. 1990. "The Transformation of Organizational Forms: How Useful Is Organization Theory in Accounting for Social Change?" In Friedland and Robertson, *Beyond the Marketplace,* pp. 301–329.

———. 1991. "Expanding the Scope of Institutional Analysis." In Powell and DiMaggio, *The New Institutionalism in Organizational Analysis,* pp. 183–203.

Powell, Walter W. and Paul J. DiMaggio, eds. 1991. *The New Institutionalism in Organizational Analysis.* Chicago: University of Chicago Press.

Powell, Walter W. and Laurel Smith-Doerr. 1994. "Networks and Economic Life." In Neil Smelser and Richard Swedberg, eds., *The Handbook of Economic Sociology,* pp. 368–402. Princeton: Princeton University Press.

Powell, Walter W., Kenneth W. Koput and Laurel Smith-Doerr. 1996. "Interorganizational Collaboration and the Locus of Innovation: Networks of Learning in Biotechnology." *Administrative Science Quarterly* 41:116–145.

Putnam, Robert D. 1993. *Making Democracy Work: Civic Traditions in Modern Italy.* Princeton: Princeton University Press.

Reich, Robert B. (1991) 1992. *The Work of Nations: Preparing Ourselves for 21st-Century Capitalism.* New York: Vintage.

Rinaldi, Ronald J. 1990. "Radically Altered States: Entering the 'Revlon Zone.'" *Columbia Law Review* 90:760–782.

Ringer, Fritz K. (1969) 1990. *The Decline of the German Mandarins: The German Academic Community, 1890–1933.* Hanover, NH: University Press of New England, Wesleyan University Press.

Rosenhan, D.L. 1973. "On Being Sane in Insane Places." *Science* 179:250–258.

Rothschild-Witt, Joyce. 1979. "The Collectivist Organization: An Alternative to Rational Bureaucratic Models." *American Sociologial Review* 44:509–527.

Roy, William G. 1997. *Socializing Capital: The Rise of the Large Industrial Corporation in America.* Princeton: Princeton University Press.

Rutherford, Malcolm. 1981. "Clarence Ayres and the Instrumental Theory of Value." *Journal of Economics Issues* 15:657–673. Reprinted 1988 in Samuels, *Institutional Economics,* vol. 3, pp. 7–23.

Sabel, Charles F. 1982. *Work and Politics: The Division of Labor in Industry.* Cambridge, UK: Cambridge University Press.

Samuels, Warren J., ed. 1988. *Institutional Economics,* 3 vols. Hants, UK: Edward Elgar.

Samuelson, Paul A. 1948. *Economics: An Introductory Analysis.* New York: McGraw-Hill.

Scheff, Thomas J. (1964) 1975. "The Societal Reaction to Deviance: Ascriptive Elements in the Psychiatric Screening of Mental Patients in a Midwestern State." In Ronald L. Akers and Richard Hawkins, eds., *Law and Control in Society,* pp. 237–249. Englewood Cliffs, NJ: Prentice-Hall.

Schmitter, Philippe C. 1974. "Still the Century of Corporatism?" In Fredrick B. Pike and Thomas Stritch, eds., *The New Corporatism,* pp. 85–131. Notre Dame, IN: University of Notre Dame Press.

———. 1981. "Interest Intermediation and Regime Governability in Contemporary Western Europe and North America." In Suzanne Berger, ed., *Organizing Interests in Western Europe,* pp. 285–327. Cambridge, UK: Cambridge University Press.

———. 1983. "Democratic Theory and Neocorporatist Practice." *Social Research* 50:885–928.

Sciulli, David. 1992. *Theory of Societal Constitutionalism: Foundations of a Non-Marxist Critical Theory.* New York: Cambridge University Press.

———. 1995. "The Scope of Donald Black's Positivist Approach to Law and Social Control." *Law and Social Inquiry* 20:805–828.

———. 1997a. "Corporate Power in Civil Society." Unpublished manuscript, 11 chapters.

———. 1997b. "Organizational Forms and Intermediary Associations." Unpublished manuscript, 40 pages.

———. 1997c. "'Rationalization' and 'Institutionalization' in the New Institutionalism." Unpublished manuscript, 51 pages.

———. 1997d. "Fiduciary Law in the Balance: Narrowing the Corporate Judiciary's Social Vision." Unpublished manuscript, 90 pages.

———. 1997e. "Critical Functionalism: Etzioni's Social Theory." Unpublished manuscript, 13 chapters.

Sciulli, David, ed. 1996. *Comparative Social Research,* Supplement 2, *Normative Social Action.* Greenwich, CT: JAI Press.

Sciulli, David and Dean Gerstein. 1985. "Social Theory and Talcott Parsons in the 1980s." *Annual Review of Sociology* 11:369–387.

Scott, W. Richard. 1981. *Organizations: Rational, Natural and Open Systems.* Englewood Cliffs, NJ: Prentice-Hall.

———. 1983. "The Organization of Environments: Network, Cultural, and Historical Elements." In Meyer and Scott, *Organizational Environments,* pp. 155–175.

———. 1987. "The Adolescence of Institutional Theory." *Administrative Science Quarterly* 32:493–511.

———. 1991. "Unpacking Institutional Arguments." In Powell and DiMaggio, *The New Institutionalism in Organizational Analysis,* pp. 164–182.

———. 1994. "Law and Organizations." In Sim B. Sitkin and Robert J. Bies, eds., *The Legalistic Organization,* pp. 3–18. Thousand Oaks, CA: Sage.

Scott, W. Richard and John W. Meyer. 1991. "The Organization of Societal Sectors: Propositions and Early Evidence." In Powell and DiMaggio, *The New Institutionalism in Organizational Analysis,* pp. 108–140.

Scull, Andrew. 1989. *Social Order/Mental Disorder: Anglo-American Psychiatry in Historical Perspective.* Berkeley: University of California Press.

Seligman, Adam B. 1992. *The Idea of Civil Society.* New York: Free Press.

Sellers, Charles. 1991. *The Market Revolution: Jacksonian America, 1815–1846.* New York: Oxford University Press.

Selznick, Philip. 1992. *The Moral Commonwealth: Social Theory and the Promise of Community.* Berkeley: University of California Press.

———. 1996. "Institutionalism 'Old' and 'New.'" *Administrative Science Quarterly* 41:270–277.

Simon, William H. 1990. "Contract Versus Politics in Corporation Doctrine." In David Kairys, ed., *The Politics of Law: A Progressive Critique,* rev. ed., pp. 387–409. New York: Pantheon.

Sitkin, Sim B. and Robert J. Bies, eds. 1994. *The Legalistic Organization.* Thousand Oaks, CA: Sage.

Smith, Steven D. 1990. "The Pursuit of Pragmatism." *Yale Law Journal* 100:409–449.

Sobel, Robert. 1984. *The Age of Giant Corporations: A Microeconomic History of American Business, 1914–1984,* 2d ed. Westport, CT: Greenwood Press.

Soltan, Karol Edward. 1993. "What Is the New Constitutionalism?" In Elkin and Soltan, *A New Constitutionalism,* pp. 3–19.

Soltan, Karol Edward and Stephen L. Elkin, eds. 1996. *The Constitution of Good Societies.* University Park: Pennsylvania State University Press.

Stewart, James B. 1991. *Den of Thieves.* New York: Simon and Schuster.

Stinchcombe, Arthur L. 1990. *Information and Organizations.* Berkeley: University of California Press.

Stone, Christopher D. 1982. "Corporate Vices and Corporate Virtues: Do Public/Private Distinctions Matter?" *University of Pennsylvania Law Review* 130:1441–1508.

Strauss, Anselm. 1978. *Negotiations.* San Francisco: Jossey-Bass.

Streeck, Wolfgang and Philippe C. Schmitter. 1985. "Community, Market, State—and Associations? The Prospective Contribution of Interest Governance to Social Order." In Streeck and Schmitter, eds., *Private Interest Government: Beyond Market and State,* pp. 1–29. London: Sage.

Stryker, Sheldon. 1980. *Symbolic Interactionism: A Social Structural Version.* Menlo Park, CA: Benjamin/Cummings.

Summers, Robert S. 1982. *Instrumentalism and American Legal Theory.* Ithaca, NY: Cornell University Press.

———. 1984. *Lon L. Fuller.* Stanford: Stanford University Press.

Sunstein, Cass R. 1990. *After the Rights Revolution: Reconceiving the Regulatory State.* Cambridge, MA: Harvard University Press.

Sutton, John R. et al. 1994. "The Legalization of the Workplace." *American Journal of Sociology* 99:944–971.

Tool, Marc R. 1981. "The Compulsive Shift to Institutional Analysis." *Journal of Economic Issues* 15:569–592. Reprinted 1988 in Samuels, *Institutional Economics,* vol. 3, pp. 108–131.

Ullmann, John E. 1983. *Social Costs in Modern Society: A Qualitative and Quantitative Assessment.* Westport, CT: Quorum Books.

Useem, Michael. 1984. *The Inner Circle.* New York: Oxford University Press.

———. 1993. *Executive Defense: Shareholder Power and Corporate Reorganization.* Cambridge, MA: Harvard University Press.

Vromen, Suzanne. 1996. "The Politics of Monuments." In Sciulli, *Comparative Social Research,* Supplement 2, pp. 31–38.

Walzer, Michael. 1983. *Spheres of Justice: A Defense of Pluralism and Equality.* New York: Basic.

Warner, R. Stephen. 1978. "Toward a Redefinition of Action Theory: Paying the Cognitive Element Its Due." *American Journal of Sociology* 83:1317–1349.

Waters, Malcolm. 1995. *Daniel Bell.* London: Routledge.

Weinrib, Ernest J. 1975. "The Fiduciary Obligation." *University of Toronto Law Journal* 25:1–22.

White, G. Edward. 1993. *Justice Oliver Wendell Holmes: Law and the Inner Self.* New York: Oxford University Press.

Wilber, Charles K. and Robert S. Harrison. 1978. "The Methodological Basis of Institutional Economics: Pattern Model, Storytelling, and Holism." *Journal of Economic Issues* 12:61–89. Reprinted 1988 in Samuels, *Institutional Economics,* vol. 2, pp. 95–123.

Williamson, Oliver. 1985. *The Economic Institutions of Capitalism: Firms, Markets, Relational Contracting.* New York: Free Press.

————. 1988a. "The Logic of Economic Organization." *Journal of Law, Economics and Organization* 4:65–93.

————. 1988b. "Corporate Finance and Corporate Governance." *Journal of Finance* 43:567–591.

Williamson, Oliver et al. 1975. "Understanding the Employment Relation: The Analysis of Idiosyncratic Exchange." *Bell Journal of Economics* 6:250–278.

Witte, Edwin E. 1954. "Institutional Economics as Seen by an Institutional Economist." *Southern Economic Journal* 21:131–140. Reprinted 1988 in Samuels, *Institutional Economics,* vol. 1, pp. 28–38.

Wolfe, Alan. 1989. *Whose Keeper? Social Science and Moral Obligation.* Berkeley: University of California Press.

Yago, Glenn. 1991. *Junk Bonds: How High Yield Securities Restructured Corporate America.* New York: Oxford University Press.

Yale Law Journal. Symposium. 1988. *The Republican Civic Tradition.* Symposium. *Yale Law Journal* 97: 1493–1846.

Zucker, Lynn G. 1983. "Organizations as Institutions." *Research in the Sociology of Organizations* 2:1–47.

————. (1977) 1991. "The Role of Institutionalization in Cultural Persistence." In Powell and DiMaggio, *The New Institutionalism in Organizational Analysis,* pp. 83–107.

————. 1988. *Institutional Patterns and Organizations: Culture and Environment.* Cambridge, MA: Ballinger.

Zukin, Sharon and Paul DiMaggio. 1990. *Structures of Capital: The Social Organization of the Economy.* Cambridge, UK: Cambridge University Press.

Index

Antitrust law, 92
Arbitrariness: and citizen vigilance, 40; of collective power, 32, 33, 82, 98; mediation of, in formal democracy, 39, 40, 62; of positional power, 2–3, 5, 34–35, 36–38, 40–41, 62, 69; of retroactive laws, 2; in structured situations in civil society, 51–52
Arnold, Thurmond, 133
Articles of incorporation, 91–92
Artificial entity theory, 85
Artificial person, corporation as, 84–85, 87, 88
Association governance. *See* Corporate governance structure
Authoritarian regimes, 26
Ayres, Clarence, 137–138

Bell, Daniel, 3, 6
Berle, Adolf, 148, 176, 178, 181
Brown decision, 121
Bureaucratic organization, fidelity in, 60
Business judgment rule, 96, 146–147; as basis for doctrinal continuity, 171–172

Cardozo, Benjamin, 129, 132–133
Citizen vigilance: and arbitrary corporate governance, 40, 62; in democratic social order, 32, 39, 50; judicial instruction in, 61; as product of institutional design, 32, 38, 39; and republican virtue, 82–83
Civil society: basic institutionalized arrangements in, 2; citizen vigilance in, 32, 82–84; imbalances of private wealth in, 83–84, 91; limited government in, 82–84; private governance structures in, 43–44
Collegial form of organization, 36, 53; and institutional design, 61–62; managers' fidelity to threshold of procedural norms in, 59–60; reasons for, 62–65
Common law courts, English, 111, 112, 113, 114, 115, 117, 119–120
Common law duty, 120
Commons, John, 137–138
Consolidated democracy. See Formal democracy
Contract law, 108, 109
Corporate agent/agency: and the courts, 92–95; and fiduciary duties, 86, 93, 94, 95, 172–175; identification of, 81, 88, 90; in multidivisional form, 163; normative restrictions on, 93–94, 96; sitting management teams as, 146–147, 176–177
Corporate boards, 151; and corporate agency, 147; positional power exercised by, 35–36
Corporate charters: history of, 81–82, 85–88; republican principles in, 86–88; standardization of, 90–92, 97–98
Corporate governance disputes, 35–36, 38, 54–55, 61, 93, 170
Corporate governance structures: arbitrary actions in, 2–3, 33, 34–35, 38, 39, 40–41; collegial formation in, 59–60, 61; defined, 1; and institu-

About the Book

This original book looks methodically at corporate law, corporate governance, and judicial practice from the perspective of social theory.

Sciulli explores whether there are identifiable limits—legal or normative—to corporate power in any democratic society; when the corporate judiciary in the United States maintains those limits, despite the pressures of intensifying global economic competition; and when the judiciary drifts, as an institution, away from bearing this responsibility.

Assessing both the promise and the limits of the new institutional approach to the sociology of organizations, Sciulli considers the influence of England's Chancery Courts in the United States, especially with regard to private power in civil society. His study, moving from the eighteenth century to the present, provides a comprehensive analysis of corporate power and judicial restraints.

David Sciulli is professor of sociology at Texas A&M University. His publications include *Macro Socio-Economics: From Theory to Activism* and *Theory of Societal Constitutionalism: Foundations of a Non-Marxist Critical Theory.*